Adam McNicol is a Ballarat-based journalist and author. He has written a number of books, including *The Danihers*, the authorised biography of the four brothers who played for Essendon, and *Manangatang*, a social history of the iconic town in northern Victoria's Mallee region. He has also co-written *All Bets Are Off*, the autobiography of former Melbourne AFL player and reformed gambler David Schwarz, and *In My Own Words*, the autobiography of former Carlton and Brisbane Lions AFL star Brendan Fevola. Along with writing books, Adam is a reporter at AFL Media, where he works on the Australian Football League's official website, afl.com.au, and its match-day magazine, the *AFL Record*.

Other books by Adam McNicol
The Danihers
Manangatang
All Bets Are Off (with David Schwarz)
Fev: In My Own Words

US vs THEM

ADAM McNICOL

GREAT
AUSTRALIAN
SPORTING
RIVALRIES

The Five Mile Press

The Five Mile Press Pty Ltd
1 Centre Road, Scoresby
Victoria 3179 Australia
www.fivemile.com.au

Part of the Bonnier Publishing Group
www.bonnierpublishing.com

Copyright © Adam McNicol, 2013
All rights reserved. No part of this book may be reproduced, stored in a retrieval system, or be transmitted by any form or by any means, electronic, mechanical, photocopying, recording or otherwise, without the pior written permission of the publisher.

Adam McNicol asserts his moral rights to be identified as the author of this book.

First published 2013

Printed in Australia at Griffin Press.
Only wood grown from sustainable regrowth forests is used in the manufacture of paper found in this book.

Page design and typesetting by Shaun Jury
Cover design by Luke Causby, Blue Cork
Internal photographs: p84 Philip Brown/Corbis; pp32, 56 and 120 © Newspix; P4 Gary Merrin © Newspix; pp70 and 148 George Salpigtidis © Newspix; p176 Geoff McLachlan © Newspix; p218 Brett Faulkner © Newspix
Indexing by Carly Brooks

National Library of Australia Cataloguing-in-Publication entry
   McNicol, Adam, author.
   Us vs Them: Great Australian Sporting Rivalries /
   Adam McNicol.
   ISBN: 9781743461914 (paperback)
   Includes index.
   Sports rivalries–Australia.
   Sports–Australia.
   796.0994

For Chub and Barnesy, my first sporting heroes

Contents

Introduction	1
MOTORSPORT **Holden vs Ford**	5
AUSTRALIAN RULES **Collingwood vs Carlton**	33
AUSTRALIAN RULES **Wayne Carey vs Glen Jakovich**	57
CRICKET **Shane Warne vs Daryll Cullinan**	71
CRICKET **Australia vs England**	85
YACHTING **Australia vs the United States**	121
NETBALL **Australia vs New Zealand**	149
RUGBY LEAGUE **New South Wales vs Queensland**	177

RUGBY UNION
Australia vs New Zealand   219

Statistics at a Glance   249

Acknowledgements   255

References   257

Index   259

Introduction

THERE ARE COUNTLESS COMPELLING rivalries in Australian sport. Some, such as the rugby league rivalry between New South Wales and Queensland, are followed fervently by hundreds of thousands of people. Others, such as Wangaratta versus the Wangaratta Rovers in Australian Rules football, captivate small rural communities. But what is it that makes a *great* rivalry? The most important ingredient is tumult, closely followed by time.

Many of Australia's most famous sporting rivalries have histories that date back more than a century. For instance, Australia and England took part in the first recognised cricket Test match in 1877, although Test series between the nations did not become known as 'the Ashes' until 1882, when the Aussies beat their colonial masters at the Oval in London. A mock obituary was subsequently published in *The Sporting Times*, which proclaimed that English cricket had died and 'the body will be cremated and the ashes taken to Australia'. All these years on, the cricketing rivalry between the nations runs so deep that it is defying the general waning interest in the game's longest form.

Australian Rules football's greatest adversaries, Carlton and Collingwood, played their first match in the same year as that history-making cricket Test at the Oval. Friends during their early years, the clubs soon became bitter enemies, their clashes drawing larger and larger crowds until a record attendance of 121,696 crammed into the Melbourne Cricket Ground to see them square off in the 1970 VFL grand final. The most extraordinary chapter in their rivalry was written that afternoon, when the Blues came from 44 points down at half time and swamped the Magpies in a dramatic finish. Carlton would defeat Collingwood in two more grand finals during the following 11 seasons, those classic contests cementing the rivalry in Australian sporting folklore.

It has also taken more than a century to build the rugby union rivalry between the Wallabies and the All Blacks into the fabled battle it has become. Similarly, New South Wales and Queensland have been squaring off since 1908. Matches between the Blues and Maroons have come to represent the broader animosity between the states and their people, and this is a key reason why the clashes have become such passionate expressions of state pride.

When it comes to tumult, it is hard to top the rivalry between Australia and New Zealand in netball. So closely matched are the teams that every match they play is like a world championship final. The fact the teams have been ranked number one and two in the world for the best part of 80 years just adds to the intensity and passion on display, on and off the court, whenever the Diamonds take on the Silver Ferns.

Great sporting rivalries between individuals last for a much shorter period of time, but they are no less passionate or compelling. It is not hard to find footy fans in Melbourne pubs who want to regale you with stories of the great Carey–Jakovich battles during the 1990s and early 2000s; similarly, cricket fans still talk about the way Shane Warne cast a spell over one of South Africa's most talented batsmen, Daryll Cullinan, during the same period.

Great rivalries can't be created overnight by a marketing wiz on a computer, although plenty of attempts are made as new clubs are added to century-old competitions. Rather, it takes a mixture of time and dramatic events to build up the passion and engagement that leads a sportsperson or fan to grit their teeth and mutter, 'It's us against them.'

Racing drivers Dick Johnson and Peter Brock were fierce rivals for more than three decades. During most of that time, Johnson was Ford's main man and Brock was Holden's pin-up boy.

MOTORSPORT
Holden *vs* Ford

IF YOU STRIKE UP a conversation with a few passionate Holden or Ford fans in your local pub, they might bend your ear with some considered points of debate such as these:

> What do you call a Ford at the top of a hill?
> A mirage.
> What do you call two Fords at the top of a of a hill?
> A miracle.
> What do you get if you cross an Aussie with a lawnmower?
> A Holden.
> What's the difference between a Holden and an elephant?
> One is big and slow and the other is an elephant.

Those jokes might seem rather silly to people who are not interested in cars – or in watching others drive cars at high speed around famous racetracks such as Bathurst and Sandown – but the fact that there are countless websites dedicated to them demonstrates the parochial nature of the Holden and Ford rivalry, which has dominated Australian motorsport for more than six decades.

The rivalry began away from the racetracks, in the early 1900s, when General Motors and Ford, two of the biggest American car manufacturers, began to make their presence felt Down Under.

In the early years both GM and Ford exported fully built cars from North America to Australia, but they soon came to the conclusion that building cars in Australia would be cheaper and would allow for the development of vehicles better suited to Australian conditions. GM initially did a deal with an Adelaide-based operation called Holden Motor Body Builders, which eventually led to a merger and the formation of the General Motors Holden business that we know today (its cars have sported the simple 'Holden' name since the merger in 1931). In contrast, Ford started a new business of its own, Ford Australia, and built a state-of-the-art factory in Victoria's second-largest city, Geelong. The move inspired GMH to respond by building its own factory at Fishermans Bend, in Melbourne's inner south.

During their early years of operation, both factories assembled cars from parts made overseas. But soon after the end of the Second World War, the federal government set about trying to create a race among carmakers to build the first 'Australian car' – a vehicle not only assembled in Australia but also constructed from locally made parts. General Motors Holden won the highly publicised race in a canter. As Steve Bedwell has written in *Holden versus Ford: The Cars, the Culture, the Competition*: 'On 29 November 1948, with 18,000 advance dealer orders held sight unseen, the Holden 48-215 was revealed to 1000 invited guests at Fishermans Bend. Forty-four radio stations broadcast [Prime Minister] Ben Chifley's speech launching the Holden; his description must go down as the most famous words in Australian automotive history: "She's a beauty!"'

Holden's sales boomed after the release of its Australian-made vehicle, and by the mid-1950s it was leaving Ford in its wake. In response, Ford's administrators, led by managing director Charlie Smith, launched a campaign to come up with a car that would capture the imagination of Aussie buyers. The car would be built at a new assembly plant in Broadmeadows, on Melbourne's northern fringe.

To choose the design, Smith travelled to Ford's global headquarters in the American city of Detroit, where he was shown a clay model of an updated version of the Zephyr, a vehicle that was being built and sold in the United Kingdom. However, as Smith later told motoring historian John Wright, 'When they wheeled out the Zephyr at the design studios, I simply didn't like the look of it, and I said so.' Smith and his team of executives knew Ford was planning to release a new 'compact' car – to be known as the Falcon – in North America, so they asked to see a model of it. Smith was immediately won over. 'That's the car I want for Australia,' he declared.

It proved to be a very wise choice. The first Falcon, the XK, was released in September 1960 and sold almost 70,000 units in around nine months. Although Holden sold more than 200,000 units of its FB and EK models during the same period, Ford was back in the game. Its rivalry with Holden was alive once more. Bedwell quoted a motoring writer of the day: 'For the first time since 1948, Australians are being offered the type of car they want without it having to be a Holden. The Falcon is a car designed for this year, unlike the Holden, which is a rehashed version of an already long established model.'

Both Holden and Ford soon realised that being involved in motorsport – and winning races, in particular – could play a key role in their sales war. Both were won over by the 'win on Sunday, sell on Monday' idea. The holy grail at the time, as it remains today, was the endurance race now known as the Bathurst 1000.

The race was initially held at Phillip Island, Victoria, and the original distance was 500 miles. Known in its early years as the Armstrong 500 (it was sponsored by Armstrong, a manufacturer of shock absorbers), the race was designed to test the speed, performance and reliability of Australian-built cars. As a result, the rules restricted entries to 'standard, unmodified saloons built or assembled in Australia'. To put it simply, the early races did not involve purpose-built race cars. Rather, they were the exact vehicles that were on sale to the public in showrooms around the nation (although safety features, such as roll cages, were allowed to be fitted). The cars competed in four classes, which were based on the purchase price of the vehicle in Australian pounds.

The first Armstrong 500 was held on 20 November 1960. A large number of Holdens and Fords were entered, yet the race was won by a Vauxhall Cresta. A Mercedes Benz – driven by Harry Firth and Bob Jane, who would both become legends of the sport – won the following year. It was not until the third race, held in November 1962, that Ford landed the first blow in its emerging motorsport rivalry with Holden.

Ford had signalled its intention to take motorsport very seriously by forming its own team, which was listed in race programs as 'Ford Motor Co. of Australia'. The team was formed early in 1962, with Jane and Firth, who served as both a driver and as team manager, among its first recruits. That year, the pair notched Ford's first victory at Phillip Island, in an XL Falcon, in a record time of eight hours and 15 minutes.

A year later the race moved to its current home, the Mount Panorama circuit at Bathurst, New South Wales. Holden responded by building a car with the specific intention of winning the race and boosting sales. The EH S4 Special Sedan featured a larger fuel tank, better brakes and a much-improved gearbox. But although the vehicle proved very popular among revheads, it didn't achieve Holden's aim of taking home the Bathurst crown.

Instead, Ford quickly developed a reputation as a motorsport powerhouse by winning the first three events held at Bathurst. Those races were won not by a Falcon but by a lighter and less powerful car, the Cortina, a model that was very popular in the United Kingdom and Europe. Firth, who wanted to win the race rather than simply use the event to advertise the Falcon, had decided that the four-cylinder Cortina was a better option at Mount Panorama. 'Everyone was saying you've got to have V8s,' Firth recalled in an interview with AAP in 2007. 'And I said: "No, this new little car with disc brakes will go just as fast around a track as what a V8 will, and it won't wear itself out. It weighs nothing and you'll never have brake trouble with it."'

Firth was a very cunning operator – he was even nicknamed 'the Fox'. During qualifying for that first race at Bathurst, in 1963, Firth was happy to encourage his opponents' view that the Cortina was a bit of a joke. 'We did half laps,' he recalled. 'Quick on one half, then slow. Then slow on the first half, and quick on the second, so no one would actually know how fast we could go.' Firth and Jane qualified in 20th position but after just five laps were leading the race. 'Bob just pulled out down the end of the straight and passed them, and off he went into the distance,' Firth remembered. 'At the first pit stop I get in the car and we are 28 seconds in front. When we finished up we were a lap and a half in front of them, and they were livid.'

A Cortina, with Jane and George Reynolds sharing the duties behind the wheel, duly took the Ford team to its second race win in 1964. Barry Seton and Midge Bosworth made it a Cortina hat-trick when they steered their privateer entry (although sponsored by a Ford dealer) home in 1965. If you include the Phillip Island years, the scoreboard by the end of that year's 'Great Race' read Ford 4, Holden 0.

Holden and Ford's rivalry was put on the backburner for a year, in 1966, when the Morris Cooper S, a vehicle made by the British Motor Corporation, became the must-have car in Australian motorsport. At Bathurst that year (with the race now known as the Gallagher 500 after a change in sponsor), the first nine cars to cross the line were Morris Cooper S models.

Ford returned to the top of the tree the following year, thanks to the development of Australia's first 'muscle car', the XR Falcon GT, which was the first Falcon to feature a V8 engine – the 289-cubic-inch engine that powered the Ford Mustang in the United States. As with Holden's EH S4, the Falcon GT was a road car that could be purchased by the public, but it was built with the primary aim of boosting the Ford brand by winning at Bathurst. And it certainly delivered, with the blue oval's factory-backed team, now known simply as Ford Australia, scoring a one–two finish in the 1967 Gallagher 500 at Mount Panorama. Harry Firth and Fred Gibson steered the first Falcon GT across the line, and they were closely followed by the team's second entry, driven by brothers Ian and Leo Geoghegan. In showrooms across Australia Holden was still outselling Ford by about two to one, but on the racetracks Ford was a true powerhouse. Firth and Gibson's victory in 1967 meant Ford had now won at Bathurst five times, while Holden was yet to break its duck.

The balance of power on the racetracks finally tilted Holden's way in 1968, when the HK was released. It was marketed as Holden's most high-tech vehicle to date, and it came in a number of configurations that would become household names. The more family-friendly versions of the car were known as the Belmont, Kingswood and Premier, but it was the two-door coupé version that would win over countless revheads and power Holden to countless race victories. The Monaro GTS was Holden's answer to the Falcon GT, and it certainly packed a punch. It was powered by a gurgling V8 motor sourced from Chevrolet, which was larger and more powerful than the machinery under the GT's bonnet. The Monaro's arrival signalled the start of an arms race that would see Holden and Ford build more and more powerful cars, before they were finally, in the early 1970s, subjected to more stringent regulations.

On 6 October 1968 the Holden Monaro and Ford's GT Falcon went toe to toe at Bathurst in the race now titled the Hardie-Ferodo 500. It was landmark day for Holden. Not only did Bruce McPhee and Barry Mulholland score Holden's first win, but Monaros also finished second, third and fifth. The first Falcon GT to see the chequered flag was in a disappointing seventh place. Ford's official team had an even more ordinary day; its three Falcon GTs finished 12th, 31st and 42nd.

Holden further upped the ante in 1969, when it formed its own factory-backed team. The outfit was branded the 'Holden Dealer Team' because General Motors did not approve of its subsidiaries entering 'official' teams in circuit racing. This had been GM's position since the so-called Le Mans Disaster of 1955, in which more than 80 people had died after poor safety standards resulted in the debris from a smash ended up in the crowd. In fact, Holden's bosses had gained approval for the formation of HDT only because they told their superiors in Detroit that it would be owned and funded by dealers from around Australia. In reality, the team was financed by Holden's head office – which was in no doubt that winning races on a Sunday boosted sales on Monday – until it sold the operation in 1980.

HDT landed an early blow against Ford when it recruited Firth to be its team manager. Despite the fact that he had been responsible for much of Ford's success in motorsport during the 1960s, Firth had been sacked as Ford Australia team boss – at 50, he was regarded as being too old for the job. Thus, he became one of the few legends of Aussie motorsport to switch from Ford to Holden.

Not only had Firth been a brilliant driver and a cunning team manager at Ford, but he was also a brilliant mechanic and engineer. HDT was soon being run out of his workshop in Melbourne, which had previously been the headquarters of Ford's factory-backed outfit. As AAP explained in 2007: 'He would do his calculations in chalk on the floor of his workshop, then oversee every aspect of development and preparation, even down to hand-cutting tyre treads on the morning of the race so they would exactly suit the conditions.'

Firth also had an eye for talent. Among the first drivers he recruited was a hot-headed and brash young man from Melbourne's northern fringe by the name of Peter Brock, whose father was a Holden dealer. Firth would hand Brock the hardware he needed to win races, and Brock would pay Firth back with some of the most skilful driving Australian motorsport has ever seen. Brock spoke to the ABC's Peter Thompson about Firth in 2006: '[Harry] knew that he would cause you to dig deep. He didn't like it when you scratched a car. And so it taught you a lot about the respect for the machinery and, I guess, the very rigid disciplines you had to impose upon yourself if you were going to be rewarded with the result. And the result was pleasing Harry, winning the race and feeling good within yourself that you actually gave it your best shot.'

Brock made his debut at Bathurst in 1969, driving a Firth-prepared HT Monaro GTS 350. That race proved to be the first classic Holden versus Ford battle, as the two manufacturers filled the first seven placings – three Holdens and four Fords. Firth's golden touch was evident from that very race, as HDT finished first, third and sixth. Colin Bond and Tony Roberts took the chequered flag, while Brock and his co-driver, Des West, finished third. One spot behind Brock was a Ford Australia XW Falcon GTHO, driven by Allan Moffat and Alan Hamilton.

The narrow gap between Brock's Holden and Moffat's Ford was a sign of things to come. Over the following decade, they would emerge as the pin-up boys of Aussie touring car racing, with Channel 7 using its pioneering coverage to telecast their deeds straight into the lounge rooms of Holden and Ford fans all over the country. Brock spoke to Andrew Denton on the ABC's chat show *Enough Rope* in 2006 about the emerging rivalry:

> [Moffat] was the toughest competitor that I ever faced. The rivalry was so intense we never flew on the same airline together. Now, along with Moffat, who was a very strong-minded individual with a group of people around him, they didn't talk to the Holden people. We felt like we were the white hats and they were the black hats. Gradually, that really grew up into a real tribal situation, where nowadays it's the red and the blue. It's the red team versus the blue oval guys type of thing. If you're a Ford person, you don't talk to a Holden person. If you switch camps – if you said, 'Oh I used to be a Holden fan,' the answer is, 'Well you never were.'

Moffat became the first of the two to win Bathurst when he single-handedly drove his XW Falcon GTHO Phase II to victory in 1970 (a number of leading drivers completed the entire race on their own between 1970 and 1972, before the rules were changed and having a co-driver became mandatory). Driving a Holden Torana at Mount Panorama for the first time, Brock finished a disappointing 37th.

Brock's boss, Harry Firth, had made the decision to switch from racing V8 Monaros to the smaller and lighter but less powerful six-cylinder Torana in the months leading up to the 1970 race. Harking back to the days when he turned the four-cylinder Ford Cortina into a racetrack weapon, Firth believed the Torana would be more nimble and reliable. He would eventually be proved right, but in its early iterations the Torana simply didn't have the straight-line speed to match either the Falcon or the new muscle car on the scene, the Chrysler Valiant Charger. which had been eagerly adopted by the Geoghegan brothers. With Holden somewhat sidelined, Moffat continued his domination of Brock at Bathurst, winning the Hardie-Ferodo 500 again in 1971, this time in an XY Falcon GTHO Phase III. That year the big Falcons filled five of the first six places. Ford had now recorded six victories in the Great Race, while Holden had won it only twice.

Despite all his success, Moffat never quite captured the public's imagination. A serious and studious man who had spent his early years in Canada, he was perceived by many racing fans – even the Ford supporters who loved the nerveless way be drove his dangerously powerful Falcon – as being somewhat aloof and cold. In contrast, Brock – a chain-smoking, beer-drinking, womanising 'Aussie' bloke from a battler background – soon emerged as a folk hero.

The key for Brock was winning at Bathurst for the first time, which he did in an updated Torana in 1972. Rain fell during much of that race, and the Holden fans on the mountain marvelled at the way he skilfully negotiated the tough conditions. Brock reminisced about the race with motorsport writer Peter Clark in 1997:

> I was in a car with lightly grooved slick tyres. I had this tremendous tussle with Allan Moffat and it went on for an hour and a half, and finally I was hassling him at the top the mountain. As we went through Reid Park, he was looking in his rear view mirror at me and I remember to this day, seeing the whites of his eyes looking at me as I was driving down the inside. The tail of his Falcon just slid wide in the excess moisture, which tends to collect on the outside of corner, and it spun home like a top and I was through.

Brock finished a lap clear of John French's Falcon, with Doug Chivas and Damon Beck coming home third in a Charger. In fact, this would be the only time that Australia's three largest manufacturers at the time – Holden, Ford and Chrysler – all featured on the podium at Bathurst. Having endured problems with his brakes, Moffat finished ninth. Holden had now scored three wins at Mount Panorama to Ford's six.

Brock and Moffat engaged in one of their most famous duels at Bathurst the following year, although their ding-dong battle came after what were some tumultuous months for Australian motorsport. The drama began during the second half of 1972, when the Aussie public and the nation's politicians became gripped by the so-called supercar scare. The issue related directly to the fact that only cars being sold to the public could be entered in the big race at Bathurst; the same rules also applied to another high-profile endurance race at Sandown, in Melbourne's south-eastern suburbs. Basically, the three big manufacturers had to make faster and faster cars to keep winning at the mountain, and they had to keep making at least 200 of these vehicles, which had blistering top speeds, available to the average Joes who wanted to buy them. Fearing an explosion of dangerous driving, and with the nationwide road toll soaring, a number of state governments pledged to ban the supercars.

In response to the public-relations disaster that appeared to be brewing, Holden canned its plan to build a V8 Torana and sell it to the public, Ford called a halt to the development of its Falcon GTHO Phase IV, which had been expected to dominate at Bathurst, and Chrysler stopped work on a more powerful Valiant Charger.

The Confederation of Australian Motor Sport (CAMS) decided to introduce a new category of touring car racing – Group C – featuring 'specially modified race vehicles derived from a production vehicle'. The Group C rules were basically an amalgamation of the regulations that had previously been used for the Australian Touring Car Championship (which until 1968 was a single race, rather than a series). Whereas the race at Bathurst had been an event specifically for production cars, purpose-built race cars had been competing in the ATCC since its first running in 1960. The new rules meant that in 1973 the same cars could compete in the ATCC and at Bathurst for the first time. The introduction of Group C, which meant manufacturers no longer had to sell their vehicles to the public in order for them to be eligible to race at Bathurst, were a win for safety. But they were a loss for the blokes who loved the fact that you could go out and buy an exact replica of the winning vehicle the day after the race at Bathurst.

Allan Moffat and his factory-backed Ford Falcon XY GTHO Phase III dominated the 1973 ATCC. Moffat won five of the eight races and finished 23 points clear of Peter Brock, whose Holden Torana LJ GTR XU-1 was neither fast enough nor reliable enough to keep up with his arch rival. As a result, Moffat was a hot favourite to win at Bathurst as well. The 'Great Race' had changed a lot in the 12 months since Brock had taken the chequered flag in 1972. Not only did the new Group C rules change the specifications of the cars competing in the 1973 race, but the length of the event was also changed from 500 miles (around 804 kilometres) to 1000 kilometres, in keeping with the nation's transition from the imperial system to the metric system, and it became known as the Hardie-Ferodo 1000. The number of laps of the Mount Panorama circuit rose accordingly from 130 to 163.

Moffat did win the race, but only after one of the great Ford versus Holden battles. In fact, Brock and his teammate, Doug Chivas, probably would have won if the Holden Dealer Team hadn't made a tactical error during the middle of the race and allowed the number-one Torana to run out of fuel; Chivas was forced to push the car along the pit lane to be refuelled. The skill of Brock came to the fore during the latter stages of the race. Pushing himself and his car to the limit, Brock managed to finish second behind Moffat and his co-driver, Ian Geoghegan.

HOLDEN vs FORD

However, bad news for Moffat and the legion of Ford fans came three months after the race. Although the blue oval now had eight Bathurst wins to its name, compared to three for Holden, Ford announced that it was shutting down its factory-backed team. The decision – made in January 1974 and brought on by a number of reasons, including the supercar scare and the 1973 oil crisis – robbed Moffat and his teammates of valuable expertise and, more importantly, funding. Moffat formed a new team, Allan Moffat Racing, and continued his relationship with Ford by racing Falcons, but he would struggle to compete with the cashed-up HDT over the following two seasons.

Ford wasn't the only manufacturer to pull out of racing at the time. Chrysler dropped its support for the teams that had been running its Valiant Chargers. The supercar scare and the ballooning fuel prices that resulted from the oil shock had badly dented the car's sales figures, so Chrysler decided to build smaller four-cylinder vehicles instead. With Ford offering little support to Moffat's new team and Chrysler nowhere to be seen, Holden happily picked up the slack. Not only did Holden continue to offer factory support to the HDT, but it also gave Harry Firth the support he needed to build the V8 Torana, which had been cancelled after the supercar scare. The new motor he developed made the Torana almost unbeatable, especially when Peter Brock was behind the wheel.

Brock cantered to victory in the 1974 Australian Touring Car Championship, winning five of the seven races. He had begun the series in his old LJ GTR XU-1, before switching to the seriously fast V8 Torana, the LH SL/R 5000. When the time came for the endurance races, it was expected that Brock would have no trouble winning at Bathurst for the second time, and the first 118 laps of the race panned out exactly as Holden supporters had hoped. After starting from pole position, Brock defied the wet weather by surging to a big lead. His co-driver, Brian Sampson, then capitalised on Brock's brilliance. With less than a third of the race remaining they were six laps in front.

But just when it seemed that a Brock–Sampson victory was inevitable, the Torana's mighty V8 gave way. The thousands of Holden supporters at Mount Panorama, not to mention the countless Holden executives and HDT staff at the circuit, shook their heads as the car was forced to withdraw from the event. Salt was rubbed into their wounds a couple of hours later when the privateer Ford Falcon of John Goss and Kevin Bartlett survived the atrocious conditions and crossed the line first. It was a famous against-the-odds win for Ford. The only consolation for Brock was that he'd lasted longer than Moffat, who had also been forced to withdraw from the race.

There was drama in the lead-up to the 1975 touring racing season, with Peter Brock quitting the Holden Dealer Team after setting up Team Brock with his brother Phil, but that didn't stop Colin Bond winning the ATCC for HDT. Holden then enjoyed a clean sweep of the podium places at Bathurst, although it was Brock and Sampson, whose team had far fewer resources than HDT, that won the race in a reliable and fast Torana. The victory was great reward for the winning drivers after their heartbreaking DNF (did not finish) the year before. Once again, Moffat failed to finish.

Driving a Falcon XB GT Hardtop, Moffat returned to form in 1976, winning the ATCC, but Holden struck back in the endurance races. Brock won at Sandown (the race was then called the Hang Ten 400), then Holden filled the first seven places at Bathurst, while Moffat failed to finish for the third year in succession. By the end of 1976 Holden was the dominant force on Australia's racetracks, although the battle in its showrooms was far closer, with the Falcon edging towards the lead in the sales war. The balance of power soon shifted Ford's way when it came to racing, with the key change being the formation of the Moffat Ford Dealers Team. The new team didn't enjoy quite the same level of support as the old Ford Australia team, but it was given some factory backing, and this helped Moffat reassert himself. He drove his XC Falcon GS500 to victory in seven of the 11 rounds of the 1977 ATCC, finishing well clear of his team's star recruit, former HDT gun Colin Bond.

Brock, who was driving a Torana A9X that was being funded by Holden dealer Bill Patterson, struck back to win the Hang Ten 400 at Sandown. However, Moffat's team proved to be in a class of its own in the 1977 Hardie-Ferodo 1000 at Mount Panorama. Not only did the team's two entries finish first and second, but they were also so far in front by the end that they were able to take the chequered flag in a one-two formation finish. Moffat, who shared his car with Belgian endurance racing legend Jacky Ickx, won the race, with his Falcon crossing the line half a length in front of Colin Bond and Alan Hamilton's identical car. Images of the famous formation finish were soon plastered all over the walls of Ford dealerships around the nation, and the smiles on the faces of the Ford bosses grew by the day as sales of the Falcon continued to soar.

Over in the Holden camp, there was much consternation as 1977 drew to a close. Something had to be done to get the lion roaring again. Most people involved with the Holden Dealer Team knew there was only one answer to their malaise: bring back Peter Brock. A change of team manager – Harry Firth stepped aside for the younger John Sheppard – paved the way for Brock to return.

It proved to be a brilliant recruiting move, as the combination of Brock and HDT was to dominate Australian touring car racing for the following decade. Brock cemented his position as an Aussie folk hero by enjoying a hat trick of wins at Bathurst between 1978 and 1980, each of them with calm Kiwi Jim Richards as his co-driver. Brock also won the ATCC twice during that period, but it was his Bathurst victories that earned him the nickname 'King of the Mountain'.

Brock and Richards' win at Mount Panorama in 1979 was particularly amazing. Brock started from pole position and grabbed an early lead, before Richards pulled further away during his stint in the middle of the race. The vehicle was then handed back to Brock, who proved so fast that the car sporting the number 05 on its door (Brock had been promoting Victoria's anti-drink-driving message – the blood-alcohol limit being 0.05 per cent – since 1975) was six laps in front by the time it took the chequered flag. Extraordinarily, Brock had set a new lap record on the final lap of the race. It was a brilliant send-off for the Torana as a top-line race car. The following year Brock and Richards delivered a brilliant advertisement for Holden's new family car when they drove a VC Commodore to victory. By the end of the 1980 Hardie-Ferodo 1000, Brock had scored five of Holden's eight wins at the mountain. Yet Ford still led the overall tally at Bathurst, having recorded ten wins in the Great Race, with Moffat responsible for four of them.

Ford might actually have won in 1980 if Queenslander Dick Johnson, who had begun his career racing a Holden Torana, had not suffered one of the worst pieces of luck in Bathurst history. Johnson's XD Falcon, which had started from second place on the grid, was 40 seconds in front when, on lap 18, he swerved to miss a tow truck and collided with a large rock that had rolled onto the track; it turned out that the truck had been despatched to pick up the rock. Although the rock was only the size of a soccer ball, it managed to badly damage the front end of his car.

The incident not only forced Johnson out of the race but also looked set to end his promising career. Johnson had taken on a huge debt in an attempt to assemble a car good enough to win the Hardie-Ferodo 1000, and the rock had now shattered his dream. Ford fans immediately sensed a Holden-led conspiracy, believing their man had been deliberately put out of the race by some passionate Brock supporters. In fact, as Johnson revealed in an interview with AAP to mark the 30th anniversary of the incident, nothing of the sort had taken place:

> You're not going to believe this but about two years ago I got an email from a guy who said he was a resident of Bathurst and if I wanted to ring him he would give me the full story. They were sitting at that spot where the rock was and these two guys who had obviously been out on the turps all night came and sat right down in front of them. One guy sat on a rock with his head in his hands because he obviously wasn't feeling that well and the other lay down with his head on a rock and played with another rock with his feet. He dislodged this rock and it rolled down the hill on to the bloody track. They got up and took off at 100 miles an hour, never to be seen again.

Funnily enough, Johnson souvenired the rock and put it in a glass case; it's now on display in his office.

Rather than end his career, the crash with the rock actually proved to be the making of Johnson. Shortly after the incident, he conducted an emotional interview with Channel 7 in which he made public his financial situation. This resonated with Ford fans across the nation, and donations soon poured in. When Ford decided to match the donations dollar for dollar, Johnson was back in business. Over the following decade he would achieve all of his goals and more, starting with the ATCC–Bathurst double in 1981. After his victory at Mount Panorama that year, in a race that was shortened due to a six-car accident on lap 121, he was officially Ford's number-one man. And – like Brock, but unlike Moffat, who by then was racing a Mazda – he had become a genuine hero of the battlers. Johnson also became a hero with Ford's head office, as his success on the racetrack boosted sales of the Falcon, helping Ford outsell Holden for the first time.

The personal battle between Dick Johnson and Peter Brock drove the Ford versus Holden rivalry. And although Johnson had enjoyed his moment in the sun in 1981, Brock soon put the Holden Dealer Team back on top, especially when the race was at Bathurst. Brock earned himself a new nickname, Peter Perfect, when he scored another hat trick of wins at Mount Panorama between 1982 and 1984. All three were won alongside ex-Formula 1 driver (and renowned mechanical genius) Larry Perkins. The first and third of these wins were relatively straightforward, with a combination of brilliant driving and mechanical excellence ruling the days. However, the pair won the 1983 race – which by then was known as the James Hardie 1000 – in controversial fashion.

As per the rules of the time, Brock and Perkins were allowed to enter themselves in each of the HDT cars that were competing in the race. When the 05 machine suffered mechanical troubles, they simply transferred to the other car and helped drive it to victory. The controversy was that Brock's brother Phil, who was to be John Harvey's co-driver in the second car, was not required to do a single lap. But the Holden fans cared little about such minor details. By the end of the 1984 race the men in red had finally levelled the Bathurst scoreboard: Holden 11, Ford 11.

Johnson scored a couple of blows through this period of Holden dominance at Bathurst, winning the ATCC in 1982 (in an XD Falcon) and in 1984 (in an XE Falcon). In late 1984, however, the Confederation of Australian Motorsport decided that local touring car racing should be held under the Group A regulations that governed the sport throughout continental Europe, Great Britain and Japan. The decision to scrap the old Group C regulations impacted Aussie racing in two key ways: European entries became common in local races, especially the higher-profile events such as Bathurst, and the rivalry between Holden and Ford was diminished. Between 1985 and 1987 the ATCC was won by BMW (twice) and Volvo. In 1987 Holden's fabled Commodore didn't win a single championship race.

Yet it was Ford's decision not to build a Group A-spec Falcon that was the major reason for the rivalry being put on the backburner for a few years. Holden, in contrast, fully supported the development of a Group A Commodore for Brock's HDT, but when Johnson lined up in the 1985 James Hardie 1000 in a Ford Mustang – a car not freely available in Australia – rather than a Falcon, it just wasn't the same. Ford and Holden fans looked on in bewilderment as a pair of Jaguars, from a team owned by a Pom by the name of Tom Walkinshaw, finished first and third. A Venezuelan and an Italian, driving a BMW 635, finished second. Brock had been on the lead lap during the closing stages before his Commodore suffered mechanical problems.

Although the Jaguars struggled with reliability issues the following year, Ford's many supporters were again left bemused when their one-time favourite, Allan Moffat, signed up to be Peter Brock's co-driver for the 1986 race at Bathurst. Seeing Moffat tearing around Mount Panorama in the 05 car was enough to make a fan of the blue oval cry.

As it turned out, Moffat didn't enjoy his finest weekend behind the wheel. Although Brock had recorded the second-fastest time during Friday's practice session, Moffat crashed the car later that day and the HDT mechanics were unable to repair it in time for Saturday's Top 10 shootout. As a result, it had to start the race from 11th place on the grid. Brock flew through the field during the early laps, and his ninth win at Bathurst seemed to be on the cards. But Moffat cost the team valuable time when he drove too fast over a speed hump in the pit lane and shattered the oil filter. The car eventually finished fifth, only one lap down on the winning Commodore (sponsored by Chickadee Chicken), which was driven by Alan Grice and Graeme Bailey. Johnson finished fourth in his Mustang, but his was the only Ford to finish the race.

The rivalry between Holden and Ford changed again in 1987. Among the reasons was Ford's decision to stop development of the Group A-spec V8 Mustang, and instead encourage its teams to race a turbocharged European hatchback known as a Sierra. Dick Johnson Racing was among the teams that adopted the Sierra, which was seriously fast, very nimble and posed a serious threat to Brock and his fellow Commodore drivers. Given that the Sierra was not available to the Australian public, however, Ford fans had very mixed feelings about it.

There were Sierras aplenty on the grid at Bathurst in 1987, when the James Hardie 1000 was included – for the first and only time – in the World Touring Car Championship. A huge number of international teams and drivers descended on Bathurst, with the Sierras run by the Swiss-based Texaco team running rings around the local drivers and manufacturers in qualifying. There was much murmuring of disapproval in the grandstands when the two Texaco Sierras finished first and second in the race, although Peter Brock saved some local pride by driving the Holden Dealer Team's second Commodore (the 05 car had suffered mechanical problems early on) into third place. At the traditional post-race presentation, the hundreds of fans gathered below the podium gave Brock a hero's reception, then booed loudly when the European Texaco drivers accepted their trophies.

Remarkably, there was a further twist in the tail. When the scrutineers looked over the cars after the race, the Texaco cars were found to have illegally modified wheel arches. They were summarily disqualified, and Holden fans celebrated when Brock was awarded his ninth Bathurst win.

The Holden supporters' joy was short-lived, however. Brock's relationship with Holden, which had been steadily deteriorating for a number of years, crumbled in the months after that famous win at Mount Panorama. Much of the tension had been brought on by a mysterious addition that Brock was making to the hotted-up Holdens that he sold under the HDT brand. Brock was by now a far different man to the smoking, drinking party boy of the 1970s. He had changed his lifestyle in many ways, which included adopting vegetarianism and taking an interest in spirituality. As part of this personal change, he had come to believe in the benefits of the Energy Polariser, which was basically a small box of magnets and crystals, whose benefits were supposedly proven by some very suspect pseudoscience. Brock was convinced that the polariser could make a car's engine perform better; Holden, on the other hand, thought it was nothing more than a con. Fearing a backlash, Holden's bosses demanded that HDT stop using the polariser. Affronted, Brock cut ties with the manufacturer that had made his career, and the name Holden Dealer Team disappeared from race programs.

After renaming his team Mobil 1 Racing, Brock raced a BMW in 1988, before making the extraordinary decision to switch to a Ford Sierra. Ford fans suddenly had both Brock and Johnson, the two greatest drivers of the 1980s, on their team. The switch to a Sierra helped Brock regain his verve. In 1989 he won a round of the ATCC for the first time since 1986; he also took pole position at Bathurst for the newly renamed Tooheys 1000, although a mechanical failure forced him out midway through the race.

Ford's Sierra – which was almost unbeatable in short races, winning every round of the ATCC in 1988 – was an even better friend to Johnson. 'Tricky Dicky' took out the ATCC in 1988 and 1989, and also won at Bathurst in 1989. Ford fans certainly enjoyed Johnson's success during this period, but the rivalry with Holden just wasn't the same. It seemed crazy that while the battle in the showrooms was Falcon versus Commodore, the duels on the track involved a European car that was never seen on Australian roads.

Finally, in 1993, motorsport's administrators bowed to public pressure and created a new category of touring racing, banning the Sierra and the Nissan Skyline GT-R in the process. The Skyline, a turbo-charged all-wheel-drive monster that, like the Sierra, was not freely available to Australian consumers, had proven wildly unpopular with local race fans.

Its unpopularity was first laid bare when one-time Holden hero Jim Richards and young gun Mark Skaife drove their Skyline to victory at Bathurst in 1991. The Nissan crossed the line to just a smattering of applause, with the roar of approval reserved for a Holden Racing Team Commodore driven by Win Percy and Alan Grice, which finished second. A year later, the reception was even worse when Richards and Skaife were declared the winners of the 1992 Tooheys 1000 after heavy rain had forced the officials to stop the race. Richards and Skaife were jeered wildly when they were presented with their trophy; Richards responded by leaning into a microphone and saying, 'I'm just really stunned for words. I can't believe the reception . . . this is bloody disgraceful. I'll keep racing, but I tell you what, this is going to remain with me for a long time. You're a pack of arseholes.' He later apologised for the outburst.

Richards was soon back in favour when he began driving a Commodore after the new rules for Aussie touring car racing were introduced for the 1993 season. The rules favoured V8 cars that were locally made. Ford promptly backed the development of an eight-cylinder EB Falcon, and soon the battle that most race fans had been baying for – V8 Falcon versus V8 Commodore – was back on. To top it all off, Peter Brock was driving a Holden again.

He had returned to the red lion in 1991, fielding a team in conjunction with his old teammate Larry Perkins. After a couple of mediocre seasons, his career went full circle when he rejoined the Holden factory-backed outfit, which by then was known as the Holden Racing Team. However, a tenth Bathurst title proved elusive for Brock, even with the resources of Holden's head office behind him. In fact, it was Perkins who, along with Russell Ingall, drove a Commodore to victory in the first race at Bathurst held under the new V8-friendly rules.

In 1994 the ATCC and Bathurst 1000 became events exclusively for Holden Commodores and Ford Falcons powered by V8 engines. Then, three years later, a marketing deal with the powerful International Management Group spurred the creation of the V8 Supercars brand, sparking a boom time for the sport. Crowds in their hundreds of thousands began turning out for new and innovative race meetings, such as Adelaide's Clipsal 500, which was held on the streets that had previously played host to the Australian Formula 1 Grand Prix. The series also headed overseas, with races held in New Zealand, Bahrain, the United Arab Emirates and China. And it was the fans' deep passion for the Holden versus Ford rivalry that underpinned all this growth.

The parity between the Holdens and Fords competing in the various races was another key reason that the popularity of the sport exploded. The close racing was engineered by a number of regulations, which were designed to ensure that meant all the cars on the grid, regardless of whether they were Holdens or Fords, used many of the same parts. Control tyres were also introduced as a way of evening up the racing. It meant the racing was consistently close and featured countless passing moves – a far different scenario to the mundane racing that has blighted Formula 1. But even though the cars became virtually the same under their skins, the fans were unfazed. To them, a car carrying a lion badge was a Holden, a vehicle sporting a blue oval was a Ford, and that was that.

The arrival of some marketable and very talented new drivers also boosted the profile of the V8 Supercars. As Brock and Johnson entered middle age and stepped back from full-time racing, Brock's protégé, Craig Lowndes, was among the young guns to emerge.

A lightning-fast and fearless driver who had grown up in Melbourne, Lowndes shot to prominence when, at the age of 20, he went toe-to-toe with Dick Johnson's co-driver, John Bowe, in the closing stages of the 1994 Tooheys 1000. In a classic Holden versus Ford duel, Lowndes, who was driving a Commodore for the Holden Racing Team, grabbed the lead with a daring overtaking manoeuvre, before Bowe managed to put his Falcon back in front. Although Bowe held on and won the race for the blue oval, it was clear that Lowndes was going to be a star. Two years later, in 1996, he won the ATCC, and then the again renamed AMP Bathurst 1000 (with Greg Murphy as his co-driver). During what was a very successful seven-year stint with the Holden Racing Team, Lowndes also won the ATCC, in 1998 and 1999, the year that the ATCC was renamed the V8 Supercars Championship Series. At the end of the 2000 season, however, he stunned Holden's many fans by defecting to Ford. It was the most high-profile move since Brock had quit Holden in 1987.

Lowndes initially drove for Gibson Motorsport, then in 2003 switched to the blue oval's number-one factory-backed team, Ford Performance Racing. After consecutive second-place finishes at Bathurst, he moved to Triple Eight Race Engineering, a British-based team that had decided to enter the V8 Supercars after receiving substantial backing from Ford's head office.

Initially, Lowndes found it difficult to compete with another darling of the Ford fans, Marcos Ambrose, who twice won the V8 Supercar Championship Series in the early 2000s. But in 2006, when

Ambrose headed to the United States to try to crack the lucrative NASCAR circuit, and after Triple Eight had fixed the reliability issues with its Falcon, Lowndes became Ford's brightest star since Dick Johnson. From that year, he and co-driver Jamie Whincup won three consecutive races at Bathurst.

The first of those victories was a career-defining moment for Lowndes. Still grieving after his hero and mentor Peter Brock had died in a rallying accident in Western Australia, Lowndes produced a faultless drive. He and Whincup were subsequently awarded the inaugural Peter Brock trophy in an emotional post-race ceremony. Lowndes' effort to win that race drew respect from fans of both Holden and Ford.

Later that year, the old rivalry flared again when the final round of the championship took place at Phillip Island. Lowndes went into the last race of the year narrowly trailing Holden's Rick Kelly. But the day ended in acrimony after the pair collided when Lowndes tried to overtake his rival. Lowndes was furious, believing Kelly had deliberately run him off the road. Protests were lodged and hearings held, but, to the delight of Holden supporters and the manufacturer's bosses, Kelly was cleared of any wrongdoing and declared the champion. Kelly's teammate, Garth Tander, won the championship for Holden the following year, before Whincup emerged from Lowndes' shadow and began his own period of dominance.

A former go-kart driver, Whincup put Ford back on top by driving his Falcon to victory in the 2008 and 2009 V8 Supercar Championship Series. But fans of the blue oval were sent into a spin when Ford withdrew its support for Triple Eight Racing; the team promptly switched to Holden, taking Whincup and Lowndes with it. In 2011 Whincup became only the second man (Norm Beechy was the first) to have won ATCC/V8 Supercar Championship Series in both a Ford and a Holden. He backed that up by winning his fourth title in 2012, which capped off a remarkable period of dominance for the red lion – Holden scored four consecutive wins at Bathurst between 2009 and 2012.

Nevertheless, the rivalry between Holden and Ford was very much alive during 2012, with allegations of race-fixing levelled at Triple Eight Racing during the final round of the series, which was held on the streets of Sydney Olympic Park. Tensions had flared after Whincup allowed Lowndes to pass him during race one, a move that meant Lowndes leapfrogged Ford's Mark Winterbottom into second place in the championship.

After 20 years of V8 touring car racing involving only Holden Commodores and Ford Falcons, the rivalry has been watered down again. The 2013 racing season saw the introduction of the new 'Car of the Future' rules, which aim to substantially reduce the amount of money it costs to run a V8 Supercars by largely standardising the vehicles. As a result, a team backed by Nissan entered the 2013 International V8 Supercars Championship Series (the new name was adopted because races are now held in a range of overseas locations, including the US state of Texas), while Stone Brothers Racing, previously a loyal Ford team, switched to Mercedes. As when the Group A rules had been introduced back in 1985, the latest changes failed to please the passionate Holden and Ford fans. In fact, brothers Todd and Rick Kelly received hate mail after they announced they were switching from Holden Commodores to Nissan Altimas.

The Holden versus Ford rivalry is also under threat away from the track. There was once a time when more than 50 per cent of cars sold in Australia were Holdens or Fords, but these days imported vehicles made in Asia by Mazda and Hyundai are far more popular. Sales of the Falcon have plummeted since the glory days of the early 1980s; as recently as 1995, an average of nearly 7000 Falcons were being sold each month, but in February 2012 just 931 were sold, the lowest monthly figure in the Falcon's 51-year history. Sales of the Commodore are not holding either, with Australian buyers now favouring smaller imported models.

Not only are the big Aussie-made sedans almost things of the past, the entire local car industry – which is now heavily reliant on government support to keep it afloat – appears unlikely to survive in the long term. Just how this will impact on the passion that has fuelled the competition between Holden and Ford on Australia's racetracks remains to be seen, but it seems probable that the glory days of the rivalry between the red lion and the blue oval are now in the past.

HOLDEN vs FORD (1960–2012)
Australian Touring Car Championship/ V8 Supercar Championship Series
Ford: 23 wins: 1964–69, 1973, 1976–77, 1981–82, 1984, 1988–89, 1993, 1995, 1997, 2003–05, 2008–10
Holden: 17 wins: 1970, 1974–75, 1978–80, 1994, 1996, 1998–2002, 2006–07, 2011, 2012

Phillip Island 500/Bathurst 500/Bathurst 1000
Holden: 29 wins: 1968–69, 1972, 1975–76, 1978–80, 1982–84, 1986–87, 1990, 1993, 1995–97, 1999–2005, 2009–12
Ford: 17 wins: 1962–65, 1967, 1979, 1971, 1973–74, 1977, 1981, 1988–89, 1994, 1998, 2006–08

Carlton's Alex Jesaulenko takes his famous high mark over Collingwood's Graeme 'Jerker' Jenkin in the 1970 Victorian Football League grand final at the MCG.

AUSTRALIAN RULES
Collingwood vs Carlton

CARLTON AND COLLINGWOOD HAVE not met in a grand final since 1981, and they have not met in a final of any type since 1988, but the reaction to Mick Malthouse's appointment as Blues coach in late 2012 showed that their long-standing rivalry remains as fierce as ever.

In the days leading up to Malthouse being officially unveiled as Carlton's new boss, fans of both clubs took to talkback radio and social media to voice their passionate views on the Blues' all-but-certain decision to hire the man who had led Collingwood to a premiership just two years prior. Some Blues fans perceived Malthouse as a saviour; others were disgusted that a man so closely tied to the Magpies was now the most important person at their club.

Mick's move was just as hard to swallow for Collingwood supporters, as passionate Pie fan William Shack wrote on his blog 'The Sporting Religion':

> He knows what it means to love the black and white. He grew up supporting them so I really don't think he could coach Carlton. If he does, then that's it for me. He will be enemy number one. His entire character will be called into question and I will be forced to hate him. To coach Carlton after coaching Collingwood to a premiership, and after reneging on a contract to stay at

Collingwood until 2015 would be a stain on his wonderful Collingwood legacy. It would be showing complete disdain for the Collingwood Football Club and its fans. This is Carlton, the land of the arrogant and expecting. The club who has broken Collingwood's heart more than any other. 1915, 1938, 1970, 1979, 1981. This club broke Mick's heart! How could you coach them after growing up supporting Collingwood?

But Malthouse did take the job, and Shack, like thousands of other Magpies supporters, was forced to confront the reality of seeing his man kitted out in navy blue.

Despite the passionate rivalry that exists today, the relationship between Carlton and Collingwood was decidedly civil from their first meeting in the Victorian Football Association in 1892 until the early years of the 20th century. Fitzroy, winner of the VFA premiership in 1895 and Victorian Football League premierships in 1898, 1899, 1904 and 1905, was the power club of that time, boasting better players, better facilities and more money than just about all of its rivals. Carlton and Collingwood, also located in Melbourne's inner-northern suburbs, saw benefits in helping each other compete with their dominant rival.

The early tradition of civility began after their initial contest in 1892, which was in fact Collingwood's first official match. By that time Carlton had been in operation for 28 years, so the Blues felt they should give the new boys a leg-up. 'While the match was billed as "a tug of war between the old and the new",' Michael Roberts and Glenn McFarlane write in *The Official Collingwood Illustrated Encyclopedia*, 'Carlton magnanimously agreed to donate its share of the gate takings to the new club. The offer was gratefully accepted.' The Magpies' coffers were bolstered considerably by the Blues' generosity, as the crowd at Victoria Park was around 16,000 people.

Five years later, in the first season of the VFL, Collingwood came to the aid of Carlton when the Blues found themselves in financial trouble. 'The man who captained Collingwood's very first VFL team in 1897, Bill Strickland, was a Brunswick boy who'd led Carlton in the VFA and played in its 1887 premiership team,' Peter Hanlon wrote in an article about the rivalry that was published in *The Age* in late 2012. 'Blues historian Tony De Bolfo notes that, in missing the last game of the 1892 VFA season, Strickland avoided the first Collingwood win over Carlton in what would become football's greatest rivalry.'

Even after the Blues emerged from their troubles to win three successive premierships in 1906, 1907 and 1908, the two clubs remained 'friendly' competitors. The rivalry that we know today, however, which is very much grounded in animosity, dates back to 1 October 1910, when the Blues and the Magpies met in what remains one of Victorian football's most infamous grand finals.

The lead-up to the game had been filled with controversy. Not only were most clubs clandestinely breaking the rules that banned payments to players, but a match-fixing scandal had also cast a shadow over the finals series. This concerned Carlton's loss to bottom team St Kilda in the final round of home-and-away matches. One Blues player subsequently accused three of his teammates – Alex Lang, Douglas Fraser and Doug Gillespie – of accepting money from gamblers to play dead. Gillespie was subsequently cleared of any wrongdoing, but Lang and Fraser were banned for five years.

The other problem afflicting the VFL was on-field violence. Brawls had marred a host of games throughout the 1910 season, which led most pundits to predict a spiteful conclusion to the season. As McFarlane wrote in *Grand Finals, Volume 1, 1897–1938*: 'There were more ominous signs on the eve of the big game that tensions were running deep. The *Herald*'s cartoon depiction of season 1910 had a Collingwood player and a Carlton player brawling, scratching and slinging punches. No one knew just how prophetic this would be. Less than 24 hours after the paper had rumbled off the presses and found its way onto the streets of Melbourne, what had been predicted was coming true at the MCG.

Despite the predictions of mayhem, the first three quarters were played in a hard but largely fair manner, with Collingwood holding sway, thanks to the skilful play of full-forward Dick Lee and the bullocking defending of Jock McHale. But any friendliness between the Magpies and Blues went up in smoke just a few minutes into the final quarter, when a clash between Carlton half-forward Jack Bacquie and Collingwood rover Tom Baxter sparked a wild brawl that threatened to become a full-scale riot. The following day's *Argus* newspaper recounted the scene in graphic detail: 'Bacquie, standing opposite the Harrison Stand, rose for a mark. Baxter rose a second later. As the two men regained their feet, their arms locked about the ball. Bacquie wrenched and twisted. Baxter hung on tenaciously. Bacquie fell back and Baxter was still gripping the ball. Bacquie released one hand and Baxter freed one of his hands. Bacquie, hot with rage at his possession being so obstinately disputed, raised his hand and in a second the two men fell to the ground fighting.'

From there, it was on for young and old. Players ran from all over the field as the fracas developed into a brawl. Not only were many of the players landing blows upon one another, but they also unleashed tirades of verbal abuse that could be heard from the sidelines. Soon, club officials became involved, and the situation threatened to erupt into a riot when the acrimony spread to the crowd. As *The Argus* reported, 'policemen bolted from the sides and 20 or 30 men from the rival camps jumped over the fence and set out to take part'.

The field umpire, Jack Elder, saved the day by throwing the ball up in the middle of the ground and declaring the game back on. The players suddenly remembered there was a premiership to be won and, as Elder recounted in the *Sporting Globe* some years later: 'the swinging rights and lefts stopped like magic. I feel certain that if I had failed to get the game going that day the crowd would have swarmed onto the ground and the rival camps of barrackers would have been at each other's throats.'

Collingwood held its nerve in the closing stages and won by 14 points, yet its victory was tarnished by what had taken place during the final quarter. The VFL tribunal came down very hard on the chief protagonists, Baxter and Bacquie, who were both suspended for a season – although Collingwood later managed to have Baxter's ban overturned. Two others, Collingwood's Jim Shorten and Carlton's Percy Sheehan, were banned for a season and a half. The football writers of the day almost universally described the game, and especially the brawl, as a disgrace. Although it remains an infamous afternoon in the long and distinguished history of Australian Rules football, it is these days also celebrated as the day when one of the code's greatest rivalries was ignited.

The Magpies celebrated their 1910 premiership long and hard, which was just as well, as Carlton would beat them in the next five grand finals contested by the two clubs. The first of those took place in 1915, only a few months after a number of former VFL players, including former Carlton defender Fenley John McDonald, had died during the Gallipoli landing in Turkey. In fact, the war had almost resulted in the season being called off. It only went ahead because, as Carlton's 1915 annual report recorded: 'it was felt that the playing of football on Saturday afternoons had no adverse effect on recruiting, was a relaxation for the public from the serious problems of business and war, and that it would be unwise to deprive thousands of people of that source of recreation.'

The Blues and the Magpies were the top two teams for most of the 1915 season, and each of the games they played that year captivated

Melbourne's ever-growing band of football fans. A huge crowd turned out when they clashed for the first time at Carlton's home ground, Princes Park, in Round 7. It proved to be a classic contest. Dick Lee kicked nine goals for Collingwood, yet the Blues won by two points in what *The Argus* claimed was 'as even and as brilliant a contest as could possibly be seen'. The return match, played at Collingwood's Victoria Park fortress, was just as good. The result was the same, although this time Carlton prevailed by just one point.

Despite those two losses to its arch-enemy, Collingwood finished the 1915 home-and-away season on the top of the ladder, and the Magpies went into the much-anticipated grand final against Carlton as warm favourites. The lead-up to the big game was filled with drama and intrigue. For a start, Collingwood captain–coach Jock McHale decided to lure his former teammate Ted Rowell out of retirement to play. Next, as passionate Carlton men Tony De Bolfo and Howard Kotton write in one of their contributions to *Grand Finals, Volume 1, 1897–1938*: 'Controversy also enveloped Collingwood players Paddy Rowan and Malcolm 'Doc' Seddon. Both men were enlisted in the army. On the morning of the match they had to complete a 16-kilometre march called by the drill sergeant at their Seymour barracks. Collingwood secretary E. W. Copeland chauffeured the pair back to the city for the match, while the rumour mill kicked into action. There was a rumour that the commanding officer was a Carlton fan. Although under duress, Seddon and Rowan took their places in the team.'

A crowd of almost 40,000 poured into the Melbourne Cricket Ground to witness the contest. Given the violence that had marred the previous grand final meeting between the clubs five years earlier, an air of tension hung over the famous ground. But any fears that the violence seen in 1910 would be repeated were allayed once the game began.

COLLINGWOOD vs CARLTON

It turned out to be a low-scoring affair, yet the scribes who reported on it were adamant that it was another brilliant and fair exhibition of the Australian code. Carlton led for most of the afternoon, but Collingwood rallied early in the final quarter, closing to within a point with around 15 minutes to go. But the Blues, who had appeared demoralised, regained their purpose and won by 33 points after booting the last five goals of the game. Their victory meant that, with Carlton and Collingwood having played in two grand finals, the score was one all.

It wasn't until 1938, when the clubs played in their third grand final, that the rivalry reached its next peak. As had the other two, the match captivated Melbourne. Collingwood was by then the power club of the VFL, having won eight premierships in the 23 years since losing the 1915 grand final to Carlton. During the same period, the Blues had not won another flag.

The capacity of the Melbourne Cricket Ground had recently been enlarged by the construction of a concrete monolith, known as the Southern Stand, around the outer side of the ground. However, the stadium still wasn't big enough to handle the number of people who wanted to watch the 1938 premiership decider.

The official crowd was 96,486, which was around 10,000 more than should have been allowed into the venue. So many people were sitting between the boundary line and the fence that the players had to dodge around them to get on and off the field. Hundreds of people were reported to have fainted during the match; some had been rushed to hospital when, prior to the opening bounce, the surging crowd caused a part of the fence around the oval to collapse. It was a miracle that no one died. As a scribe known as 'Forward' wrote in *The Age* the following Monday, 'Just before the great game opening the ground authorities shut the gates to prevent further accidents. This led to an angry outburst by hundreds who arrived late, and scores attempted to storm their watch into the Melbourne Cricket Club reserve.' Thankfully for the VFL, the game was largely clean and fair. If it had been anything like 1910, and if the crowd had turned violent, then spectators would almost certainly have been killed, such was the overcrowding.

Carlton went into the match as a hot favourite. The Blues had finished on top of the ladder, whereas Collingwood had made the grand final from fourth place. In that regard, the clash panned out as expected. Although Carlton's gun forward Harry Vallance kicked only one goal, the Blues led from start to finish. Yet the Magpies never gave up, and the final margin was just 15 points.

Blues fans celebrated heartily, revelling in the fact that Carlton had broken its drought against the club they loved to hate. Their victory also meant that, although Collingwood had won eight premierships, none had been over Carlton. There was, however, a tragic postscript for Carlton five years later, when its star full-back Jim Park was killed during a Second World War battle in New Guinea.

Carlton and Collingwood would not meet in another grand final until their famous battle in 1970, and this hiatus enabled VFL followers to revel in a number of other great rivalries. Richmond and Collingwood – which were both slum-ridden, working-class suburbs in the first half of the 20th century – already boasted a fearsome rivalry by then, with the animosity between them dating back to the late 1920s, when they met in three successive grand finals, the Magpies winning them all; that Collingwood team had in fact won four successive flags, earning itself the nickname The Machine. Richmond legend Jack Dyer, who played 312 games for the Tigers between 1931 and 1949, often quipped: 'I hate Collingwood so much I cant even watch black and white TV.'

After Dyer hung up his boots, becoming a much-loved media performer and commentator, Richmond's rivalry with Collingwood diminished for a period, largely because Melbourne emerged as the Magpies' greatest challenger during the 1950s and 1960s. The Demons and Collingwood enjoyed a rivalry that encapsulated the class and sectarian divides in Victoria's capital city. Melbourne was largely a Protestant club, backed by graduates of prestigious private schools who voted for the right-wing Liberal Party. Collingwood, in contrast, was a predominantly Catholic club whose supporters were Labor-voting battlers.

For around 15 years, every clash between Melbourne and Collingwood was like a grand final. In fact, the crowd of 99,256 that watched the Demons defeat the Magpies by 11 points in Round 10 of 1958 remains the record attendance for a home-and-away game in VFL/AFL history. Ultimately, Melbourne and Collingwood did battle in five grand finals between 1955 and 1964. The Demons won four of them – 1955, 1956, 1960 and 1964 – but the Magpies' victory in the 1958 decider was a particularly famous result: it prevented Melbourne from equalling Collingwood's record of four successive flags, which still stands today.

Melbourne and Collingwood continue to have a rivalry of sorts, with the clubs playing a match at the Melbourne Cricket Ground on the Queen's Birthday holiday each season. But the last chapter in their intense rivalry of the 1950s and 1960s was played out when they did battle in a thrilling grand final in 1964.

The final quarter of that game was extraordinary. Collingwood had trailed by 11 points at the final change, but the Magpies found themselves in front after hulking ruckman Ray Gabelich booted two brilliant goals. The first came after he snared the ball at a boundary throw-in, while the second is regarded as one of the greatest goals in grand final history. Gabelich won the ball on the half-forward flank and began galloping towards goal. He had four bounces – almost losing the ball on each occasion – and then, with a number of Melbourne players bearing down on him, put his running shot straight through the big sticks. The drama was not yet over, however, and Melbourne defender Neil Crompton then followed his opponent up the field and put the Demons back in front by kicking his only goal for the season. Melbourne subsequently hung on and won by four points. The result proved to be the first of many heartbreaking grand final defeats for Collingwood coach Bob Rose.

A champion player with the Magpies before he took up coaching, Rose, who died in 2003 after a long battle with cancer, experienced a number of great Australian Rules rivalries first-hand. He played for Collingwood in countless heated clashes against the likes of Carlton, Richmond and Melbourne, but he was also involved in the creation of one of the greatest rivalries in grassroots football. Rose quit the Magpies after the 1955 grand final loss to Melbourne and headed bush, becoming the playing coach of the Wangaratta Rovers in the Ovens and Murray League, a competition in Victoria's north-east. (Amazingly, he was paid far more to play for the Rovers than he had previously received to run around for Collingwood in the nation's elite competition.)

Before the arrival of Rose, the Wangaratta Rovers had lived in the shadow of their powerful local rival, the Wangaratta Football Club, which wears Collingwood's famous black and white stripes and is also known as the Magpies. Although their home grounds are separated by just a thin strip of bitumen, the two clubs were not on-field rivals until 1950, when the Rovers were promoted from the local district league to the powerful OMFL.

In the early days, all the results went one way, as Wangaratta won four premierships in a row, becoming known as the Magpies of the bush. Rose helped the Rovers turn their fortunes around, guiding the club to premierships in 1958 and 1960; in fact, he won the league's best and fairest award, the Morris Medal, in both premiership years.

Wangaratta, a town that these days has a population of around 18,000 people, now had two strong football clubs, and their evenness encouraged the development of a fearsome rivalry. Kevin Allan, a premiership player for the Wangaratta Magpies, told *The Age* in 2005: 'Our supporters in those days, they absolutely hated them [the Rovers]. They wouldn't walk into a shop owned by Rovers people and they wouldn't go into a pub where the Rovers drank. A bloke owned a fruit shop and half his family were Magpies and half were Rovers. On the Saturday when the Rovers played the Magpies there was absolute division. They wouldn't even eat together.'

Allan recalled a 75-year-old man being taken away from a Magpies–Rovers derby in a divvy van one afternoon after becoming enraged by the action off the field. Betting on the derbies also became serious business for the local men. 'In the early days they'd give the Rovers 15 or 20 to one just to get a bet,' Allan said. 'When the Rovers improved and made games out of it there was big money invested.'

In 1976 the Rovers were aiming for their third consecutive premiership, only for the Magpies to beat them in a famous local derby grand final. However, Rovers turned the tables in 1977. Nowadays, their rivalry remains strong, although it doesn't quite pack the ferocious punch that it did a couple of decades ago.

There are countless such rivalries in grassroots sport all over the nation. The story of how the football community in the western Victorian town of Hamilton became split down the middle, for example, is quite a tale. The drama began early in the 1947 season, when the Hamilton Football Club was languishing near the foot of the Western District League ladder. The club's administrators decided to sack the coach, Ken Block, and replace him with former Melbourne ruckman Jack O'Keefe, who was appointed caretaker coach for the remainder of the season. O'Keefe worked wonders with the team; Hamilton not only made the finals, it won the premiership with a one-point victory over Casterton in the grand final. Ted Kenna, who had won the Victoria Cross two years earlier for his bravery during a Second World War battle in Papua New Guinea, booted the winning behind.

Not surprisingly, O'Keefe, who had originally declared he would not be returning to Hamilton in 1948, changed his mind. During the season, however, Hamilton's vice-president, Pat Condon, had approached star Melbourne full-forward Fred Fanning, with a view to him becoming the Magpies' coach for their 1948 campaign. Fanning had married a girl from Hamilton and was planning to set up a business in the town. He was promised £12 per game – a big increase on the £3 per game he had been receiving to play for the Demons. O'Keefe's success inspired a change of heart in Condon. Three days after the 1947 grand final, he proposed that O'Keefe be reappointed coach, but this idea was summarily dismissed. The key reason was that Fanning had been promised money to join Hamilton, and the rules at the time stated that only the coach could be paid.

So enraged by the situation was Condon that he decided to start a new club, Hamilton Imperial, which set up its base opposite Hamilton's change rooms at Melville Oval. O'Keefe was appointed the new club's inaugural coach, and it didn't take long for a strong rivalry to spark up between Imps (nicknamed the Bulldogs and regarded as the Catholic working man's club) and Hamilton (regarded as the club of the Protestant graziers and 'toffs'). 'It was incredible,' three-time Melbourne premiership player Ian Ridley, who played for Imps in 1953, told *The Age* some years ago. 'Barrackers didn't talk to each other... it was "pull down the curtain" in the week before that game.' However, the rivalry between Hamilton and Hamilton Imperials has not endured. With both clubs struggling to survive, their animosity was cast aside in late 2012, when they merged to form the Hamilton Kangaroos.

It is unlikely there will ever be a truce of that kind called between Carlton and Collingwood. They remain bitter rivals, with their modern-day rivalry dating back to the famous 1970 grand final, when Bob Rose was in his eighth season at the helm of the Magpies and the legendary Ron Barassi was leading Carlton.

Rose had already led Collingwood to heartbreaking grand final losses in 1964 (to Melbourne by four points) and 1966 (to St Kilda by one point), but for about 99 per cent of the 1970 season it seemed the Magpies would finally put those disappointments behind them and secure a premiership of their own. Collingwood finished on top of the ladder, having won 18 of its 22 games, then beat Carlton by ten points in the second semi-final. When the Blues beat St Kilda a week later, the stage was set for the first Collingwood–Carlton grand final since 1938.

The contest created such a buzz that it attracted a crowd of 121,696 people, which remains the greatest attendance at an Australian Rules game. There was plenty for the huge crowd to cheer about in the first half, including Alex Jesaulenko's towering mark over Collingwood ruckman Graeme 'Jerker' Jenkin, which many years later was declared the mark of the century. It also produced one of the century's great pieces of commentary: Mike Williamson's cry of 'Jesaulenko, you beauty!'.

Yet Jesaulenko's great grab failed to inspire the Blues, and by half-time the game looked over, as Collingwood, spearheaded by five goals from star full-forward Peter McKenna, led by 44 points. In fact, the Magpies should have been further in front, having registered 23 scoring shots to just nine.

There are conflicting versions of what happened in the Collingwood and Carlton change rooms during the half-time break, although it seems that some of the Magpies' players and supporters certainly engaged in premature celebrations. In his seminal book about the match, *1970 & Other Stories of the Australian Game*, revered journalist and author Martin Flanagan tried to find out. According to Flanagan, champion Collingwood ruckman Len Thompson recalled:

> [that] raucous supporters – he says several hundred of them – that were 'somehow' admitted to the Collingwood rooms. He says the person who let them in should be shot. Twiggy Dunne remembers voices shouting, 'We've got 'em! We've got 'em! This is the one, this is our year!' He identifies one of the supporters as lawyer Frank Galbally. Fullback Jeff Clifton, who'd been positive and purposeful in the first half, dismisses as nonsense the story that champagne was flowing in the Collingwood rooms at half-time. So too – with barely suppressed anger – does Bob Rose. He sees it as being typical of the rumours that bedevilled his time as coach of Collingwood. Various players remember Rose moving to quell the euphoria, but Jenkin recalls 19-year-old Johnny Greening joining in the gleeful chorus and shouting, 'Crack the champagne, we've got 'em!'

A vastly different mood filled the Carlton rooms, as the players pondered the prospect of a huge defeat. Never one to accept such a situation, Barassi initially exploded in a fit of rage, apparently 'grabbing the wooden table carrying the half-time drinks and upending it against a wall'. Just before the Blues ran back out for the third quarter, however, Barassi addressed them again, this time with a cool and measured tone. In a last-ditch effort to fire up his men, he drew upon the great rivalry between the clubs. 'Barassi said if the match continued as it had and Carlton lost by 14 goals, they could never be able to forget it,' wrote Flanagan. 'Why? Because the loss would be to Collingwood.'

The events of the second half had long-lasting repercussions for both clubs, and cemented their rivalry as the most zealous in the game. Inspired by Barassi's speech and his insistence on more handball, Carlton hit the ground running. The Blues kicked seven goals in a touch over ten minutes and were just four points down midway through the third quarter. Collingwood suddenly looked tired.

The Magpies' predicament was worse than simple fatigue, however. Two of their gun players, McKenna and centreman Des Tuddenham, were injured after colliding during the second quarter. Tuddenham had accidentally collected McKenna with a hip to the head, leaving 'Tuddy' bruised and his star goal kicker badly concussed. McKenna was later unable to remember anything about the second half, even through he was on the field the whole time and even kicked a goal, taking his tally for the game to six.

After Carlton's onslaught, the Magpies steadied late in the third quarter and took a 17-point lead into the final change. But it was not enough. With small forward Ted Hopkins, who had been substituted into the game at half-time, running riot, the Blues edged in front. With the scoreboard clock showing that 27 minutes had elapsed in the quarter, Collingwood had one last crack at winning the game, as rover Barry Price delivered a pass in the direction of McKenna. The ball momentarily stuck in the big forward's hands just before a gang of Carlton defenders crashed into him. The Magpies thought a mark should have been paid, but it was not.

Instead, Blues full-back Sergio Silvagni was able to boot the ball back to the middle of the ground. It eventually reached Jesaulenko, who evaded a number of defenders and booted his third goal – the sealer. Carlton won by ten points.

The result created many legends, none bigger than that of Barassi, who would be known as a 'supercoach' from then on. His call for more handballing is now seen as having paved the way for the fast and furious modern style of play, while his decision to replace Burt Thornley with Hopkins at half-time led to him being hailed as both a master tactician and a brilliant man-manager. Carlton, which had also won the 1968 flag, went on to win another premiership in 1972. The Blues became a club that demanded success, and they enjoyed plenty of it.

In stark contrast, the 1970 grand final left a scar on Collingwood, and on Rose, that took many years to heal. The captain of that Magpies team, Terry Waters, told Flanagan: 'I don't think anybody could believe it or wanted to believe it or could imagine how they were going to live with it.' Barry Price added: 'The 1970 grand final had devastating consequences for our club.' Heartbroken by his run of near misses, Rose quit the club at the end of the 1971 season and became coach of Footscray.

Rose had been tormented yet again by Carlton just a couple of weeks before deciding that his time at the club was up. In the last round of the 1971 home-and-away season, the Magpies had played Carlton at Princes Park. Collingwood led by exactly seven goals at half-time (10.5 to 3.5), yet the Blues booted 13 goals to three in the second half and won by 19 points. Rose would later return to Collingwood, as senior coach for the 1985 and 1986 seasons.

Carlton continued to torment Collingwood over the following decade. Magpies supporters were devastated when one of their heroes, Peter McKenna, signed with the Blues for the 1977 season. McKenna had left Collingwood at the end of the 1975 season after suffering a kidney injury, and had then spent a season playing with Devonport in Tasmania. 'I had a two-year contract at Carlton,' he told *The Age* in 2012, 'but I left after one because I found it very, very hard – even though I loved the players and they were a great club – I found it very difficult playing against Collingwood.'

COLLINGWOOD vs CARLTON

The Magpies and Blues met in another grand final in 1979, by which time McKenna was enjoying his retirement and was very much a Collingwood man again. The game was played on a wet and muddy Melbourne Cricket Ground before a crowd of 113,545 people. Carlton, which had lost only three games during the season and had cruised straight into the grand final with an easy win over North Melbourne in the second semi, entered the match as a hot favourite. The Magpies, in contrast, had taken the longest route possible, having lost their qualifying final to North, before defeating Fitzroy in the first semi and overcoming the Roos in the preliminary final.

The game began in an unexpected fashion. With rain falling, Collingwood, which was under the guidance of Tom Hafey – who had coached Richmond to four premierships during the late 1960s and early 1970s – surged to a 28-point lead by the 20-minute mark of the second quarter. Remarkably, Carlton had not scored a goal. But just when the Magpies' huge band of followers began to sense that their grand final curse might be over, the Blues changed their approach. Their captain–coach, Alex Jesaulenko, moved himself out of the centre and shifted young bull Wayne Harmes into the middle of the ground. Harmes helped Carlton pile on five goals in ten minutes, and the Blues were a point in front when the half-time siren sounded. Harmes and his teammates continued their surge in the third quarter, kicking five goals to two, and by the last change Carlton was 21 points up and seemingly cruising towards another premiership.

Then the game changed again. Spurred on by some inspirational words from Hafey, and with their much-loved and admired centre half-back Billy Picken controlling the play, Collingwood kicked three successive goals, narrowing the margin to four points. It was during the following couple of minutes that one of the most famous incidents in the history of the Carlton–Collingwood rivalry took place.

The storied passage of play began when Harmes grabbed the ball on the half-forward flank and aimed a kick towards Carlton's goal. The ball wobbled off the side his boot and floated towards the right pocket at the city end of the Melbourne Cricket Ground. Sensing that there was no one between him and the ball, Harmes started chasing his own kick, haring after the Sherrin in an attempt to grab it before it trickled over the boundary line. When he came within a couple of metres of the ball, Harmes dived forward and knocked it towards Carlton's goal square.

Collingwood fans leapt out of their seats and roared their disapproval, believing the ball had crossed the boundary line, but the umpires had ruled that it was still in play. Then, to the dismay of the black and white army, Harmes' teammate Ken Sheldon picked up the ball unopposed and run into an open goal. The margin was back out to ten points, and the Blues supporters were dancing in the aisles.

Both teams had their chances during the final ten minutes of the match. Collingwood kicked what proved to be the last goal of the game, which once again brought the margin back to four points. But Carlton then surged forward one last time, Alex Marcou snapped a point, and the Blues won by five points.

In the decades since that famous contest in 1979, the Harmes incident has been replayed and pored over countless times. Universities have done studies to determine whether the ball was in or out, while Harmes is asked to recount his thoughts on the matter during most grand final weeks. Carlton supporters maintain it was in; Collingwood fans remain adamant it was out.

Two years after Harmes entered football folklore, Carlton and Collingwood qualified for another grand final. By 1981, however, the nerves of the Magpies' supporters were just about shot. The club had been in seven grand finals since its last premiership in 1958 and had failed to win any of them. The Pies' closest result during that run of outs had come in 1977, when they blew a 27-point three-quarter-time lead and drew with North Melbourne; they then lost the replay by 27 points. The loss to Carlton in 1979 was another bitter pill to swallow, but the 81-point defeat they suffered at the hands of Richmond in the 1980 decider had been embarrassing.

Nevertheless, another massive crowd – 112,694 people – turned up at the Melbourne Cricket Ground to see if Hafey could finally guide Collingwood to a grand final win over its fiercest rival. 'The supporters were fantastic,' Hafey said in a documentary about the game, *The Final Story – 1981*, produced by AFL Media in 2011. 'They could see no wrong in their own. One of the players could murder his mum and they'd probably say, "Oh well, she had it coming."' Half-back Graeme Allan said: 'I didn't know anyone on the Collingwood board, but when we played Carlton they'd all be in the rooms before the game and after the game, and when we won, I've never seen a happier group.'

Once again, the Magpies went in as underdogs, even though they had beaten Carlton twice during the home-and-away season. The Collingwood team, captained by star ruckman Peter Moore, contained plenty of talented players, among them evergreen centre half-back Billy Picken and youngsters Peter Daicos and Tony Shaw, but it was regarded as an unfashionable line-up that lacked flair. As in in 1979, the Pies had taken the long route to the grand final, having lost the qualifying final then won the first semi and their preliminary.

Not only was Collingwood rated the outsider, but there was also a dark cloud hanging over Moore's fitness. The 1979 Brownlow medallist had suffered a hamstring strain during the second semi-final, an injury that usually requires a recovery period of at least three weeks. Yet Moore was arguably Collingwood's best player. Not only was he brilliant around the ground, but he could also push forward and kick goals. Hafey desperately wanted him to play, while Moore himself, having played in three losing grand finals and the draw of 1977, was desperate to line up in the big game. On the Thursday night before the match Hafey put his team through a long and testing training session. Moore looked less than fit throughout, but he was selected in the team anyway.

There were no such problems in the Carlton camp, and the Blues – now coached by former Hawthorn captain and coach David Parkin – were desperate to inflict more pain on Collingwood. 'The rivalry between the two clubs was unbelievable,' Parkin said in the documentary about the game. 'People got the shakes, people said and did nasty things, people changed.'

Having finished on top of the ladder, the Blues had enjoyed a rest on the opening weekend of the finals, and then had beaten Geelong in the second semi, which earned them a berth in the big one and another weekend off to boot. The Blues' side was star-studded. It featured great players such as dynamic centreman Wayne Johnston, mercurial half-forward Peter Bosustow, never-say-die backman Bruce 'the Flying Doormat' Doull, skilful and tough rover Rod Ashman and ruckman Mike Fitzpatrick (who would later become chairman of the AFL).

Yet the game did not pan out as expected. Despite Moore being largely anchored to the goal square, Hafey's men managed to stay in touch and were just one point down at half-time. The Magpies then exploded in the third quarter, kicking five of the first six goals and grabbing a 21-point lead. As they had done so many times before, the club's players and supporters began to wonder if they were finally going to enjoy a grand final victory. 'At the 25-minute mark of the third quarter I remember thinking, "Boys, we're nearly there now,"' recalled Tony Shaw. Those watching at home heard Channel 7 commentator and former Collingwood captain Lou

Richards say, 'But don't start celebrating yet, fellas, because it's a long way from over.'

There was genuine concern in the Carlton camp. 'We were in trouble,' admitted the Blues' key forward Mark Maclure, who had an enthralling duel with Collingwood defender Billy Picken. 'Absolutely you get worried.' But Carlton refused to lie down. The Blues booted the last two goals of the third term, narrowing the margin to nine points, and when the teams paused for the final break it appeared that Collingwood was running out of steam. Carlton went on to break the hearts of the Magpie faithful yet again by kicking four answered goals in the last quarter. The final margin was 20 points. Rubbing salt into the black-and-white army's wound was the fact that Carlton's victory saw it draw level with Collingwood on 13 premierships – the Magpies had held the outright VFL record for flags won since 1929.

The VFL had decided to award runner-up medals that year, but Moore was so gutted about playing in his fourth losing grand final that he threw his into the crowd. 'I didn't want to be seen to accept coming second,' he said. 'I certainly don't want it back. Whoever's got it can have it.' Tony Shaw threw his medal in a bin in the rooms. Largely as a result of the Collingwood players' reaction, runner-up medals were never awarded again.

Collingwood's third straight grand final loss led to the term 'Colliwobbles' being used to describe the club's lack of ability to get the job done on the biggest day of the season. It also caused the club to implode: Hafey was sacked, Moore later left and joined Melbourne, and there were upheavals at board level. It was not until 1990, when the Magpies broke their 32-year premiership drought by thrashing Essendon in the grand final, that the Colliwobbles were finally laid to rest – a funeral was actually held for the Colliwobbles at Victoria Park during the premiership celebrations.

Since then, the rivalry between Carlton and Collingwood has simmered, rather than boiled. Between 1982 and 2012 the clubs met in only one finals match— in 1988, when the Blues beat the Magpies by 38 points in a qualifying final at the Melbourne Cricket Ground. In the past decade it has been West Coast and Sydney and Geelong and Hawthorn that have enjoyed the two great modern-day rivalries.

The Eagles and Swans did battle in the 2005 and 2006 grand finals, which were decided by a combined margin of five points, with Sydney winning the first and West Coast triumphing in the second. In fact, the clubs had a run of six matches between 2005 and 2007 that were all decided by four points or less.

The rivalry between the Cats and the Hawks, meanwhile, dates back to the 1989 grand final, which Hawthorn won by six points and which is regarded as one of the greatest games of Australian football ever played. Their rivalry was reignited in 2008, when they did battle in another grand final. That day the Hawks caused a major upset, defeating a Geelong team that had previously lost only one game for the season. Geelong was stung so badly by that defeat that it won all nine games the two sides played between 2009 and 2012.

Mick Malthouse's decision to join Carlton as its senior coach is sure to breathe some fire back into the rivalry between the Blues and the Pies. As the journalist, author, historian and Collingwood fan Paul Daley wrote on the website 'The Hoopla' in the days after Malthouse was appointed: 'Sometimes having a partner who is a football and, worse, a Collingwood, agnostic, can bring a new dimension to obsession. I was huffing, agitatedly texting, and puffing about the potential impact on Collingwood morale of the likely move by Mick Malthouse to the Carlton coaching job. "What's the fuss?" she asked. I replied: "Well, imagine if a First World War general had defected to the other side. Something like that."'

For supporters of the two clubs, the rivalry between Collingwood and Carlton really is that big.

CARLTON vs COLLINGWOOD, AUSTRALIAN RULES (1897–2012)

Matches played: 245
Carlton wins: 125
Collingwood wins: 116
Draws: 4

VFL/AFL premierships

Carlton: 16: 1906–08, 1914–15, 1938, 1945, 1947, 1968, 1970, 1972, 1979, 1981–82, 1987, 1995
Collingwood: 15: 1902–03, 1910, 1917, 1919, 1927–30, 1935–36, 1953, 1958, 1990, 2010

North Melbourne champion Wayne Carey takes a mark in front of his greatest rival, West Coast defender Glen Jakovich, during a match at Subiaco Oval in 1998.

AUSTRALIAN RULES
Wayne Carey *vs* Glen Jakovich

THE WAY AUSTRALIAN RULES is played at the elite level these days, head-to-head battles are rare. They still happen – Sydney defender Ted Richards usually plays on Hawthorn star Lance 'Buddy' Franklin when the Swans do battle with the Hawks – but, due to the increasing number of interchange rotations, the days when two players would do battle for an entire match are largely gone. That is why there is much nostalgia for the way North Melbourne centre half-forward Wayne Carey and West Coast centre half-back Glen Jakovich went head-to-head through the 1990s and early 2000s, in what were some of the greatest heavyweight stoushes the AFL has seen. Carey regularly dominated just about every defender he played on, yet things were very different whenever he took on Jakovich.

The pair first matched up on each other when the Kangaroos hosted the Eagles on a cold Friday night at the Melbourne Cricket Ground in June 1992. Only 10,165 people were there to see what was reported as being a largely forgettable contest, in which West Coast, which would go on to win the premiership that year, overcame some woeful kicking for goal to win in a canter, 14.26 (110) to 10.6 (66).

Although the game was a blowout on the scoreboard, the battle between Carey and Jakovich was far closer – it was indeed a taste of things to come. Carey, then aged 21, tried his best to keep his struggling team in the game, and he recorded a narrow victory over the man who would prove to be his toughest opponent. He finished the evening with 18 possessions and 11 marks, but only one goal. Jakovich, then just 19, collected 14 touches of his own, took four marks and snuck forward to boot a behind. None of the newspaper reporters who wrote about the game took much notice of the clash between Carey and Jakovich, but, as we now know, a famous rivalry had begun.

Carey and Jakovich were, and remain, very different men. The former came from a rough rural background and played just as hard off the field as on it. 'I don't think there was a weekend when I didn't have a beer, or three, during my entire career,' Carey wrote in his autobiography, *The Truth Hurts*. Jakovich, in contrast, was much more of a straight man, as he told Ben Collins in *Champions: Conversations with Great Players & Coaches of Australian Football*:

> I was against doing anything that jeopardised my footy. I never ate junk food, never smoked, and I knew that drinking gallons of alcohol wasn't the way to go, even though plenty of footballers did. I wanted to become a professional footballer, and those things could have no place in my life if I was to get there and succeed. I'd do anything, no questions asked, if I thought it would help me play better. I made a rule not to drink between New Year's Eve and the end of the footy season. I broke that rule only a couple of times in 14 years.

On the field, however, the two men were similar. Both were towering players – Carey stood 192 centimetres tall and weighed 97 kilograms, while Jakovich was 193 centimetres and 100 kilograms – and fierce competitors. Carey was a key forward right from his first game in the AFL. Jakovich was initially played all over the park by Eagles coach Mick Malthouse, even rucking against Jim Stynes in a final in 1991. Sent to defence by Malthouse at the start of the 1992 season, he teamed with John Worsfold and Guy McKenna to form a brilliant Eagles half-back line.

Having had the better of Jakovich in their first meeting, Carey easily took the honours in their second, which occurred on a Friday night at the WACA ground in Perth midway through the 1993 season. North Melbourne silenced the sell-out crowd of more than 30,000 by scoring an upset six-point victory, and Carey, who would be regarded as the best player in the AFL by the end of that year – in which he won the Kangaroos' best and fairest and was named All-Australian captain – was among the key contributors. Carey looked too powerful for his opponent, finishing with 21 possessions, 11 marks and three goals, although he only polled one Brownlow Medal vote for his effort. (The three votes went to North midfielder John Blakey, and the two votes were awarded to another Roo, full-back Mick Martyn, who held Eagles forward Peter Sumich to only four kicks.)

Less than three months later, Jakovich turned the tables and shut Carey down for the first time. The game was an elimination final at Waverley Park. The Eagles went into the game as underdogs; they were the reigning premiers but had struggled through the season, finishing sixth and only scaping into the finals, thanks to their decent percentage. North Melbourne, under the guidance of new coach Denis Pagan, had enjoyed a far more impressive home-and-away campaign. Pagan had made Carey his captain despite his young age of 21, and the positive relationship between skipper and coach was seen as being a key force behind the Kangaroos' surge up to third place on the ladder. But the Roos' revival was halted when West Coast scored a thumping 51-point win over them and knocked Pagan's team out of the 1993 premiership race.

Jakovich was the star for West Coast. He held Carey scoreless, and limited him to just six possessions and one mark. At the same time, the Eagle exposed Carey's lack of defensive skills, gathering 26 touches and setting up numerous goals for his side. During an interview for the 'rivalry round' of 2005, Jakovich told the AFL website: 'I think the one thing that I valued most was that Mick Malthouse kept me on Wayne in that period when he was all over me. Mick purposely kept me on Wayne during those formative years because I had to build a strength and resolve from it. I was grateful to Mick for doing that because it was very good as far as my development was concerned.'

Carey and Jakovich split their two duels the following year. Carey dominated the first – a Saturday-afternoon clash at the Melbourne Cricket Ground early in the season. Although North Melbourne lost the match by 37 points, Carey kicked 5.3 and took 15 marks as he ran his man ragged. It was an effort that would earn him two Brownlow Medal votes.

Jakovich responded with a best-on-ground performance when the Eagles prevailed by nine points at the WACA in Round 21. The gun backman not only held Carey to one goal and 14 disposals, but he also attacked relentlessly for his side, amassing a career-best 29 possessions. By now people were going to the footy just to watch Carey and Jakovich take each other on, and the two champions went within a whisker of meeting in the 1994 grand final.

West Coast, which was clearly the best team in the competition that season, advanced to the premiership decider thanks to a narrow win over Collingwood in a qualifying final and a big win over Melbourne in a preliminary final. Carey did all he could to drag North Melbourne into the big game by putting on an epic display against Geelong in the other preliminary final, which drew a crowd of over 80,000 fans to the Melbourne Cricket Ground. But the Kangaroos fell six points short after Leigh Tudor's wobbling left-foot pass drifted over Mick Martyn's head and landed in the lap of Gary Ablett, who was standing in the goal square. With only seconds remaining on the clock, Ablett won the game for the Cats by kicking truly.

Years later, while sitting alongside Carey to discuss the match, Jakovich lamented: 'When they lost to Geelong in '94 . . . I was actually watching that game and barracking for North because . . . I would have loved to play against this great man on the biggest stage on the last day of September. That was probably the only thing that I missed in our duel, I reckon – was to play each other in a grand final.'

A week after North's heartbreaking loss to Geelong, the Eagles thrashed the Cats in the grand final and Jakovich was able to celebrate his second flag. Thanks to his great form, the footy media and many fans were suddenly asking themselves if Jakovich was in fact the best player in the competition. He certainly had plenty to celebrate, as in the lead-up to the big game he had been named at centre half-back in the All-Australian team; Carey was named at centre half-forward. On top of all that, Jakovich won the Eagles' best and fairest for the third successive year.

At that point, the head-to-head scoreboard read Carey 3, Jakovich 2. But the Eagle took the upper hand in their rivalry with three brilliant performances during the 1995 season. In those three games – a Round 3 clash at the WACA that West Coast won by 48 points, a Round 18 match at Princes Park in Melbourne that North won by 62 points, and a semi-final at the Melbourne Cricket Ground that North won by 58 points – Jakovich restricted Carey to a combined total of just 35 possessions and only two goals. In fact, Jakovich held Carey goalless in the first and third of those matches. He later told Ben Collins:

Wayne Carey was my barometer. He drove me to levels that other players couldn't. Mick [Malthouse] got the best out of me, but Wayne got the super-best out of me. There's no bigger compliment than someone saying: 'You beat the best when they were at their best', but the truth is, I had to play that well to beat Wayne. He dragged it out of me. It was either that or be swallowed up like most of his other opponents. It was a big game pretty much whenever we played on each other because we dominated the early '90s and the Kangaroos dominated the late '90s and both sides played finals throughout the whole decade. Wayne gave me a few sleepless nights during the week, but I loved playing against him. I loved that edge, that confrontation. He beat me a few times and each time I decided: 'That's not going to happen again.' I worked on myself more than I worked on him.

Although he'd been beaten by Jakovich in 1995, Carey was still an outstanding player over the course of the season. For the second year in a row he was selected at centre half-forward in the All-Australian team, while Jakovich was named at centre half-back.

The pair resumed hostilities in Round 7 of the 1996 season at Subiaco Oval in Perth. The Eagles won the game by 11 goals but the honours in the key personal battle went to Carey, who gathered 19 possessions, took ten marks and had seven scoring shots, which yielded 3.4. Jakovich was still a very effective player, collecting 22 touches of his own, but Carey had taken the points over his toughest opponent for the first time since 1994. That left the head-to-head score as Jakovich 5, Carey 4. Later that year Carey led North to its first premiership since 1977.

Their next meeting was not until the 1997 finals series, and injuries to both players were the reason. Jakovich went down first, suffering a serious knee injury during a game against St Kilda in

WAYNE CAREY vs GLEN JAKOVICH

Round 12 of the 1996 season. After having a knee reconstruction, he didn't play again until Round 6 of 1997. Carey, meanwhile, suffered a shoulder injury early in the Roos' 1997 campaign. Both men missed North Melbourne's only home-and-away game against West Coast.

By the time the finals rolled around, however, Carey was not only fit but also in top form. Under the top-eight system in use at the time, the top team played the eighth-placed team in week one, while number two played number seven and so on. The Kangaroos had finished seventh, so they went in as rank outsiders against Geelong, which had finished second. But on a wet night at the Melbourne Cricket Ground, Carey, sporting about five rolls of tape on his shoulder, put on a masterclass. He booted seven of his team's 11 goals, ran a series of opponents ragged and led his men to a brilliant win.

North Melbourne was subsequently granted a home semi-final against West Coast, which had lost its qualifying final to Adelaide the previous week. More than 55,000 people turned up to see the game, with many pundits predicting the Carey vs Jakovich match-up would decide the result. As it turned out, they were wrong.

Jakovich produced a performance that he rates as one of the best in his career. He restricted Carey to 16 touches, five marks and two goals, while gathering 23 possessions of his own. *The Age* reported on the match: 'It took just 15 minutes before Pagan conceded the Carey vs Jakovich duel. Carey was moved to the backline after Jakovich completely outplayed him. Jakovich was superb in both clearing the ball from defence and keeping Carey quiet. In fact Jakovich looked impassable at centre half back – and assisted by runners such as Kemp, Peter Matera and Banfield – West Coast was able to run the ball at will out of defence.'

But Jakovich was left devastated at the end of the game: North Melbourne had overcome a 20-point half-time deficit to win by 13. As Carey observed in 2005: 'If you look back and look at all the times

Glen and I played on one another, the actual duel had no bearing on the actual game. If he'd beaten me, usually the Kangaroos won quite convincingly and vice versa. So it was weird.'

North Melbourne hosted West Coast in the first match of the 1998 season. Heading into the Friday-night clash at the Melbourne Cricket Ground, the personal match-up scoreboard for the teams' biggest stars now read Jakovich 6, Carey 4. This time, they became locked in another highly entertaining struggle. Carey, who was just shy of his 27th birthday, finished with 18 touches but only three scoring shots. Jakovich, who had turned 25 earlier that week, collected 19 possessions, combining his defensive and attacking roles with aplomb. The scribes at the game gave the nod to Jakovich, although it was a close call. The final result on the scoreboard was similarly close, with the Kangaroos kicking four goals to two in the last quarter to win a thrilling contest by two points.

Carey, who had by now earned the nickname 'the King', finally got back on top of Jakovich when he led his team to a 14-point win over the Eagles at Subiaco in Round 16. Carey ended the match with five goals, his effort narrowing the head-to-head score to Jakovich 7, Carey 5.

The rivals met only once in 1999, as Carey led the Kangaroos to their second premiership in four seasons. The game in question was part of North Melbourne's first push to play home games interstate, and it took place at the Sydney Cricket Ground. Carey didn't kick a goal but did gather 12 touches, while Jakovich had only eight. Neither was named among the best players, but it seems reasonable to award Carey a narrow win. Jakovich 7, Carey 6.

The King had the chance to level things up when the Roos and the Eagles opened the 2000 season on a Friday night at the Melbourne Cricket Ground. However, it was a double victory for Jakovich: West Coast won the game – its first under new coach Ken Judge – by 43 points and he kept Carey to just 11 touches and two goals. Jakovich 8, Carey 6.

When the teams met at Subiaco Oval in Round 16, it proved to be another one of those quirky games: North Melbourne won by 61 points, yet Carey was comprehensively outplayed by Jakovich. Carey finished with only six disposals and two goals, whereas Jakovich picked up 23 kicks, two handballs and took six marks. Jakovich 9, Carey 6.

Speaking to Collins for the *Champions* book some years later, Jakovich reflected on why he was so successful against Carey: 'North Melbourne's structure and game plan suited me. 'Pagan's Paddock' [North coach Denis Pagan's tactic of leaving the forward 50-metre zone open so Carey could lead towards the Roos' goal] revolved around one player, Wayne Carey, so I thought: "If I just sit on his shoulder, he's going to take me to 20 more contests than I would normally get." I saw the opportunity to get more of the ball. But I hoped we'd put midfield pressure on them too, because if the ball was delivered well it wouldn't matter if I was [Australian sprinter] Patrick Johnson, I wouldn't be able to stop it.'

Because both sides missed the finals in 2001, their only meeting that year took place at Subiaco Oval in Round 15. Carey narrowed the head-to-head score to 9–7, kicking five goals as North Melbourne cruised to a 44-point win. As it happened, this was the last time that Carey took on Jakovich while wearing a Kangaroos guernsey. Six months later, on the eve of the 2002 season, the champion forward was forced to quit the club after his affair with the wife of teammate Anthony Stevens became public. Carey subsequently stood out of football for a year; his absence from the AFL saw the rivalry between Geelong full-back Matthew Scarlett and Essendon full-forward Matthew Lloyd emerge as the new must-see battle.

Scarlett was given the big job on Lloyd in his first game, which came in the final round of the 1998 home-and-away season. At the age of 20, Lloyd was already a star; Scarlett was a 76-kilogram teenager. Lloyd regularly outmuscled Scarlett that afternoon, hauling in seven marks and kicking six goals. When they next did battle, in Round 11 of the 1999 season, the star Bomber booted another five, and he kicked another seven against the Cats the following year. 'I remember him being pretty light, in terms of his body-weight and size,' Lloyd told the *AFL Record* in 2012. 'He wasn't too strong. I never thought he'd be one of the best full-backs the game's ever seen.'

While Lloyd continued to dominate most of the competition's best defenders for another decade, he had few easy games on Scarlett from then on. The Essendon star later said: '[He] went on to become no doubt the best player that I ever played on. Every shot at goal I got on Matty Scarlett I really wanted to kick the goal, because I knew it might be a fair while until I got my next shot. That's how hard he was to get a kick on.'

In the early 2000s there were few more entertaining match-ups than Scarlett vs Lloyd. Yet their rivalry didn't capture the public's imagination like the battles between Carey and Jakovich, who faced off for the final time during the 2003 season.

By this time, the King was playing for Adelaide and was staring at the end of his grand career. Jakovich narrowly took the honours in Round 4, but there was a bit of life left in Carey, who rediscovered his strut when the Crows travelled to Subiaco Oval in Round 19. Veteran footy scribe John McGrath wrote in his match report for *The Age*:

> West Coast fans got their wish when local hero Glen Jakovich ran to his great rival Wayne Carey before the start of yesterday's match against Adelaide at Subiaco. The two have enjoyed some wonderful battles over the years with Jakovich the only player in the league who could claim to have some kind of advantage over

the former Kangaroos great. But it was evident early in yesterday's match that this was not going to be one such occasion. The King, even at the age of 32, had come to play. He might not move as gracefully as he once did, or hold the sensational pack marks, but Carey still has enough footy smarts to keep even such a great backman as Jakovich on his mettle.

Carey ended up taking the honours, his brilliant first quarter – during which he booted one goal and had a hand in four others – helping Adelaide record an easy win. But he remained behind on the overall scoreboard, which finished Jakovich 10, Carey 8.

When the two men sat down to reflect on their battles in the interview with the AFL's website in 2005, Jakovich said: 'We've come up with a final outcome. Wayne was quicker than I was. I was stronger than he was. I was more durable – I played 276 games. He played 272.'

But Carey graciously acknowledged that Jakovich had indeed beaten him over the course of their careers. 'In the overall tally, I think Glen might have won by one, he says maybe two,' he admitted. 'I've always said it's a lot easier to punch it than mark it and turn around and do something with it. But I can't say that about Glen because his greatest strength was the fact that he got a lot of the ball and put pressure on.'

WAYNE CAREY vs GLEN JAKOVICH, AUSTRALIAN RULES

Wayne Carey

Clubs: North Melbourne (1989–2001), Adelaide (2003–04)
Position: Centre half-forward
Matches played: 272
Goals kicked: 727
Premierships: 1996, 1999
Club best-and-fairest awards: 4: 1992–93, 1996, 1998
Number of times selected in All-Australian team: 7: 1993–96, 1998–2000

Glen Jakovich

Club: West Coast (1991–2004)
Position: Centre half-back
Matches played: 276
Goals kicked: 60
Premierships: 1992, 1994
Club best-and-fairest awards: 4: 1993–95, 2000
Number of times selected in All-Australian team: 2: 1994–95

Legendary Australian leg-spinner Shane Warne torments South African batsman Daryll Cullinan by bowling him during a Test match at the MCG in 1997.

CRICKET
Shane Warne *vs* Daryll Cullinan

GIVEN THAT SHANE WARNE took 708 Test wickets and another 293 in international 50-over cricket, it's fair to say he had the edge over most of the batsmen he came up against. But when Aussie cricket fans ponder Warne's ability to dominate opponents, one name almost inevitably comes up: Daryll Cullinan.

In the mid-1990s Warne and Cullinan emerged as two of the most talented young cricketers on the planet, and between 1993 and 2000 they went head-to-head in some of the most riveting Tests and limited-overs matches played during the past three decades. The problem for Cullinan was that his confrontations with Warne usually ended with the Aussie leg-spinner celebrating as the South African trudged back to the pavilion with only a handful of runs to his name. In all, Warne dismissed Cullinan four times in Tests matches and on eight occasions in one-dayers. Their rivalry was largely one-sided, yet it remained utterly captivating.

A brash and combative player, Cullinan was a batting prodigy in his youth. He made his first-class debut for his province, Border, at the age of 16 in 1983, and soon became the youngest batsman to make a century in South Africa's premier domestic competition. Cullinan was subsequently lumped with the tag 'the next Graeme Pollock', which is akin to an Australian youngster being branded the next Don Bradman.

At that time, South Africa was banned from international sport because of its policy of apartheid, so many of Cullinan's talented countrymen – players such as Kepler Wessels, Alan Lamb and Robin Smith – went to England or Australia to try their luck. But Cullinan stayed at home, dominating the local bowlers during stints with Impalas, Western Province and Transvaal, and setting more records – including the highest ever first-class score in South Africa at the time, 337 not out.

South Africa was welcomed back into international cricket in time for the 1992 World Cup. Cullinan was overlooked for that tournament but made his Test debut the following year against India at Cape Town, scoring 46 in his first knock. He averaged 47 in his first six innings – an impressive start that included his first Test century, which he scored against Sri Lanka on a turning pitch at Colombo in September 1993. Cullinan's effort in taming Sri Lanka's tweakers – a line-up that included a young Muttiah Muralitharan – demonstrated that he had the ability hold his nerve against top-class spinners. But his reputation was soon dented by his first round of battles against Shane Warne.

Cullinan faced Australia's spin king for the first time in the opening match of the 1993–94 Benson & Hedges World Series Cup, which took place on a balmy night at the Melbourne Cricket Ground. Having knocked over the Aussies for 189 (Michael Slater top-scored on debut with a whirlwind 73 off 69 balls), South Africa was in a very strong position by the time Cullinan strode to the crease. Although the visitors needed only 46 more runs to win, the 60,000 people in attendance remained in full voice, hoping that Warne, the hometown hero, would produce another miracle.

Since making a rather lacklustre debut against India at the Sydney Cricket Ground during the summer of 1991–92 (his figures in his first Test were 1 for 150), Warne had emerged as one of the hottest stars

SHANE WARNE vs DARYLL CULLINAN

in the game, single-handedly reviving the supposedly lost art of leg-spin bowling by bamboozling batsmen the world over. Among his many highlights were his match-winning haul of 7 for 52 against the West Indies at the Melbourne Cricket Ground in late 1992, and his first ball in a Test on English soil – a sharply turning leg-break that bowled English batsman Mike Gatting and subsequently became known simply as the Gatting ball.

The big crowd roared as Cullinan took guard and prepared to face Warne for the first time. He nervously survived three deliveries, as the Australians stepped up the pressure with a verbal attack, before Warne decided to unleash one of his trademark variations. The ball, nicknamed the flipper, pitched around middle stump. Cullinan expected it to curve towards the off side, like a typical leg break, but instead it veered straight ahead and crashed into his stumps. Warne saluted the Aussie fans as Cullinan, out for a duck, shook his head in dismay. South Africa ended up winning the match with eight balls to spare, thanks largely to Hansie Cronje's unbeaten 91. But Warne had put his first dent in Cullinan's mental armour. Their rivalry was on.

When Cullinan lined up against Australia in a Test match for the first time – it was the 1993 Boxing Day Test at the Melbourne Cricket Ground – he avoided a confrontation with Warne because he fell cheaply to fast bowler Craig McDermott early in his team's only innings; the game was marred by rain. But in the New Year Test at the Sydney Cricket Ground the following week, Cullinan found himself taking on Warne on a spin-friendly track; it was during this game that Warne cast his spell over the talented South African.

Cullinan survived just 11 balls and made nine runs in the first innings before Warne bowled him with a perfectly placed flipper. In South Africa's second innings he managed only two runs off 13 deliveries before Warne trapped him lbw with another slider.

Warne finished the match with ten wickets, yet it was Cullinan and his mates who were celebrating at the end after Australia lost 9 for 60 in their second dig and crashed to a five-run defeat.

Cullinan wasn't smiling for long. When the Benson & Hedges World Series Cup resumed in January, he endured a horror run. Previously such a composed player, he suddenly seemed unsure of himself; the low points of his involvement in the tournament came when part-time bowlers Mark Waugh and Allan Border knocked him over during the preliminary games.

In the second final, played at the Sydney Cricket Ground, a match South Africa had to win to take the competition to a deciding game, Cullinan arrived at the crease with his team at 3 for 102, chasing 248 for victory. The stage was set for Cullinan to make a stand. He poked and prodded his way to three runs off 12 balls, but with Warne working the sell-out crowd into a frenzy, the pressure grew by the minute. Warne was at the peak of his powers, and his various deliveries had taken on cult status, with the flipper garnering the greatest reputation. That night at the Sydney Cricket Ground countless Aussie fans waved blow-up dolphins and held banners extolling the virtues of the flipper. Try as he might, Cullinan couldn't survive. His 13th ball, delivered by Warne, took the outside edge of his bat and flew to Steve Waugh in the slips. Warne had done it again.

Cullinan spoke to the website Cricinfo in 2007 about his approach to batting against spin:

> It's one of the first things you tell a kid: watch the ball. But it's probably the last thing on most professional players' minds. I know this was something I did not pay much attention to, and that cost me dearly. When I think of my first-class days, we had only one spinner who was playing first-class cricket – Denys Hobson, who was a genuine leg-spinner, and he had recently

SHANE WARNE vs DARYLL CULLINAN

retired. And we had Alan Kourie, who was basically a left-arm roller. Other than that we had mostly finger-spinners. Wrist-spin was something we never completely understood, and I think that's what distinguished the better players from the others – the ability to watch the ball completely out of the hand and then play accordingly.

After his miserable run in the one-day matches against Australia, Cullinan then failed twice in the Third Test, which was played in Adelaide in late January, although Steve Waugh and Craig McDermott combined to dismiss him rather than Warne.

Warne's next chance to torment Cullinan came when Australia and South Africa took part in a triangular one-day tournament in Pakistan in October 1994. Cullinan went into the series with renewed confidence, having recently made 99 runs in two limited-overs innings in England. He had also made a stylish 94 in a Test against the English at the Oval. But after making just 12 against the Aussies in the first game, in Lahore, he fell to Warne yet again when the teams next did battle in Peshawar. Once again, it was a straight ball that did the trick, with Warne bowling Cullinan before he had scored.

Three months later, in February 1995, South Africa took on Australia in another one-dayer on neutral territory, the venue on this occasion being the Basin Reserve in Wellington, New Zealand. For Cullinan, the game was another disaster. His seventh ball was a leg-break from Warne, and he lunged forward to try to nudge it into the off side. As the ball swerved past his bat, he stumbled forward and found himself out of his crease. Quick as a flash, Aussie wicketkeeper Ian Healy gloved the ball and whipped the bails off. Cullinan was out – stumped Healy, bowled Warne – for a duck.

At least Cullinan had something to laugh about when he went home to South Africa and spent some time playing for Transvaal in the local first-class competition. Cullinan was batting in a game at Paarl when he hit fellow international player Roger Telemachus for six. The ball crashed into a food stand and was eventually found in a frying pan full of sizzling calamari. As was noted in the 1996 edition of the *Wisden Cricketers' Almanack*: 'It was about ten minutes before the ball was cool enough for the umpires to remove the grease. Even then, [the bowler] was unable to grip the ball and it had to be replaced.'

Cullinan at last made an impression against Australia in the Titan Cup, which was held in India in late 1996; he made 71 not out and 43 not out. Yet it seemed that the key reason for Cullinan's success was the absence of Warne, who missed the tournament due to an injury. Everything changed when Warne returned to the Australian team for its tour to South Africa in February–April 1997.

Cullinan went into the Test series in great form, having made a stylish 122 not out against India in the weeks before Australia's arrival. He made a painstaking 27 off 73 balls in the first innings, then fell for a duck – caught Healy, bowled Warne – in his second dig. The Aussie press began delighting in referring to Cullinan as Warne's number-one bunny – the term being an extension of a poor performer often being called a 'rabbit'. Cullinan didn't get out to Warne again during the remainder of the Test series, but that was his only consolation.

He finally enjoyed a win over Warne in the first match of the seven-game one-day series that followed the Tests. He survived numerous flippers and sharply turning leg-breaks and made 85 not out, guiding South Africa to a six-wicket victory. Although Warne dismissed him in two of the matches, that series proved to be Cullinan's finest period against Australia. He made four half-centuries, including a best knock of 89. That was a rare occasion when the champion leggie had to admit he'd been beaten by his bunny.

SHANE WARNE vs DARYLL CULLINAN

Warne and Cullinan renewed their rivalry when South Africa toured Australia in the summer of 1997–98. In the lead-up to the arrival of the South Africans, an Aussie newspaper ran a double-page feature in which it stated that Cullinan had been so scarred by his past failures against Warne that he was seeking therapy. 'I couldn't believe it,' Warne later wrote in *Shane Warne: My Autobiography*. 'I knew Daryll was a bit fragile at times, but never imagined he would go to a shrink to learn how to read a googly.'

When Cullinan was interviewed for a feature story in Adelaide's *Sunday Mail* in 2007, he said the matter had been 'blown all out of proportion. It wasn't a case of going to see someone. The fact is that I had a relationship with a sport psychologist who played a massive role in my career from day one. [But] suddenly, someone jumped on the bandwagon and said: "He's going for special treatment. [Warne] has put him on the couch."'

The first battle between Warne and Cullinan during that summer took place in an early match of the one-day series. South Africa batted first, and Cullinan made a composed 33 before being run out. Australia struggled early in its chase, and South African captain Hansie Cronje decided to give Cullinan a bowl. Sending down some rather innocuous off-breaks, Cullinan dismissed Aussie wicketkeeper Adam Gilchrist caught and bowled. He then enjoyed one of his greatest moments against the Australians when he trapped Warne leg before wicket. Cullinan celebrated long and hard as Warne trudged back to the pavilion. South Africa went on to win the game.

The pair's next meeting took place during the Boxing Day Test at the Melbourne Cricket Ground, the first match of a three-Test series. Having enjoyed such a great record against Cullinan, Warne now relentlessly sledged him every time they crossed paths in a game. But the South African often fought back, as his former teammate Allan Donald recalled in a television feature produced by *Fox Sports* in 2012. Donald recalled an incident in which Cullinan sledged Warne while the Australian was batting at the Melbourne Cricket Ground. 'I remember Warnie, at the end of the over, walked with Daryll across the pitch and said to him: "Mate, if I were you I'd zip it because when you come into bat it's going to be the same old, same old,"' Donald said.

But Cullinan never backed down, as the much-quoted events that took place during the 1997 Boxing Day Test attest. Never the skinniest of men, the Aussie spinner had been battling weight issues during the previous months, although his portly appearance had not reduced his confidence. The legendary tale goes like this: when Cullinan strode out to bat in the first innings, Warne turned to him and said that he'd been waiting a long time to embarrass him again in a Test match. Cullinan is said to have retorted, 'Looks like you spent it eating.'

Cullinan likes to play down the story. 'That was actually a bit of mixed reporting,' he told the *Sunday Mail* in 2007. 'At the time I was batting with Gary Kirsten and we had a chuckle about it, but I was attributed to the comments.' Nevertheless, the sledge has become part of cricketing folklore.

As so often happened, however, Warne had the last laugh, bowling Cullinan for a duck during the final innings of the match; the previous two balls had spun past his reaching bat. Cullinan was subsequently dropped for the following Test in Sydney. In fact, he never played another Test against Australia. 'For such a good batsman against other countries, and a bloke with a triple-hundred in first-class cricket to his name, I have never figured out his problem against us,' Warne wrote in his autobiography. 'He is an intense, prickly guy, and I can only imagine he developed a bit of a phobia.'

Cullinan's former teammate Fanie de Villiers had his say in the aforementioned *Fox Sports* television feature. 'The fact [Cullinan] talked back was the wrong choice,' de Villiers said. 'He's a clever guy but [that] wasn't very clever. That got hold of him and that became too much for him in the end.'

Cullinan himself has never publicly expressed any bitterness towards his adversary. '[Warne] was too good for me in terms of Test cricket,' Cullinan added in the *Sunday Mail* interview in 2007. 'I thought I played him a lot better in one-day cricket, which has been overlooked. But one thing I can always say about him is it never was nasty. There were the mind games and subtle sledging but often where people got it wrong was that it was never, ever nasty. If you spend time with him off the field, you like him. That's the kind of guy he is. He's certainly not a vindictive cricketer. He's actually quite a nice guy.'

Cullinan played eight more one-dayers for South Africa against the Aussies. In one, a Carlton & United Series match at the WACA ground in Perth, he made the most of Warne's absence by making 35 not out and helping guide South Africa to a seven-wicket win.

But when Warne returned for the first final of that series, played at the Melbourne Cricket Ground, normal transmission resumed: after opening the batting, Cullinan was stumped Healy, bowled Warne for 26. The one positive for Cullinan was that his team won a brilliant game by six runs, which meant South Africa needed just one more victory to win the tournament. However, Australia fought back to win the second final during which Warne was involved in Cullinan's dismissal again, taking a catch from Mark Waugh's part-time off-spin. Cullinan was then dropped for the third final. He watched from the stands as South Africa attacked the game in typically combative style but fell 14 runs short at the finish.

In June 1999 Cullinan and Warne went head-to-head during the crucial Super Six match between South Africa and Australia at the World Cup in England. South Africa batted first, and Cullinan made a stylish 50 before he fell to his nemesis yet again, bowled. Still, Cullinan's knock helped his team put together a very competitive total of 271. Australia had to win the game to stay in the tournament: it was a heroic knock of 120 not out from skipper Steve Waugh that enabled the Aussies to keep their dream of taking out the tournament alive.

The result also meant South Africa and Australia met in a semi-final four days later. The Aussies looked in all sorts of trouble when they were bowled out for 213. But Cullinan was one of many South African batsmen who failed to handle the pressure in the run chase. As it turned out, his wicket wasn't taken by Warne – he was run out instead. Yet Warne proved Australia's hero, taking 4 for 29 off his ten overs as the game ended in a tie, which meant the Aussies progressed to the final, thanks to their previous victory over the South Africans.

According to Warne, he and Cullinan had their first meaningful discussion after that famous game. Warne wrote in his autobiography. 'It was a bit uneasy. As we exchanged shirts he said: "I expect this will take pride of place in the bunny's section." I just laughed at him and said it would go on the wall with the others. I would never humiliate a guy and if you look at Daryll's record against other countries he is a very talented batsman. Once you get to know him he is OK.'

The last time Cullinan took on Warne was when South Africa travelled to Australia for a three-game one-day series at Melbourne's new Docklands stadium in August 2000. Cullinan was not dismissed by Warne in any of the matches, yet his misery against the Aussies continued. He made 29 in the first contest, then failed to score in games two and three. In the second match he was caught by Warne off the bowling of Andrew Symonds.

Cullinan's international playing career came to an end in 2001. Having made 14 Test centuries, including a top score of 275 (which was the highest score made by a South African in Test cricket at the time), he finished up with a Test average of 44.21. But in his seven Tests against Australia he made only 153 runs at 12.75. He fared a little better in one-day cricket, averaging 32.6 against Australia, compared to 33 against all opponents.

Statistically, the rivalry between Warne and Cullinan was nothing to get too excited about. Warne knocked over Cullinan only four times in Test cricket, a number that pales to insignificance when compared to the stranglehold that Australian paceman Glenn McGrath had over England batsman Mike Atherton. McGrath dismissed Atherton on 19 occasions in Test matches, their one-sided rivalry contributing to Australia's domination of the Ashes series during the 1990s and early 2000s. Yet the battles between McGrath and Atherton never quite captured the public's imagination like Warne versus Cullinan.

Despite their fierce rivalry, Cullinan and Warne have since crossed paths on a number of occasions over the past decade. Cullinan told Cricinfo in 2004: 'He was guest of honour at my benefit dinner banquet during the World Cup in South Africa [in 2003]. He stole the show and was a great credit to the game. Quite simply, Warne was too good for me. In hindsight, the focus on me was a compliment. I, however, only caught on towards the end that I did not do the simplest of things well – and that is watch the ball out of the hand. But by then it was too late.'

Warne summed up his rivalry with Cullinan in his book *Shane Warne: My Illustrated Career*, published in 2006. Under a picture of him bowling Cullinan for a duck at the Melbourne Cricket Ground in 1997, Warne wrote: 'I gave him a terrible time down the years. He set himself up for a fall with his sledging from slip but when he batted, things got worse and worse. At one point he went to a psychiatrist to help deal with leg-spin. I hope for his sake he played it better from the couch.'

SHANE WARNE vs DARYLL CULLINAN, TEST CRICKET

Shane Warne
Team: Australia
International career span: 1992–2007
Test matches played: 145
Test wickets: 708
Test bowling average: 25.41
Best Test figures: 8 for 71 vs England, 1994
ODI matches played: 194
ODI wickets: 293
ODI bowling average: 25.73
Best ODI figures: 5 for 33 vs West Indies, 1996

Daryll Cullinan
Team: South Africa
International career span: 1993–2000
Test matches played: 70
Test runs: 4554
Test batting average: 44.21
Test average versus Australia: 12.75
Highest Test score: 275* vs New Zealand, 1999 (* denotes not out)
ODI matches played: 138
ODI runs: 3860
ODI batting average: 32.99
Highest ODI score: 124 vs Pakistan, 1996

A replica of the tiny urn that is the most famous trophy in cricket.

CRICKET
Australia *vs* England

MOST SPORTING RIVALRIES TEND to wane after great players retire or great teams lose their winning edge, but the cricketing rivalry between Australia and England has certainly stood the test of time. The sporting expression of the relationship between the colony and the 'mother country', contests between the nations have been fiercely played and fiercely followed for more than 150 years, regardless of whether the Aussie or English teams have been considered great line-ups or have been evenly matched. 'It's the convicts' revenge, isn't it?' quipped an England fan at the start of *Ashes Fever*, a documentary produced to commemorate the enthralling Ashes series of 2005. 'Let's be candid. It's unquestionably all those old prisoners coming back up from down under to slaughter the vicious pigs that despatched them there in the first place!'

The rivalry between Australia and England began in the summer of 1861–62, 15 years before the first official Test match and 20 years before Tests between the Aussies and the English were nicknamed 'the Ashes'. A cricketer from Surrey by the name of Heatherfield Harman Stephenson – he was better known simply as H. H. Stephenson – was responsible for organising the first matches. An all-rounder with a distinctive round-arm bowling action, Stephenson had several claims to fame: he was the first cricketer to be awarded a hat for taking three wickets in consecutive balls, which led to the coining of the term 'hat-trick' to describe the feat, and he was part of cricket's first ever overseas tour, to North America in 1859.

Two years later Stephenson captained the first English team to tour Australia. The party was put together by a pair of English-born, Melbourne-based businessmen, Felix William Spiers and Christopher Pond, who saw a profit-making opportunity in bringing some of England's most talented players to the southern colony, where many people were flush with money – and thus happy to pay an admission fee to watch the games – thanks to the gold rush and wool boom. Cricket had become a popular sport in Australia during the early 1800s, with the game becoming more structured after the formation of the Melbourne Cricket Club in 1838 (the MCC organised the inaugural first-class match in Australia, between Victoria and Tasmania, in February 1851).

Stephenson and his men were paid £150 each to take part in the tour, and the trip proved to be a great success. The standard of play was high, with the touring side winning six, drawing four and losing two of the 12 matches staged. In addition, the organisers pocketed a tidy profit. As a result, another English team, this one captained by gifted Nottinghamshire batsman George Parr, toured Australia and New Zealand in the summer of 1863–64. Parr's team proved to be a top-class outfit, returning home unbeaten after winning ten and drawing six of its 16 matches.

A team of Indigenous cricketers from western Victoria was the first Australian team to tour England. Led by the hugely talented all-rounder Johnny Mullagh, the team was greeted with disdain by the English press when it arrived in London in May 1868. Nevertheless, around 20,000 people turned up to see the first game between the Indigenous men and an England XI, and the spectators were surprised to find that most members of the touring party really could play the game. Despite suffering many setbacks – one player, King Cole, died from tuberculosis only a month after arriving, while Sundown and Jim Crow returned home due to ill health – the team played 47 matches over the course of six months, winning 14, losing 14 and drawing 19. Mullagh was the dominant player of the series, scoring 1698 runs – all on pitches that were considered treacherous, at best – and taking 245 wickets. A subsequent change in the laws that applied to Aboriginal people meant that such a tour was unable to be repeated in the years that followed; the cricketing rivalry between Australia and England was further developed exclusively by white men.

The next battle between the nations took place in the summer of 1873–74, when legendary all-rounder William Gilbert 'W. G.' Grace led a team of Englishmen on a tour of Australia. As they departed from Southampton, Grace declared that his team 'had a duty to perform to maintain the honour of English cricket'. However, Grace and his men suffered embarrassing early losses to Victoria and New South Wales. Grace's insistence on treating the amateur and professional members of his team differently (the amateurs were upper-class Englishmen, while the professionals were from the lower classes) meant his players were often more worried about battling each other than their opposition. Yet they eventually pulled themselves together and held their own in most of the 15 games they played.

Another privately organised English team toured Australia in the summer of 1876–77. James Lillywhite, who had been part of the tumultuous tour run by Grace, put together a team that featured only professional players that proved to be a much more harmonious outfit. During the latter stages of the tour, which also featured a number of games in New Zealand, Lillywhite's men were challenged to a match by representatives from Victoria and New South Wales who had been able to assemble of team of the best players in Australia. A pair of four-innings matches between Lillywhite's England XI and the Australian XI were subsequently played at the Melbourne Cricket Ground in March and early April 1877. Although regarded as nothing more than a curiosity at the time, the games were later handed great historical significance when they were classified as the first Test matches.

'Alfred Shaw started it all,' wrote historian David Frith in his book *Australia versus England*: 'A plump, bearded, cunning Nottinghamshire slow-medium bowler, he send down the first ever ball in test cricket just after one o'clock on Thursday, March 15, 1877, from the eastern end of the MCG. It was a fine day, but there were only about 1500 spectators present (Sixty years later just over a quarter of a million people passed through the turnstiles of the expanded MCG over the five days of the deciding Test match).'

The Australian team caused a minor sensation by winning the opening Test by 45 runs. English-born Aussie player Charles Bannerman was the hero for the home side, making both the first run in Test cricket and also compiling the first century. Medium-pace bowler Billy Midwinter, who would later play four Test matches for England, was another solid performer for Australia. The Aussies' cause was helped by the fact that Lillywhite's men had only arrived in Melbourne from New Zealand the day before the match started, and some of the English players were still struggling to overcome bouts of seasickness. But the local team had endured troubles of its own in the lead-up to the contest, most of them a result of the bitter rivalry between New South Wales and Victoria. The pre-game bickering came to a head when Fred Spofforth, who was considered the best fast bowler in the nation, boycotted the game in protest at the selection of a Victorian wicketkeeper instead of his close mate (and fellow New South Welshman) Billy Murdoch. Spofforth and

Murdoch both played in the second Test match, in which England rebounded to square the series at one win apiece.

Spofforth established his reputation as one of the greatest fast bowlers in cricket history when he was part of an Australian team that toured England in May and June 1878. No Test matches were played but Spofforth helped the Aussies defeat county teams Middlesex and Gloustershire. Spofforth's performance in the first of those matches was extraordinary. He finished with figures of 10 for 20, including the scalp of W. G. Grace for a duck in the first innings, as Middlesex was bowled out for 33 and then 19. Played at Lord's, which would come to be known as the home of English cricket, the game was all over in four hours, with the colonials winning by nine wickets. The victory over Middlesex took the cricketing rivalry between Australia and England to a new level. It was now clear that the cricketers in the colony were just as good as their more highly regarded counterparts in England.

Just two months after the Australians arrived home, an English team disembarked in Melbourne and began a tour that was organised by the Melbourne Cricket Club (it wouldn't be until 1892 that the first national cricket board was formed, although initially it only included representatives from Victoria, New South Wales and South Australia). The first game, which took place at the Melbourne Cricket Ground, has since been classified as the third Test match in cricket's history. The Aussies made yet another statement by scoring a ten-wicket victory in less than three days. Spofforth was once again the star of the show, taking 13 wickets and even making 39 runs in Australia's first innings.

Later in the tour, the burgeoning cricketing rivalry between Australia and England exploded when a riot broke out during the touring team's match against New South Wales at the Sydney Cricket Ground. England had batted first and been bowled out for 267, with

Spofforth taking five wickets. New South Wales was then bowled out for 177, although their total would have been much lower if not for a brilliant knock of 82 not out by Billy Murdoch. Because the follow-on mark at the time was 80 runs less than the opponent's first innings, the England skipper, Lord Harris, decided to make New South Wales bat again.

The drama began early in that innings, when Murdoch was controversially adjudged by umpire George Coulthard to have been run out. The decision enraged the crowd, many of whom had illegally bet on a New South Wales victory. The punters in the stands thought the decision was cheating for two reasons: Coulthard was a Victorian, and Victorians hated New South Welshmen far more than Englishmen; and Coulthard was also the umpire who had been chosen by the English to officiate in the game (the umpire chosen by New South Wales was in fact Edmund Barton, who later became Australia's first prime minister).

After Murdoch was given out, the New South Wales captain, Dave Gregory, who was also the captain of Australia, fanned the discontent by refusing to send another man out to bat unless the English changed their umpire. Harris refused, and during the stalemate hundreds of spectators, including a young A. B. 'Banjo' Paterson, surged onto the field and began assaulting Coulthard and some of the English players. It took more than 30 minutes for the field to be cleared. Barton then attempted to restart the game by encouraging Gregory to send in a new batsman. Gregory eventually agreed, only for the crowd to rush onto the field again and force the day's play to be abandoned. The game was finished a couple of days later: the England team was able to compose itself more quickly, and Lord Harris' men recorded an innings victory.

There was much hand-wringing in the aftermath of the riot. Two men, one of whom was a Victorian bookmaker, were eventually charged with instigating the disturbance, and both were fined and banned from the Sydney Cricket Ground. Meanwhile, Harris cancelled a planned game against an Australian XI in Sydney, which would have become the fourth official Test match, and took his team back to Melbourne, where they played Victoria twice before heading home to England. The cricketing relationship between Australia and England was eventually patched up after Murdoch took an Aussie team to Britain in 1880. After much encouragement from W. G. Grace, Lord Harris agreed to put together an England team to take on the visitors in what is now recognised as the fourth Test match. The Oval in south London hosted the match, and big crowds turned out to see what was an exciting contest. The English players made their supporters happy by scoring a five-wicket win, and the tradition of Australia and England touring each other's nations on a regular basis has continued ever since.

An England team came to Australia in the summer of 1881–82 and played four Test matches – two in Melbourne and two in Sydney – but the touring party was unable to match the strong local side. Two of the Tests were drawn, while Australia won the other two. It meant the colonials had won four of the eight Test matches played, while England had won only two.

The good folk back in the mother country had no doubt that their men would be too strong for the Australian team that Murdoch led to England in the northern hemisphere summer of 1882. Murdoch and his fellow players packed in an extraordinary amount of cricket on that four-month tour, playing 33 first-class matches and five other games. They proved their mettle by winning 18 of the first-class matches and all five of the other games, with Fred Spofforth taking an incredible 157 wickets, while Murdoch made 1582 runs.

Yet Australia still went into the only Test match of the tour, which was played at the Oval, as the underdog. And the Aussies' chances appeared shot when they were bowled out for 63 in their first innings (wicketkeeper John Blackham top-scored with 17). But Spofforth evened things up by taking 7 for 46 in England's first dig – his haul including the scalp of W. G. Grace for just four – as the home side was bowled out for 101. Australia made 122 in its second dig, which left England needing only 85 runs to win the game.

Although the pitch was far from being a batsman's paradise, the local boys were expected to waltz to victory. Grace made a fine 32, but he had little support: his teammates crumbled in the face of a barrage from Spofforth, who took another seven wickets. In a tense finish, England's last batsman, Ted Peate, strode to the crease with his team needing ten runs to win. He made only two before he was bowled by Aussie paceman Harry Boyle.

The spectators were stunned, finding it hard to believe that a colonial team had beaten England on its home soil for the first time. But they soon ran onto the field and chaired Spofforth and Boyle from the field, all the while praising them for their gutsy performances. Spofforth's brilliant effort gained him the nickname 'the Demon Bowler'. The game dominated the sports pages in the English press, with most publications praising the Australians for the character they had shown and giving the local players a dressing-down for their lack of fight. Two days after the match ended, a mock obituary appeared in the *Sporting Times*. It read:

In Affectionate Remembrance
of
ENGLISH CRICKET,
which died at the Oval
on
29th AUGUST 1882

> *Deeply lamented by a large circle of sorrowing*
> *friends and acquaintances*
> *R.I.P.*
> *N.B.—The body will be cremated and the*
> *ashes taken to Australia.*

A few weeks after the momentous Test match, an English team, captained by Ivo Bligh (later Lord Darnley), set off to tour Australia. With the English slated to play three Tests against the Aussies, Bligh vowed to win the series and return with the ashes. During the 1882–83 tour, Bligh was presented with a tiny terracotta urn – some historians believe it may previously have contained perfume – that has since become the most famous trophy in cricket.

The urn was said to contain the ashes that Bligh had travelled to Australia to secure, and it was presented to him after a social match hosted by Sir William Clarke at his property, 'Rupertswood', located around 40 kilometres north of Melbourne, near the town of Sunbury. Over the past 140 years there has been much debate about exactly when the match at 'Rupertswood' took place, who gave Bligh the urn and whether it indeed contained the ashes from a burnt cricket bail. According to the Marylebone Cricket Club, which has the urn on display in its museum at Lord's (it attracts tens of thousands of visitors every year), the match took place on Christmas Eve, six days prior to the start of the first Test of the series. The urn was apparently presented to Bligh, as a joke, by a number of women, including Lady Clarke.

Bligh and his men were soundly beaten in the first Test at the Melbourne Cricket Ground, but they rebounded to win the second Test, also played in Melbourne, and the third Test, which took place in Sydney. (Another match was played at the Sydney Cricket Ground between England and an Australian XI, which was won by the Aussies and has since been granted Test status, but most historians do not count it as having been part of the series.) It is believed that, at the end of the tour, Bligh and his team went back to 'Rupertswood', where they were again presented with the urn in recognition of their 2–1 series win.

Bligh and his men were feted at a farewell dinner hosted by the Melbourne Cricket Club. The renowned cricket writer Gideon Haigh wrote about the dinner in an article published in *The Australian* during the summer of 2012–13:

> As the assembled cricketers and their hosts grazed on Boiled Turkey en Becahmel, Saddle of Mutton with Red Currant Jelly, and Cabinet Pudding with Maraschino Jelly, lubricated with Moët, Guiness and Dreher's Austrian Prize Lager Beer, the formal avowals reflected the newness of the rivalry. According to an account by *The Argus*, when the acting club president offered the Englishmen congratulations on recovering 'the revered Ashes of English cricket', Bligh replied that he felt his team 'could not take them back to England'; he would prefer they were buried at the Melbourne Cricket Ground. It must be the last time Australians offered the Ashes to Englishmen, and the last time Englishmen refused them.

England dominated the rivalry with Australia for more than a decade after that successful tour. Between July 1884 and August 1893, England won 21 of the 34 Ashes Tests played. Australia won only eight, and the other five were drawn or abandoned. The only series won by Australia during this time came when the Aussies beat the English 2–1 at home in a three-Test series in early 1892.

England certainly had better players throughout this period, none of them greater than W. G. Grace, who continued making centuries well into his forties, but the English teams were also helped by the disorganised and fractious nature of Australian cricket. When England toured Australia in 1884–85, the visitors scored an easy victory in the second of five Tests after a number of the best Aussie players, including the captain, Billy Murdoch, went on strike in protest at how little they were being paid to play.

But there was also plenty of brilliant cricket played during England's 11-year period of dominance, and the First Test of that 1884–85 series was among the finest ever played. Australia looked to be on track for a big win when it made 586 in its first innings, thanks to Syd Gregory's 201. England was then dismissed for 325 and forced to follow on. The game turned dramatically when England managed to compile 437 in its second innings, leaving Australia needing 177 runs to take a 1–0 lead in the series. The Aussies cruised to 2 for 113 before heavy rain began to fall. When play resumed the following day the wicket was almost unplayable; a pair of English left-arm slow bowlers made the most of the conditions, combining to knock Australia over for just 166.

After so many years of struggle, Australia's fortunes rose under the captaincy of Harry Trott, an all-rounder from Melbourne. An assertive leader, Trott put an end to the ill discipline that had afflicted previous Aussie teams, guiding Australia to a 4–1 series win over the England side that toured in the summer of 1897–88. The men from the colony continued their winning ways when Joe Darling assumed the captaincy, with batsmen Victor Trumper and Clem Hill, who would become legends of the game, helping Australia score a 1–0 series win in England in 1899. (The other four Tests were drawn, with bad weather one of the main reasons.) W. G. Grace, who was by then 51, made his final appearance in a Test in the first game of the 1899 series. No longer able to field properly, he retired from international cricket, although he continued to play first-class cricket until after his 60th birthday.

Meanwhile, Australia won all four Ashes series played between 1897 and 1902, although the Aussies did have their share of dramas along the way. South Australian fast bowler Ernie Jones became the first man no-balled for using an illegal action in a Test match when he was called for throwing at the Melbourne Cricket Ground in 1898, while Australia suffered the indignity of being bowled out for 36 in the first innings of the First Test at Lord's in 1902; England's left-arm spinner Wilfred Rhodes, who ultimately played 58 Test matches during an international career that last 31 years, finished with figures of 7 for 17. England then regained the upper hand in the Ashes rivalry, winning four of the six series played between 1903 and 1912. The three Tests played in England in 1912 – the first two of which were drawn, while the last was won by the home side – were the final Ashes matches played prior to the start of the First World War.

Despite the many run-ins between Australia's players and the various businessmen who organised the game in those days, most of which were centred around money, the period between 1890 and the First World War is often described as the 'Golden Age' of cricket. Notable cricket writer David Frith declared in an article for Cricinfo in 2010: 'Viewed against subsequent eras through a mist of nostalgia it seems untarnished and therefore attractive. Those years were replete with dashing amateurs who did not depend on the game for a living. And since it came to a jarring end with the outbreak of the most horrific of wars, a unique poignancy attaches to the period. The stars of the Golden Age were predominantly English. Apart from the occasional shock administered by the Australians, the mother country stood supreme, spreading cricket and much else to all parts of the globe.'

But things changed after the war, and it was the Australian team that prospered by adopting a belligerent approach under the captaincy of all-rounder Warwick Armstrong. A giant of a man –

he stood 190 centimetres tall and weighed 133 kilograms – and nicknamed 'the Big Ship', Armstrong was a strong advocate for the rights of professional players during his long Test career, which began in 1902. This meant he was almost permanently at loggerheads with the Australian Board of Control for International Cricket (the forerunner to today's Cricket Australia) after it was formed in 1905, but it also meant he was widely respected by his teammates. Handed the captaincy in 1920, despite his troubled relationship with the game's administrators, Armstrong led Australia to a commanding 5–0 series win at home in 1920–21 and a 3–0 series victory in England in the northern summer of 1921.

Even after Armstrong fell ill during a tour of South Africa and Herbie Collins took over as captain, Australia continued to dominate its rivalry with England. The Aussies won four of the five Tests played in Melbourne, Sydney and Adelaide during the summer of 1924–25, with Bill Ponsford emerging as Australia's new batting star after making a century on debut. Nevertheless, the English did go some way to restoring their reputation when they won the third Test, played at the Melbourne Cricket Ground in mid-February, by an innings and 29 runs. It was England's first Test victory for 12 and a half years (of course, no international cricket had been played during a number of those years due to the war).

England finally enjoyed a series win when Australia toured in 1926. The first four Tests resulted in draws, with bad weather and the three-day limit that was applied to most Tests at the time copping the blame. The final match, at the Oval, was played as a 'timeless Test' – meaning the game could continue until there was a winner – which was then customary for series-deciding games. Australia led by 22 runs after the first innings but lost its grip on the match when England piled on 425 in its second innings, the total having been set up by a 171-run opening partnership between champion batsmen Jack Hobbs and Herbert Sutcliffe. Staring down such a huge chase proved too much for the tourists, who were skittled for 125 on day four.

By the time the England team toured Australia in the summer of 1928–29, it had few weaknesses. Although the Aussies boasted such luminaries as Bill Ponsford, Bill Woodfull and a young Don Bradman, England dominated the series, winning the first four Tests (Bradman was dropped from the Aussie team after the second Test). Wally Hammond proved unstoppable with the bat, making more than 900 runs at an average of more than 100, while fast bowler Harold Larwood terrorised the Australian batsmen. The home side's only consolation was its victory in the final match. In the following three years, two things dramatically changed the rivalry between cricket's oldest foes: Bradman emerged as a batsman without peer, and England decided that no tactic was off limits in order to stop him.

Bradman took the cricketing world by storm when he made 974 runs at an average of 139.14 on Australia's tour of England in 1930. He made 252 at Lord's, 309 in a day at Leeds and 232 in the deciding Test (another timeless match) at the Oval, which Australia won, clinching a 2–1 series victory. In response, Douglas Jardine, an upper-class, Oxford-educated batsman who became England captain in 1931 – and who had previously responded to taunts from Aussie spectators by saying, 'All Australians are uneducated, and an unruly mob' – responded by leading the discussions that created 'bodyline'.

Referred to as the 'fast leg theory' by the English press, which supported it, bodyline was a method of peppering the Aussie batsmen, especially Bradman, with short balls that pitched on leg stump and angled in at their bodies. A large number of fieldsmen were then placed behind square on the leg side in the hope that the batsmen would fend the ball in that direction and be caught out. Jardine believed that bodyline was a perfectly legitimate tactic; indeed, occasional bursts of short-pitched, leg-side bowling had been seen in Test cricket before. When England toured Australia in 1932–33, in what would become the most infamous Test series in cricket history, bodyline proved to be both extremely successful and extremely controversial. Having restricted Bradman to an average of just over 50 (around half his eventual career average), and with Larwood inflicting physical and mental damage on just about every Aussie player, England won the series 4–1. But the conduct of Jardine and his team so riled the Australian fans, the Australian cricket administrators and even the Australian government that it very nearly sparked a complete breakdown in relations between the two nations.

The situation veered out of control on the second day of the third Test, played at the Adelaide Oval. A record crowd of more than 50,000 had turned up to see the day's play, which began with the Australian supporters cheering as their bowlers knocked over England's tail-enders. But the very same people were soon outraged when Larwood struck Woodfull, the Australian captain, in the chest with a fearsome short ball. Woodfull, who had opened the batting with Jack Fingleton, doubled over in pain but eventually composed himself and took guard once more.

Jardine then stacked the leg side with fielders, and Larwood peppered the Australian with more short balls; later, in their autobiographies, the two men blamed each other for deciding that this was the right course of action. The crowd showed its disgust by booing every ball, and for a while it appeared that a full-scale riot was going to break out.

Woodfull made a courageous 22 before succumbing, and later in the day the England team manager, Pelham Warner, visited the Australian dressing room to enquire about his health. Woodfull responded by delivering one of the most famous statements in the history of Aussie cricket: 'I don't want to see you, Mr Warner. There are two teams out there, one is playing cricket. The other is making no attempt to do so.' The words were never meant to be made public, but someone in the Australian dressing room leaked them to the press.

A day later, when Aussie wicketkeeper Bert Oldfield top-edged a short ball from Larwood into his head and suffered a fractured skull, the situation came to a head. The Australian Board of Control for International Cricket sent a cable to the Marylebone Cricket Club, which ran the game in England, stating that the English team's tactics were 'unsportsmanlike'. Jardine reacted with fury, stating that he would withdraw his team from the fourth and fifth Tests if the statement was not retracted. The British public wholeheartedly supported him in his stance. A fear soon developed within the Australian government that British consumers would trigger an economic crisis by boycotting Aussie exports.

The statement was finally retracted after pressure from Australian Prime Minister Joseph Lyons. England ended up winning the Adelaide Test and the last two matches of the series as well. Jardine went home convinced that the Australians had been sore losers, yet the laws of cricket were later changed so that umpires could act against bowlers deliberately trying to injure a batsman, and so that no more than two fielders could be placed behind square on the leg side. The Australian public never forgave Jardine, although many Aussies, including a number of the batsmen he had tried to maim, later warmed to Larwood, who lived the second half of his life Down Under after falling out with England's cricketing elite.

It took much backroom wheeling and dealing before another Test series could take place between cricket's greatest rivals. When Australia eventually arrived in England for a five-Test series in

1934, Larwood and Jardine were left out of the home side. Despite insisting that he had been bowling in accordance with Jardine's orders, Larwood had been given the choice of apologising for his role in the bodyline affair or being left out of the England team. He chose the latter, and he never played for England again.

Under the continuing captaincy of Bill Woodfull, Australia won the first Test, played at Nottingham, then suffered a heavy defeat in the second match, at Lord's. The third and fourth Tests were drawn. Bradman had battled ill health and poor form during the early part of the series, but he returned to form by making 304 in the fourth Test. He then combined with Bill Ponsford for a 451-run partnership in the deciding match at the Oval, as Australia compiled a first-innings score of 701 (scored at better than four runs per over). England needed 708 in the final innings to win the game but was knocked over for just 145, with Aussie leg-spinners Clarrie Grimmett and Bill O'Reilly taking seven wickets between them.

The tour ended in dramatic circumstances when Bradman almost died after contracting appendicitis. He eventually recovered, and Australia held the Ashes until he retired in 1948, winning the four series played either side of the Second World War.

Not that the Aussies had things all their own way throughout this period. They began in terrible fashion after Bradman was appointed captain for the 1936–37 Ashes series in Australia, losing the first two matches of the five-Test series. Yet Australia came back and won the final three Tests, two of which were played at the Melbourne Cricket Ground, the other at the Adelaide Oval. Bradman's side had become the only team in Ashes history to win a five-Test series after losing the first two matches.

The first of the games in Melbourne was a tumultuous contest. Australia batted first and made only 200, with Bradman out for 13. But the home side then knocked over England for just 76 after rain had made the pitch very hard to bat on. Bradman then made his name as a tactician by mixing up his batting order, so that his best players could stay in the pavilion while the pitch dried out. By the time Bradman came in at number seven, the pitch was free of its demons and he made 270 in a 345-run partnership with Jack Fingleton. In 2001 the *Wisden Cricketers' Almanack* rated Bradman's knock as the great innings played in Test match history. Australia went on to win by more than 300 runs.

A series of flat pitches marred the 1938 Ashes series in England, which was the last played before the outbreak of the Second World War. After the first two Tests were drawn and the third was abandoned due to poor weather, Australia kept its hold on the Ashes by winning the thrilling fourth Test, played at Leeds, by five wickets. Chasing only 107 for victory, the Aussies had slumped to 4 for 61, with Bradman out cheaply. Bradman became so nervous that he was unable to watch the closing stages, but his middle-order batsmen held their nerve and guided the visitors to the target.

England squared the series by taking out the final Test after posting a remarkable first innings score of 7 for 903 declared (the total was only surpassed in 1997, when Sri Lanka made 6 for 952 at Colombo). Keen to try to take some strain off his bowlers, Bradman decided to send a few balls down himself during England's marathon innings, only for his gesture to end in disaster when he slipped and broke his ankle. With its best player sidelined, Australia slumped to defeat by an innings and 579 runs, which remains the greatest margin in a Test match.

The next series between the old rivals took place in Australia in the summer of 1946–47. Although he had battled a number of health problems during the war, Bradman, by now 38 years of age, was appointed Australian captain. He struggled to have his usual impact with the bat but his team still managed to win the series

3–0, with fast bowlers Ray Lindwall and Keith Miller doing plenty of damage with the ball.

One of the most controversial incidents in Ashes history occurred during the first Test, played at the Gabba in Brisbane. Bradman was on 28 when he appeared to have been caught low-down by Jack Ikin in the gully. But Bradman believed it had been a bump-ball and stood his ground. To the dismay of the Englishmen, the umpire ruled in his favour, and Bradman went on revive his wavering career by making 187.

Bradman then agreed to take part in one last tour to England in 1948. His team proved to be one of the best ever to represent Australia: it did not lose any of the 34 matches that it played during the tour (the final breakdown was 27 wins and seven draws), and it won four of the five Test matches played.

The Aussies' victory in the fourth Test, at Leeds, was the defining performance of their brilliant English summer. Spurred on by a record crowd, England declared early on the last day of the match, setting Australia a target of 404 to win. It seemed an impossible task, yet Bradman (173 not out) and Arthur Morris (182) guided the tourists to a seven-wicket victory with 15 minutes to spare.

When the series and Bradman's career came to an end at the Oval, 'the Don', who was just a few days shy of his 40th birthday, was famously bowled for a duck by a googly from Eric Hollies in Australia's first innings. England's batting line-up then collapsed twice, handing the Aussies an innings victory and denying Bradman the chance to bat again. Had he made just four runs in what proved to be his final knock, Bradman would have averaged 100 runs per innings. Instead, he finished with an average of 99.94. No batsman has come close to matching that figure in the many years of Test cricket that have followed his retirement.

Even after Bradman retired, Australia continued its domination, winning the 1950–51 Ashes series 4–1 at home. Little-known leg-spinner Jack Iverson burst onto the scene that summer, bamboozling an inexperienced England team and taking 21 wickets at an average of 15. However, the English did break one of their droughts. Their victory in the final Test, played at the Melbourne Cricket Ground, was their first win over Australia for more than 12 years. In a bonus for the Englishmen, Iverson quit international cricket after the series so he could take over his father's business.

England finally gained the ascendancy in 1953 – the same year as Queen Elizabeth II's coronation – although the series was a frustrating affair for both sides. The season was interrupted by rain, which meant the first four Tests were drawn, so the Ashes were on the line when the teams came together at the Oval for the fifth Test. Just a few runs separated the combatants after the first innings, but the Australians dug themselves a hole when they collapsed to be all out for 162 in their second dig. England cruised to an eight-wicket victory on the fourth day, and the result handed them the Ashes for the first time since 1933.

England won the next two series as well, with off-spinner Jim Laker proving almost unplayable in the English summer of 1956. Laker became a household name when he took 19 of the 20 Australian wickets to fall in the fourth Test at Old Trafford. Aided by a very dry pitch, which the Australian players believed had been prepared to suit him, Lake picked up 9 for 37 in the Aussies' first innings, then went one better in the second innings, finishing with the remarkable figures of 10 for 53 as England won by an innings and 170 runs.

Laker is one of only two bowlers to have taken every wicket in an innings of Test cricket – the champion Indian leg-spinner Anil Kumble is the other one – and his match figures of 19 for 90 remain the best recorded in a Test. However, his extraordinary feat failed to garner much interest in his own household. As the legendary tale goes, Laker was married to an Austrian who had no interest in cricket or understanding of the game. In the hours after the Test finished, while Laker was enjoying a few celebratory ales, she answered countless congratulatory phone calls, some of them from very important people, but she had no idea what the fuss was all about. When Laker arrived home, she quietly asked, 'Jim, did you do something good today?'

After winning three Ashes series in succession, the English were expecting more of the same when they travelled to Australia in the summer of 1958–59. But the Aussies, having been rejuvenated by the appointment of all-rounder Richie Benaud as captain, dominated the series from start to finish. Benaud's men won four of the five Tests, although their victories were not without controversy. The issue that flared most often was the action of Australian left-arm fast bowler Ian Meckiff.

The matter came to a head after Meckiff played a starring role in the home side's eight-wicket win in the second Test, at the Melbourne Cricket Ground. He took 6 for 38 as England was knocked over for 87 in its second innings, after which a number of English journalists, and even a few touring players, accused him of throwing his team to victory. Yet he was never called for having an illegal action during the series. (He was, however, no-balled for throwing in a Test match against South Africa in Brisbane in 1963, and after that he never played cricket again at any level.)

Benaud's shrewd captaincy helped Australia retain the Ashes with a 2–1 series win in England in 1961. It was a sign of things to come, as the Aussies held the Ashes throughout the 1960s. However, the cricket played between the game's oldest rivals during that decade was generally of a lacklustre standard, with the Australian captains who followed Benaud – Bob Simpson and Bill Lawry – both favouring defensive tactics that resulted in slow play, which frustrated the crowds at the games and the many people watching at home on their television sets. Of the 20 Tests played between 1962 and 1968, 13 were draws. Of the seven matches that produced a result, Australia won four and England three. The hard hitting of England batsman Ted Dexter, who captained his country between 1961 and 1964, was one of the few highlights of the period.

England finally regained the Ashes during the Australian summer of 1970–71. The series included six Test matches, yet only two of them yielded results. Among the home side's few moments of glory was Greg Chappell's century on debut in the second Test at the WACA ground in Perth. 'Now perhaps I won't just be Vic Richardson's grandson or Ian Chappell's brother,' he said after his innings. 'Now I can be Greg Chappell.' In the first of many such occurrences, millions of cricket fans in Australia's eastern states missed the moment that Chappell reached his century because ABC TV switched to its 7 pm news bulletin.

England's 2–0 series victory was largely due to the fast bowling feats of John Snow, the batting of opener Geoff Boycott and the captaincy of Ray Illingworth. Snow's fearsome short balls created plenty of drama during the series, and the issue flared in spectacular fashion during the last Test, at the Sydney Cricket Ground. Having riled the crowd by peppering the Aussie batsmen with bouncers, Snow was pelted with bottles, cans and food while fielding on the boundary, and one spectator even leant over the fence and grabbed him. Illingworth decided enough was enough and led his team off the field. Play was delayed for almost ten minutes while the oval was cleared of rubbish and the police quelled the crowd. England had the last laugh, winning the match by 62 runs and clinching the Ashes in the process.

Another notable event that took place during that series was the first one-day international. Limited-overs games had been played in domestic competitions since the early 1960s, but moves to introduce the format to international cricket had previously been blocked. The match only came about by chance: the third Test, played at the Melbourne Cricket Ground, was abandoned without a ball being bowled after rain washed out the first three days' play. In response, the Australian and English administrators did a deal to put on a 40-overs-per-side match on what would have been the fifth day, as compensation for the many cricket-loving Melburnians who had missed out on seeing any cricket. (They also agreed to hold another Test in Melbourne later in January, which is why the 1970–71 Ashes series is often regarded as being a seven-Test series.)

Around 46,000 people turned up to see the one-day match, which was played without many of the rules that have since become synonymous with one-day cricket. Fielders could be placed anywhere, while bowlers could send down as many bouncers as they wished. Also, the players wore whites and used a red ball. The ABC, which had the exclusive rights to show international cricket on television in Australia, agreed to televise the match, although it felt the need to explain the unfamiliar format to its viewers before the first ball. Legendary commentator Alan McGilvray stated at the beginning of the telecast: 'It is a splendid game. It's different to a Test match or a state game. There's more involved; there's more tactical operations, more alertness in the field, better running between the wickets. Generally, it's a spectacle that I've enjoyed in England very much.'

The Australian captain, Bill Lawry, won the toss and elected to field, after which England was bowled out in its final over for 190. The tourists' only batsman to successfully adapt to the format was opener John Edrich, who made 82 from 119 balls. 'We played badly,' former England all-rounder Peter Lever said in a feature on the match that aired on the ABC's *7.30 Report* in 1999. 'Keith Stackpole took three wickets, and he can't bowl, can't Keith. You could play him with a stick of rhubarb in your undies, no problem, but he got three wickets.'

Australia then cantered to a five-wicket win with five overs to spare, wicketkeeper Rod Marsh hitting the winning runs by smashing a pull shot to the square-leg boundary. Ian Chappell (60) and Doug Walters (41 off 50 deliveries) had earlier been the stars of the run chase, both delighting the big crowd by playing many innovative shots.

By the end of the 1970s, one-day cricket would be the most popular form of the game at international level. 'I think everyone sort of saw one-day cricket as just being an add-on and a bit of fun to be had on the side occasionally, in a situation like that, basically,' Greg Chappell added in the *7.30 Report* feature. 'I don't think anyone really had any idea of what might grow out of it.'

When it came to Test matches, Australia and England each held sway at various stages during the remainder of the 1970s. With young guns Greg Chappell, Dennis Lillee, Jeff Thomson and Rod Marsh making names for themselves, the Aussies regained the ascendancy with a 4–1 series win at home in 1974–75. Australia then retained the Ashes with 1–0 series in win England in 1975, and it also won the Centenary Test, which was played at the Melbourne Cricket Ground in March 1977.

The contest commemorated the first official Test match, which took place at the same ground in 1877. Coincidentally, Australia's winning margin in 1977 – 45 runs – was identical to that of 1877. The 1977 Centenary Test is best remembered as the match in which Aussie young gun David Hookes hit England captain Tony Greig for five fours in an over. A second Centenary Test, which commemorated the first Test played in England, in 1880, was held at Lord's in 1980. That match was badly affected by rain and ended in a draw. (Neither of the Centenary Tests are considered by historians as being Ashes matches.)

In between those two commemorative games, England had a strong grip on the Ashes, winning the series played in 1977 in

England and in 1978–79 in Australia by a combined margin of 8–1. A key reason for the one-sided nature of those series was the split created by the advent of Kerry Packer's World Series Cricket (WSC). The players who aligned themselves with Packer and the Australian team that played in WSC were left out of the 'official' Aussie side, which weakened it considerably. It was not until the 1981 English summer – by which time Packer and the Australian Cricket Board had settled their differences, with Packer gaining the rights to televise the game on his Nine Network – that the Ashes once more featured the strongest possible teams.

Despite this, the Aussies, under the leadership of Greg Chappell, lost that series as well, although it was a brilliant tussle. Australia won the first Test, at Trent Bridge, then established what appeared to be a match-winning lead in the third match, played at Headingley, in Leeds. Australia batted first and made 9 for 401 declared, with John Dyson contributing a century and Kim Hughes 89. The tourists then bowled England out for just 174 and forced the home side to follow on. England promptly collapsed again to be 7 for 135 in its second innings.

With the Aussies in a seemingly unbeatable position, the English bookmakers began offering odds of 500:1 on an English victory. Ever the practical jokers – and ever the keen punters – Australians Dennis Lillee and Rod Marsh put a £15 bet on their opponents winning the match. Little did they realise the controversy that would be sparked a couple of days later, after English all-rounder Ian Botham and paceman Bob Willis turned the match on its head.

Botham made 149 not out off 148 balls in England's second dig, in the process taking his team from 7 for 135 to 356 all out (his effort was later rated as the fourth-best Test innings ever played). The 25-year-old's heroics enabled the home side to set Australia a modest victory target of 130. Willis then tore through the Aussies, taking 8 for 43 as

England pulled off one of Test cricket's most remarkable comebacks by knocking over Australia for 111 and winning by 18 runs.

Lillee and Marsh were later forced to defend their integrity, although neither has ever been accused of being happy that England won the match. It is believed, however, that they pocketed their winnings. In 2003 the English journalist Ian Wooldrige, who worked on the *Daily Mail* for almost 50 years, wrote: 'Their team coach driver, Peter Anonymous, had spotted the bet and collected the £7500 winnings, from which Lillee and Marsh bought him a set of golf clubs, return air tickets to Australia and paid for his hotel accommodation.'

Botham's legend grew when he helped England pull off another miracle comeback in the fourth Test, at Edgbaston in Birmingham. Chappell's men needed only 151 in the final innings of the match to claim victory, and they looked to have things under control when they reached 5 for 114. But Botham then produced a spell of wizardry, taking 5 for 1 in 28 balls and bowling Australia out 30 runs short of its target.

As if that wasn't enough, Botham then came to the rescue again when England found itself in trouble in its second innings of the fifth Test, at Old Trafford in Manchester. With his team struggling to set the Australians a decent victory target, Botham blasted 13 fours and six sixes as he made 118 off 102 balls. England went on to win the game by 103 runs.

Still under Greg Chappell's leadership, Australia won back the Ashes during the Aussie summer of 1982–83, although in the fourth Test, at the Melbourne Cricket Ground, the home side – already 2–0 up at that stage – suffered a heartbreaking three-run loss. Australia needed 74 to win when its last batsman, Jeff Thomson, walked out to join Allan Border in the middle of the ground. With Border farming the strike, the pair had taken Australia within 37 runs of a remarkable victory by stumps on the fourth day. Around 20,000 people turned up to see what would happen on the fifth day, each of them knowing that there was every chance the game would be over within minutes of play commencing. Yet Border and 'Thommo' batted on.

As many of their teammates watched on with beers in hand, the pair edged to within four runs of their target. Their grand fightback came to a dramatic end, however, when Thomson edged a delivery from Botham to Chris Tavare at second slip. Thomson thought he was safe when the ball spilled out of Tavare's hands, but Geoff Miller, who had been stationed at first slip, then caught it. England duly celebrated the closest Ashes result since Australia's three-run win at Old Trafford in 1902.

Border, Thomson and their well-lubricated teammates were shattered. As Thomson told Cricinfo in 2005:

> I could not talk about it for years. It was one of the all-time low moments in my life. I was not worried about getting out. I looked up at the board and we needed only four to win. I thought I would get a single, so 'AB' could hit the winning runs. How stupid is that?! Botham could have bowled a full toss on leg stump. [The ball from Botham] was a half-tracker and a bit of an away swinger. A bad ball really. I just tried to push it out for a single rather than smash it. All I did was get an edge. I was spewing. I had lost and I couldn't believe it. I was so angry because I had decided what to do with that ball before seeing it. It really wound me up. But all the blokes in the dressing room were drinking while we were batting. When I got back they were all pissed. I went into the English dressing room and lost it. I gave them a real mouthful and told them they were going to pay for it at Sydney. That was not like me. Beefy was a good mate. I bet they all thought, 'What a dickhead.'

With players such as Botham and batting dynamos Graham Gooch and David Gower reaching the peak of their powers, and with Australia struggling to replace Thomson, Lillee, Marsh and Greg Chappell, who had all retired, England turned the tables at home in 1985, taking back the Ashes with a 3–1 series win. Under the captaincy of Gower, England came to Australia in 1986–87 and won that series as well. But the balance of power in cricket's greatest international rivalry soon shifted again, and this time it shifted decisively.

The change began when England and Australia met in the 1987 World Cup final, played at the giant Eden Gardens stadium in Kolkata, India – the first time the World Cup had been held outside England. Now skippered by burly batsman Mike Gatting, England went into the match as hot favourite. Gatting's team had been expected to do well in the tournament, whereas the youthful Aussie side (the 22-year-old Steve Waugh was among its best players), led by Allan Border, had been expected to struggle.

'We were dubbed the worst team in Australian history to leave our shores to play in a World Cup,' fast bowler Craig McDermott told a Cricinfo video series titled *How We Won the World Cup*. 'But we were well prepared because we'd been to India the year before.'

In the final, Australia won the toss and made 253 in its 50 overs, with David Boon making an impressive 75. England then looked to have the match under control when Gatting and Bill Athey guided it to 2 for 135. But Gatting fell to one of the most spectacular brain-fades in cricketing history when he tried to reverse-sweep an innocuous delivery from Border and was caught behind. England struggled to regain its momentum thereafter, and Australia prevailed by seven runs.

Two years later, in England, Border's men demoralised England by winning back the Ashes with a 4–0 series victory that featured countless highlights, including openers Mark Taylor and Geoff Marsh batting through the opening day of the Fifth Test, at Nottingham; Australia's score at stumps on day one was 0 for 301. Taylor finished the six-Test program with more than 800 runs, while Steve Waugh made 506 runs at an average of 126.5 and fast bowler Terry Alderman picked up 41 wickets, the best effort by an Aussie bowler in an Ashes series.

Australia then dominated Test matches against England for more than a decade. Between 1989 and 2003, the Aussies – under the captaincy of Border, then Taylor, then Steve Waugh – won 28 of the 43 Ashes Tests played. England won just seven, and there were eight draws.

Throughout that period, countless Australian legends were made. Champion leg-spinner Shane Warne made an audacious entry to Ashes cricket when, at Old Trafford in 1993, his first ball spun past Gatting's bat and crashed into his off stump. The delivery was soon dubbed 'the Ball of the Century'. Paceman Glenn McGrath was another Aussie who dominated his English opponents. The boy from Dubbo in central New South Wales took 157 wickets against England at an average of just under 21, those numbers including a best performance of 8 for 38 at Lord's in 1997. In particular, McGrath developed a stranglehold over England opener Mike Atherton, dismissing him 19 times in Test matches.

In the foreword to David Frith's book *Australia versus England*, Atherton wrote:

> I played in seven Ashes series, winning none. It was, in truth, a poor era for English cricket, stymied as we were by an appalling feeder system. And it was a golden era for Australian cricket, blessed with a couple of players who will go down as all-time greats. The combination ensured a more one-sided contest than I or anyone else would have hoped for. Still, to have played

against the great Shane Warne, among others, and to have tried, fallen short, mired in dust and sweat, and kept coming back for more, to try again (as Theodore Roosevelt might have said), was a thrill in itself.

Under the innovative and astute captaincy of top-order batsman Michael Vaughan, England finally broke its Ashes drought when it prevailed in an enthralling series in 2005, a contest that reinvigorated the game in the nation where it began. Australia actually won the first match, at Lord's, which kept alive the Aussies' record of not having lost a Test at the home of English cricket since 1934. McGrath, who took nine wickets, promptly declared that Australia would win the series 5–0.

Ten days later, the second Test, at Edgbaston, proved to be one of the greatest matches in the history of the Australia–England rivalry. Australian captain Ricky Ponting handed the early initiative to the home side when he won the toss and elected to bowl (12 of the previous 13 Tests at Edgbaston had been won by the team that bowled first). The Aussies hit their first hurdle when McGrath stepped on a ball during the warm-up and had to be ruled out of the game. England then made Ponting look very foolish when it made 407 on the first day, at a run-rate of more than five per over. English all-rounder Andrew 'Freddy' Flintoff shook off his underachiever tag by putting Australia's pacemen, Brett Lee, Jason Gillespie, Michael Kasprowicz, to the sword. Flintoff blasted 68 from just 62 deliveries, each of his five sixes sending the boisterous crowd into raptures. Shane Warne was the only bowler who made an impression, his four wickets ensuring that Australia at least remained in the contest.

The Aussies were bowled out for 308 in their first dig – a deficit of 99 – but Warne and Lee then combined to restrict the Englishmen to 182 in their second innings. Chasing 282, Australia slumped to

8 for 175 when youngster Michael Clarke had his stumps sprawled by Steve Harmison just prior to stumps on day three. When play resumed on day four, England needed only two wickets to square the series, while Australia needed a further 102 runs to pull off a miracle win.

A sell-out crowd of passionate England supporters turned up expecting to see their team finish the job, but their roaring and chanting diminished as Warne and Lee put on 45 for the ninth wicket. But the home fans were out of their seats when Warne took a backward step to try to fend off a short ball from Flintoff and stepped on his stumps. England now needed one more wicket, while Australia was still 42 runs shy of its target.

Unfazed by the mountainous task ahead of them, Lee and the Aussies' last batsman, Kasprowicz, began accumulating runs. As they edged closer and closer to the target, each delivery became an event in itself. By the time Australia worked its way to within ten runs of victory, most of the England fans had convinced themselves that the cricketing gods were not on their side. But with the Aussies needing only two more runs to force a tie and three more to win, Kasprowicz fended a short leg-side ball from Harmison through to the England wicketkeeper, Geraint Jones.

Amid the pandemonium that ensued, as most of the English players and all of their fans began celebrating wildly, Flintoff put his arm around Lee, who was hunched despairingly over his bat. Flintoff's act of sportsmanship summed up the whole series: the play was hard but fair, and it was almost always riveting.

Just how much public interest there now was in the series (in both England and Australia it is not possible to reserve a seat for the fifth day of a Test match) was demonstrated by the scenes at Old Trafford that preceded the beginning of play on the final day of the third Test. 'Old Trafford sell-outs are more usually associated with football but yesterday morning 10,000 fans were turned away from the cricket ground as Manchester became the latest city to fall victim to an increasingly virulent epidemic known as Ashes fever,' wrote Lawrence Booth in *The Guardian*. Booth interviewed Jim Cumbes, the chief executive of the Lancashire Country Cricket Club, which was hosting the match, and Cumbes told him: 'I've never seen interest in cricket like it. You would probably have to go back to the days of Denis Compton and Don Bradman after the war for something similar.'

England went on and won the series 2–1, its other victory coming in the fourth Test at Trent Bridge, during which Australia was forced to follow on for the first time in 191 matches. The Aussies had their chances to draw the series and retain the Ashes when they put up a brave fight in the fifth Test, at the Oval. But Warne, who enthralled the English crowds by taking 40 wickets, dropped his friend Kevin Pietersen in the slips during the home side's second innings. Pietersen went on to make 158 and the match ended in a draw.

Flintoff was named man of the series. While his batting was outstanding, his bowling was even better. He was the leading wicket-taker among England's outstanding fast-bowling quartet, which also featured Harmison, Matthew Hoggard and Simon Jones. So well did the English bowlers work as a team that champion Australian wicketkeeper Adam Gilchrist was moved to describe them as the best attack he had ever faced.

The England players were feted for days after securing the Ashes (these days the winning team is awarded a crystal replica of the original urn). The celebrations included an open-top car parade that drew hundreds of thousands of people to London's Trafalgar Square and its surrounds, and a meeting with the Queen.

A chronic knee problem meant Vaughan was unable to take part in England's defence of the Ashes in the Australian summer of

2006–07. Instead, Flintoff was appointed captain, with his superiors hoping he would lead from the front, as he had in 2005. Sell-out crowds packed the Aussie grounds, and expectations were high that another classic series would ensue. But it proved to be the most one-sided Ashes series since Warwick Armstrong's team whitewashed England in 1920–21. Harmison's shocking delivery at the start of the first Test, in Brisbane, which was so wide that it ended up in the hands of second slip, set the tone, and Australia regained the Ashes with a thumping 5–0 series victory.

There were many highlights for the home side, none better than its fightback in the second Test, in Adelaide. England had appeared in control of the game when it declared its first innings closed on 6 for 551. But some magic from Warne saw England collapse to be all out for 129 in its second innings. The Aussies, with Mike Hussey playing the lead role, then chased down their victory target of 168 in just 32.5 overs, with six wickets to spare.

The following Test, played in Perth, produced another stunning effort when Gilchrist blasted a 57-ball century. (West Indian legend Viv Richards holds the record for the fastest Test-match 100, which he achieved in 56 deliveries.) But although the Aussies' performances were emphatic, that series proved to be the end of an era for Australian cricket. Star batsman Damien Martyn retired during the series, while Warne, McGrath and long-time opening batsman Justin Langer all retired after the final Test, played in Sydney.

Since then, the balance of power has shifted again, with England winning at home in 2009 and in Australia 18 months later. Although it drew the first Test, in Brisbane, and lost the second Test, in Perth, England had complete control during the remainder of the 2010–11 series. With captain Andrew Strauss leading from the front, England won the final three matches, each of them by an innings. The English batsmen were particularly dominant, compiling totals of more than

500 on four occasions, with Alastair Cook, Jonathan Trott and Ian Bell notching numerous big scores. The home side's capitulation meant that Ricky Ponting had lost three Ashes series as Australian captain – a blot on his otherwise outstanding record.

Nevertheless, Australia remains in front when it comes to the head-to-head record since the Aussies took on England in the first Test match in 1877. And although recent Ashes series have been dominated by the mother country, history shows that the pendulum will soon swing again. It is this long history of fierce competition, some of it fair and some not so fair, that has made the Ashes the greatest rivalry in international cricket.

Even as Test cricket is being swamped by the many Twenty20 competitions now played around the world, there is no doubt that the rivalry has plenty of life left in it yet. As Justin Langer wrote in his contribution to Frith's *Australia versus England*: 'While England and Australia continue to play with such passion, then cricket will prosper for at least another 130 years.'

AUSTRALIA vs ENGLAND, TEST CRICKET (1877–2012)

Tests played: 310
Australia wins: 123
England wins: 100
Draws: 87
Ties: 0

Test series wins

Australia: 31: 1891–92, 1897/–98, 1899, 1901–02, 1902, 1907–08, 1909, 1920–21, 1924–25, 1930, 1934, 1936–37, 1946–47, 1948, 1950–51, 1958–59, 1961, 1964, 1974–75,

AUSTRALIA vs ENGLAND

1975, 1982–83, 1989, 1990–91, 1993, 1994–95, 1997, 1998–99, 2001, 2002–03, 2006–07

England: 30: 1882–83, 1884, 1884–85, 1886, 1886–87, 1887–88, 1888, 1890, 1893, 1894–95, 1896, 1903–04, 1905, 1911–12, 1912, 1926, 1928–29, 1932–33, 1953, 1954–55, 1956, 1970–71, 1977, 1978–79, 1981, 1985, 1986–87, 2005, 2009, 2010–11

Drawn series: 5: 1938, 1962–63, 1965–66, 1968, 1972

Australia II skipper John Bertrand and syndicate head Alan Bond show off the America's Cup at a welcome home parade in Perth in 1983.

YACHTING
Australia *vs* the United States

AUSTRALIA'S LOVE AFFAIR WITH the America's Cup ended in early March 1995, when *One Australia* split in two during a race in the challenger series – the Louis Vuitton Cup – and rapidly sank to the bottom of San Diego Harbour. But in the three decades before that rather embarrassing incident, Australia and the United States forged a passionate sailing rivalry that resulted in the America's Cup captivating millions of sports fans in both nations.

The first Australian attempt to win the America's Cup took place in 1962, when the holders of the trophy, the New York Yacht Club (NYYC), accepted a challenge from a syndicate headed by media baron Sir Frank Packer. Under the rules in place at the time, Packer's yacht, *Gretel*, which raced under the banner of the Royal Sydney Yacht Club, did not have to compete in a series of races to win the right to challenge for the cup. Instead, the NYYC was allowed to accept any challenge that it liked. *Gretel* subsequently became the first boat from the southern hemisphere to compete in the America's Cup.

The New Yorkers believed that the best-of-seven race series with the boys from Down Under – to be held over a 24-mile triangular course off Newport, Long Island – would be a cakewalk. And their attitude was hardly surprising: the NYYC had held the trophy, known colloquially as the 'Auld Mug', since a boat named *America* defeated a number of British rivals to win a race around the Isle of Wight in 1851. (It was after that victory that the gentlemen from New York named the trophy the America's Cup in honour of their boat.) Prior to the challenge mounted by Packer, 17 British or Canadian syndicates had tried to take the cup away from the NYYC, but few had even come close to realising their goal.

Sir Thomas Lipton, who created the Lipton tea brand, was the most persistent. A Scot of Irish heritage, he took on the Americans five times between 1899 and 1930, representing the Ireland-based Royal Ulster Yacht Club. His boats, named *Shamrock* through to *Shamrock V*, were no match for the state-of-the-art American vessels they came up against. Yet Lipton became a much-admired figure in America, and he was eventually presented with a special cup for being 'the best of all losers'. More importantly, Lipton's sailing feats made his tea brand famous and extremely popular in the United States. Lipton's attempts to win the America's Cup also have a strong link to Australia's later success in the event. Thomas Pearkes, the grandfather of Australia's cup-winning skipper John Bertrand, was Lipton's chief engineer when two of the *Shamrock* boats were constructed.

In the days when Lipton raced against the Americans, the yachts involved were giant vessels, but by the time *Gretel* came along, the rules – known as the Deed of Gift – called for 12-metre boats. The NYYC was so confident that it chose *Weatherly* – a reconditioned vessel that had performed poorly in the 1958 defenders series (although there was no challenger series, the Americans usually held a regatta to determine which boat should defend the cup) – to represent it. In contrast, Packer had *Gretel* built especially for his challenge, and the boat featured all the latest sail and rigging technology. 'The only yacht designer working in Australia, [Packer's designer Alan] Payne was as tactful and attentive to basic issues as his backer was gruff

AUSTRALIA *vs* THE UNITED STATES

and freewheeling,' wrote John Rousmaniere in *The America's Cup: 1851–1983*; 'not only did he persuade the [NYYC] to let him use the New Jersey test tank, but he also talked them into allowing his boat to use sails made of American sail cloth, which was far superior to Australian and British cloth.'

Nevertheless, *Weatherly*, under the control of champion helmsman Emil 'Bus' Mosbacher, who was renowned as the finest yachtsman in the United States, won the first race by a touch under four minutes. As Rousmaniere later wrote, *Gretel* was not helped by its owner's pre-race antics: 'Frank Packer, an autocrat who was uncomfortable when out of the limelight, seemed unwilling to lose control of *Gretel* when she left her dock. He did not name the skipper, Jock Sturrock, until the eve of the match and he changed navigators on the morning of the first race, when *Gretel* went out with a crew of 12 men who had never sailed as a team before.'

But three days later, on 18 September 1962, Sturrock and his crew delivered a huge shock to the Americans when, aided by a huge wave, they surfed straight past *Weatherly* in the closing stages of the second race and won it by 47 seconds. An enthusiastic broadcaster described the finish in a *Movietone News* reel that was shown in cinemas around the world: 'On the second leg, with balloon spinnakers broken out on both yachts, the *Gretel* storms forward, the *Weatherly* suffers a broken spinnaker pole. Yes, it's the challenger's day today, and she exults in the heavy going that is more like the down waters her crew is used to. The *Gretel* never relinquishes her advantage, and the diggers do it, winning number two to draw even in the series.'

The Australians partied through the night, with the strains of 'Waltzing Matilda' ringing out around the docks. Their upset victory meant there was a huge amount of interest in the third race, but the light winds suited *Weatherly*, and the American boat won easily.

123

In the fourth race, held on 22 September, the Australians shadowed their rival all the way. Yet the Aussies were left shattered after Sturrock was lured into a tactical blunder by some gamesmanship from Mosbacher, which enabled *Weatherly* to win the race. 'Her 28-second margin was the smallest ever,' exulted the *Movietone* broadcaster. 'The equivalent of a nose finish in horseracing.' Needing just one more win to take the match, *Weatherly* cruised to an easy victory in the last race, as president John F. Kennedy and his wife Jacqueline watched on proudly, leaving the final score at 4–1 in favour of the Americans. Nevertheless, with the knowledge that the series had been far closer than those numbers suggested, a number of Australian syndicates, Packer's included, began putting together new challenges.

Having thrashed a British challenger in 1964, the NYYC decided to accept another Aussie challenge in 1967. With two Australian syndicates vying to travel to Rhode Island for the match, a regatta was held to determine whether Packer's refurbished *Gretel* or a new boat, *Dame Pattie* – named for the wife of the former prime minister Sir Robert Menzies – would travel to Newport for the match.

Ultimately, *Dame Pattie*, a vessel that was backed by numerous businessmen and corporations and that represented the Royal Sydney Yacht Squadron, became the twentieth challenger for the Auld Mug. As in 1962, 'Bus' Mosbacher skippered the defender and John Sturrock was at the helm of the Australian challenger. Memories of the close tussles in '62 meant that Mosbacher went into the match feeling very nervous. But his multi-million-dollar boat, *Intrepid*, whose hull boasted a revolutionary new shape that was the brainchild of legendary yacht designer Olin Stephens, proved much too good in the big swells and fresh winds blown up by a hurricane out in the North Atlantic, and the Americans prevailed 4–0.

'Aloft, *Intrepid*'s sails provided the drive necessary to slash through the turbulence below,' journalist Carleton Mitchell, who covered all the races, wrote in *Sports Illustrated*. 'Sails provide the horsepower for a racing yacht, and Sail Cutter Ted Hood had harnessed a whole stable of stallions for the defender. It was later revealed that *Intrepid's* mainsail was of 7.5-ounce fabric, against 12-ounce material in the *Dame's*. Although Hood sailcloth is available in Australia, the secret of the amazing fabric on *Intrepid* remains locked in Hood's brain.' In contrast, *Dame Pattie's* designer had gambled on making a boat that was better in light winds, and it was unable to cope with the conditions.

Still, the Aussies were far from disgraced, as Mitchell noted in his report:

> Although the weather this year played a considerable part in the proceedings, it should not be allowed to obscure the fact that Australia produced a very fine and advanced 12-meter yacht. Outsiders cannot realize that the technological requirements are of almost space-age complexity. For *Dame Pattie*, Australian industry for the first time fabricated such exotic items as bar rigging and extruded aluminium masts some 80 feet tall. So well did they succeed in all departments that it can be safely said that the Australians, on only the second try, came up with a vessel at least the equal of any 12-meter yacht ever built anywhere in the world – until *Intrepid* was launched.

Nowadays, *Dame Pattie* is used for charters around the French and Italian Rivieras.

The loss failed to dampen the Australian business and sailing communities' enthusiasm for the America's Cup, and Sir Frank Packer spearheaded the third Aussie challenge in 1970. A trio of syndicates from Britain, France and Greece also wanted to take on the Americans that year, so a challenger series – the forerunner to today's Louis Vuitton Cup – was held off Rhode Island. The Greek and British entries dropped out of the running before the first race was held, so it became a head-to-head battle between Packer's new boat, *Gretel II*, and *France*, owned by Baron Marcel Bich, who had made his fortune by exporting Bic pens around the globe.

John Rousmaniere described the travails of Bich and his crew: 'Bich brought ... to Newport ... sixty sailors, two chefs, and an immense quantity of French wine. Unfortunately, this colourful Gallic feeling also permeated the more technical aspects of Bich's campaign. He switched skipper and crews around all summer and, in the trials, tried two different helmsmen before he himself took over in the fourth race.'

Carleton Mitchell, again covering the event for *Sports Illustrated*, described the farce that followed as Bich tried to extend the best-of-seven series, which the Aussies led 3–0: 'The baron came prepared to go down in style, dressed as no racing sailor has been in this era – white blazer, white slacks, white shirt, white yachting cap, even white gloves. As he passed the astonished Aussies, he doffed his cap with a courtly gesture. The start was a tragicomic anticlimax. The baron had invented a manoeuvre surely unique in yachting annals – he planned to lure *Gretel* far to windward across the line before the starting gun, then have his crew ready with a spinnaker. He would suddenly turn back, catch *Gretel* unprepared, duck across and be off. The Aussies simply stayed between *France* and the line, dipped down first and were making knots to windward while the baron was still trying to get back under spinnaker.

Although visibility was at least a mile at the start, the haze soon thickened into fog. Progressively the race became a test of navigators. *France*, four minutes 44 seconds astern at the third mark, trailed by 24 minutes and 15 seconds at the next after a period of groping. Australian Bill Fesq hit every mark on the nose. *Gretel II* came charging out of the murk to cross precisely at the centre of the finish line. Visibility then dropped to nearly zero. After more than half an hour of fruitless searching, *France* lowered sails. It was a sad ending for the French, but indubitably navigation is part of the test of racing. Baron Bich did not agree. On Sunday he called a press conference to criticize the International Race Committee for not cancelling the race and declared that he would not return as a challenger.'

Gretel II, skippered by Jim Hardy (a member of the wine-making dynasty who later became Sir James Hardy), subsequently came up against a refurbished *Intrepid*, skippered by Bill Ficker, in the battle for the Auld Mug. Hardy's crew included John Bertrand, who would eventually lead Australia to glory some years later. The battle between *Gretel II* and *Intrepid* proved to be the hardest-fought contest in the history of the America's Cup.

Intrepid won the first race, but not before each boat lodged a protest against the other after almost colliding at the start. The protests were dismissed, although the race officials declared that the Australians had been in the wrong. The two boats did collide at the start of the second race. *Gretel II* recovered best and crossed the line first, but Ficker lodged another protest. As the rules did not require an independent tribunal to hear such matters, Ficker's protest, as were those lodged after the first race, was heard by members of the NYYC. When *Gretel II* was disqualified and the race awarded to *Intrepid* – the NYYC's own entry – the Australian camp reacted with fury.

'An American skipper protesting to the New York Yacht Club committee is like a man complaining to his mother-in-law about his wife,' Packer thundered. Martin Visser, the chief tactician on *Gretel II*, added, 'We feel we can't beat the New York Yacht Club, but we feel we can beat *Intrepid*.' Despite the outcry, the result stood, although an independent panel was formed to hear such disputes in later America's Cups.

In a further blow for the Australian entry, Hardy lost a tactical battle with Finker in the third race, which enabled *Intrepid* to claim another victory and take a 3–0 lead. *Gretel II* won the fourth race, but the New Yorkers successfully defended the America's Cup yet again by winning the fifth race by almost two minutes.

Rousmaniere wrote: 'Apparently, the Australians had repeated their 1962 mistake of never fully realising how much faster their boat was than the Americans. If they had trusted in their boat speed instead of their fierce starting-line tactics, Hardy and his crew might well have won the match four races to one. Make that a clean sweep if they had taken the time to learn the racing rules.'

Hardy reflected on that tumultuous series of races when interviewed by Peter Thompson on the ABC TV program *Talking Heads* in 2009. He recalled: 'We won two races, but we lost one under very acrimonious protest. In another race, we were leading, and it was called off in the fog. So, we were really making a fight of it and from that, we got an international jury for future America's Cup. We didn't win the war, but we won the battle, because in the finish, it was the international committee that cleared Australia to use the upside-down keel. We were on the track to winning the America's Cup after 1970.'

The sailing rivalry between Australia and the United States had previously just simmered along, but the events of 1970 brought it to the boil. In the minds of many Aussie businessmen, sailors and sports fans in general, Australia now *had* to win the America's Cup.

When Packer decided against funding another challenge, Alan Bond, a Perth-based property developer, decided to mount his own campaign as a way of drawing publicity to his property developments. Bond commissioned the construction of a 12-metre yacht that he christened *Southern Cross*. He then hired Jim Hardy to be its skipper and secured a number of others who had been part of the *Gretel II* team, Bertrand among them. As well as being part of the crew, Bertrand also worked as an assistant to *Southern Cross*'s designer, Robert Miller – a man who would later achieve fame after changing his name to Ben Lexcen.

After a number of postponements, the NYYC decided it was prepared to take on a challenger in September 1974 – the 22nd challenge since the club had taken possession of the Auld Mug in 1851. Despite the farcical nature of his campaign in 1970, Baron Bich still harboured a dream that his boat, *France*, would race against the Americans, so he decided to take on the Aussies in another challenger series. As they did in 1970, the Australians won easily.

Southern Cross's victory over the Frenchmen set up a contest against *Courageous*, a boat skippered by a brash Californian by the name of Dennis Conner, which had won the right to defend the cup by narrowly defeating *Intrepid*. Like its Australian predecessors, *Southern Cross* was regarded as being as fast as its American rival. But once again the Americans brought better tactics and organisation to the water, and they swept the match 4–0. John Bertram was unhappy with the campaign, as he told told Ben Collins in *The Book of Success*: 'I said: "Never again will I be involved in the America's Cup" because this was even worse than in 1970. It was amateur hour. [But] great credit to Alan [Bond] because that was the first of four America's Cup attempts he made. He learnt from 1974 and he came back in '77, '80 and '83.'

Bond's 1977 challenge started in positive fashion. Robert Miller was by now known as Ben Lexcen – he apparently changed his name after parting ways with the sail-making company Miller and Whitworth, which he had helped set up. He and Dutchman Johan Valentijn designed a boat for Bond that was expected to be fast in most conditions, but especially so in the light winds that usually prevailed at Newport during September, the month in which the

NYYC almost always scheduled the America's Cup races. Never lacking in hubris, Bond named his boat *Australia*.

It was skippered by Noel 'Stumbles' Robins, an inspirational figure in Australian sailing who had been made a 'walking quadriplegic' by a car accident some years earlier. Robins never recovered full movement in his arms or legs – hence his nickname – but he did regain his brilliant sailing ability. Born and bred in Perth, Robins came to know Bond through his connections in both real estate and sailing. Still, Bond surprised many people when he looked past Robins' limited physical capacity and selected him as skipper.

Representing the Sun City Yacht Club at Fremantle, *Australia* won the challenger series, but not before running into some stiff competition. For the first time, two Australian syndicates had taken part, with Packer dusting off his beloved vessel *Gretel II* for another tilt at the cup. *Gretel II* actually beat *Australia* in their one head-to-head race, making it all the way to the semi-finals, where it met *Sverige*, a sleek yacht entered by a consortium of Swedish businesses. The crew of *Gretel II* pushed their old boat to the limit, and after six races the semi-final was tied at three wins apiece. But *Sverige* held sway in the final race and set up a meeting with *Australia* in the best-of-seven final. Bond's confidence rose when *Australia* defeated *Sverige* 4–0. He now had no doubt that *Australia* was good enough break sport's longest winning streak.

Adding to Bond's confidence was the fact that the Americans had chosen the winning boat from 1974, *Courageous*, as the defender, and Dennis Conner – perhaps the best sailor in the world – was no longer skippering it. The backers of *Courageous* had been running low on cash in the lead-up to the defenders series, so they recruited a man who could both sail and cover the costs of the campaign. Although he had failed miserably in his attempt to win the right to defend the cup in 1974, media mogul Ted Turner fitted the bill perfectly.

AUSTRALIA vs THE UNITED STATES

Bond was certain that Robins and *Australia* would be too good for Turner and *Courageous*. However, it wasn't to be. The Americans, who had been training all summer on the official course, could read the fluky winds like a book. Although each race was close, *Australia* failed to record a single victory.

His sailing reputation restored, Turner wasted no time getting the celebrations started after winning the fourth race. As described in *The America's Cup: 1851–1983*: 'Turner arrived at the dock brandishing a bottle of rum with inebriated good cheer and later collapsed in a drunken stupor at the post-match press conference.'

In the Aussie camp, meanwhile, it was back to the drawing board for Bond and his men. The bitter rivalry between Australia and the United States had developed into a very one-sided affair.

Yet Bond put his hand up straight away when it was announced that the Auld Mug would be up for grabs again in 1980. And by the time *Australia* had been rebuilt and was ready for the challenger series, Bertrand, the rising star of Aussie sailing, had changed his mind and was back in Bond's team, which was again to be skippered by Jim Hardy. During his time away from the America's Cup scene, Bertrand had won a bronze medal in the Finn class at the 1976 Olympic Games in Montreal. He had also completed a masters degree in ocean engineering at the Massachusetts Institute of Technology in Boston.

Hardy and his men came up against some good competition in the challenger series. A British entry, *Lionheart*, proved very fast, while Baron Bich returned to the fray with a dynamic boat, *France 3*, and – at last – a well-organised crew. Although *Lionheart* seemed to have the most impressive technology, it was *France 3* and *Australia* that performed best during the preliminary races. The highlight of that competition was *France 3*'s effort in recording a race win; Baron Bich's syndicates had previously lost all 18 races they had entered.

France 3 even managed to defeat *Australia* in a race during the best-of-seven final, but the Aussies were able to regroup and progress to yet another clash with the Americans.

As in 1974, the battle for the Auld Mug pitted Jim Hardy against Dennis Conner, whose boat, *Freedom*, had comfortably seen off a number of rivals during the defender series. In the past, the Aussies had played the role of respectful guests of the NYYC, but they brought a harder edge to the 1980 contest. In particular, they tried to heap pressure on the Americans, especially Conner. 'The poor old defending helmsman, ouch, he's got heaps of fear of defeat,' Hardy told reporters in the lead-up to the first race.

Conner held his nerve and won the first race by almost two minutes, but *Australia* then shot out to a big lead in the second, only for the wind to die down to such an extent that the race could not be completed within the permitted time. As if that wasn't a big enough scare for Conner and his team, *Australia* then won the rerun by around 30 seconds, tying the match at 1–1. That race was also impacted by light winds, and both boats finished in near-darkness.

Shortly after they arrived back at their moorings, the competing nations' rivalry flared when Conner lodged a protest against the challengers for not carrying navigation lights. Conner was lambasted for his protest (which was thrown out the next morning), as it seemed to indicate that the pressure exerted by the Australians was getting to him.

But Conner did not have a reputation as one of the finest sailors in the world for nothing. He read the winds to perfection in the third race, scoring a narrow win. The Aussies then bungled their sail choices in the fourth race, which enabled *Freedom* to take a 3–1 advantage. Advantaged by some strong breezes, Freedom then won race five and claimed the match 4–1, a result that ensured that Conner remained a national hero and that the America's Cup remained bolted to a podium at the NYYC.

No one would have held it against Bond if he had decided that winning the America's Cup was impossible. But the risk-taking entrepreneur was convinced that he was getting closer to his goal. At the final press conference after *Freedom* claimed its match-winning victory in 1980, Bond announced that he would be launching another challenge in 1983, and he named Bertrand as his skipper.

Among Bond's first moves was to commission Ben Lexcen to design him another yacht – one that would be faster and more nimble than *Australia*. Lexcen travelled to Holland in 1981 and spent four months testing scale models at the Netherlands Ship Model Basin (now known by the acronym MARIN), working in conjunction with a team of Dutchmen led by naval architect Peter van Oossanen and Joop Slooff, the chief aerodynamicist from the National Aerospace Laboratory in Amsterdam. The design Lexcen and his helpers eventually settled on for Bond's new challenger – named *Australia II* – included many innovations, none of which proved more valuable or controversial than its radical keel, which was a far different shape to a traditional keel and also featured winglets on either side.

While *Australia II* was being designed by Lexcen and built from aluminium by Fremantle-based boatbuilder Steve Ward, Bertrand was busy putting together his crew. Unlike in other Aussie challenges, nothing was left to chance. 'We made the crew live together for three months in the old Customs House in Williamstown in Melbourne to check out the members' compatibility,' Bertrand explained to Collins in *The Book of Success*. 'The way we saw it we were going to a congested minefield and we needed everyone pulling in the same direction. We had to let a few people go because they weren't compatible.'

Bertrand's final crew included Australian Army Major Peter Costello and Olympians Colin Beashel and Brian Richardson. They trained harder than any Aussie crew had before, with some sessions overseen by members of the defence force's toughest regiment, the Special Air Service (SAS). At other times the crew worked with a sports psychologist, who also helped Carlton win the 1982 VFL premiership.

Thus, when in June 1983 Bertrand and his men arrived at Newport, Rhode Island, for the challenger series – named the Louis Vuitton Cup for the first time – they were ready for anything their opposition could throw at them. They even had their own battle flag and chose Men at Work's 'Land Down Under' as their rallying song. Bertrand said in *The Book of Success*: 'Historically, all great armies going to war have battle flags and music. We had a flag in 1980 bearing what looked like a flying rat and no sense of pride. After many consultations with an advertising agency, it was reborn as a boxing kangaroo. It had a pumped-up chest for pride and red gloves for aggression; it looked like an animal that was going to take on the world.'

Representing the Royal Perth Yacht Club, *Australia II* wasn't the only boat from Down Under that hoped to take on the Americans in 1983. A group of Victorian businessmen, led by cardboard magnate Richard Pratt, put together their own syndicate, and despite some financial and organisational troubles in the lead-up, they made it to Newport. Their boat, *Challenge 12*, was also designed by Lexcen and built by Ward, but it was a far more traditional design – more like Bond's 1980 entry, *Australia*, than the revolutionary *Australia II*. (In fact, Bertrand had initially wanted *Challenge 12* to be his boat, but he was convinced of the potential of *Australia II* by the Dutch engineers.) A third Australian entry, *Advance*, led by ocean racing champion and Bond-hater Syd Fischer, also took part in the Louis Vuitton Cup. The non-Australian challengers were *Victory '83* (Great Britain), *Azzura* (Italy), *Canada 1* and Baron Bich's *France 3*.

Desperate to keep their boat's unique design under wraps, Bond and his team transported *Australia II* to Newport in utmost secrecy, and every time the boat was taken out of the water for maintenance, dark plastic was wrapped around its keel. When the elimination trials began on 18 June, it soon emerged that *Australia II* was seriously fast. With Bertrand demonstrating great tactical and technical nous, *Australia II* blitzed its rivals, winning 36 of its 40 races in the preliminary rounds. For a while it looked as if the best-of-seven final would be an all-Australian affair, as *Challenge 12* performed very well during its early races. The third Aussie entry, *Advance*, won only two of its 24 races and was quickly eliminated. *Challenge 12* faded in the third round of the preliminary races and missed the semi-finals.

The final pitted *Australia II* against *Victory '83*, and the British boat surprised everyone by scoring a 13-second win in the first race. 'Her win prompted the dockside joke that *Australia II* was "sandbagging" to make her keel seem less threatening to the Americans,' Rousmaniere later wrote. 'But *Australia II* did not "sandbag" the next four races, which she won easily to become clearly the favoured challenger.'

The stage was now set for the next chapter to be written in the fierce America's Cup rivalry between the United States and Australia. *Liberty*, skippered by Dennis Conner, and *Australia II*, with Bertrand at the helm, would square off in the 25th battle for the Auld Mug. Bertrand later told Collins:

> I felt we could [win]. But remember, we were from 'the land down under', with a population of 17 million, and we were taking on the might of the US of A, which had 260 million people. Their budget was three times what we had, and they built three new boats. They literally had the US Navy behind them. The first time I saw the armada come in was when the US Coast Guard was

chaperoning Dennis Conner's boat. It was a formidable looking enterprise and here was our little boat with a skirt around it [to hide the keel] and a flag with a funny-looking yellow animal on a green background.

The rivalry between the two nations escalated in the lead-up to the first race between *Liberty* and the Aussie challenger. Rattled by *Australia II*'s brilliant performances in the Louis Vuitton Cup, and fearful that the boat's revolutionary keel was going to make it unbeatable, the Americans lodged a pair of protests. Their first point of objection was the wings on the keel; second, they alleged that the Dutchmen, rather than Lexcen, had played the lead role in designing the keel. (The rules at the time stipulated that the design and construction of the competing boats had to be overseen by a person from the country that it was representing.)

After days of claims and counter-claims, both protests were thrown out. Quizzed by reporters at the Newport docks, Lexcen reportedly said, 'I have in mind to admit it all to the New York Yacht Club that I really owe the secret of the design to a Greek guy who helped me out and was invaluable. He's been dead for 2000 years, bloody Archimedes...'

Nevertheless, the accusation that the Dutchmen were responsible for designing both the winged keel and *Australia II*'s hull has never really gone away, and van Oossanen threw some fuel on those flames in 2009. Sick and tired of Lexcen being given all the credit, van Oossanen gave his version of events to Dan Spurr of *Professional Boatbuilder* magazine:

> I got a telex from Warren Jones [Bond's project manager] asking me to meet him in Perth, Australia, which I did in March or April '81. Contracts were signed and details discussed, such as

confidentiality. We started work in April–May. We very quickly built a model of Australia. I had suggested a whole series of keel tests because I felt that the keel was lacking.

While this was going on I visited the National Aerospace Laboratory in Amsterdam. I met with their chief aerodynamicist, Joop Slooff, who was also a bit of a yachting bloke. He would play a very important role in what was to follow. We identified four different keels with different taper ratios and aspect ratios ... and arranged with the Australians to test different keels in the tank ... While all this was going on, Ben Lexcen wasn't in the Netherlands; he was back in Australia. I sent a telex to Warren [Jones] and Ben saying we needed to test this.

Ben came over a second time, and he and I started sketching what the winglets would have to look like on a keel. On a keel you obviously need two winglets, for port and starboard tacks, because the lift direction changes. We at MARIN made the drawings for the upside-down keel. Ben had nothing to do with it. He wasn't even here when we tested it. The numbers were miraculously better. When we saw the numbers out of the tank there was no doubt to us that the improvement was substantial: about 25% less induced drag going upwind for the same side force. Huge!

Van Oossanen also claimed to have been paid $25,000 by Alan Bond to keep quiet about his role in *Australia II*'s design. In 2009, after his controversial admission, he was asked by *The Age* if he believed that the *Australia II* syndicate had cheated in 1983. 'Yes,' Dr van Oossanen said. 'If everything had stayed the same, I would have taken this to my grave. But they are writing us out of history.' He then added: 'The America's Cup had always been plagued by accusations of cheating and espionage. Therefore, when you see it in that light, I would say, no ...'

Bertrand has time and time again defended the role that Lexcen, who died of a heart attack in 1988, played in boat's design. 'Although he had had only three years of formal education, Ben was a brilliant man – a Leonardo da Vinci,' Bertrand said in *The Book of Success*.

Not only did Bond, Bertrand and the rest of their team bring a revolutionary boat to Newport in 1983, they also brought a new attitude. As Bertrand recounted to Collins:

> I practised with sports psychologist Laurie Hayden about how to meet Dennis at the first press conference ... I said to Laurie: 'I'm representing a winning team; tell me the style of body language required.' We talked about shaking hands eyeball-to-eyeball and how the first person to blink lost the mini-battle. It was a bit of a joke because the handshake went for about 40 seconds before Dennis blinked. I always tried to walk in front of Dennis to the press launch and if I was behind, I'd always follow well behind, so I wasn't right on his heels. It's all part of the image of a winning nation. There wasn't the intimidation that I'd witnessed with my past skippers. There were a lot of things to winning other than the ability to race a yacht.

Adding to the theatre in the lead-up to the first race, Bond declared that he had brought with him a gold-plated wrench, which he would use to remove the bolt that held the Auld Mug in place in the NYYC's trophy cabinet.

Despite all that, a series of equipment failures and some superior sailing from Conner and his team resulted in *Liberty* winning three of the first four races. *Australia II*'s one victory in those four races was impressive – its winning margin of three minutes and 14 seconds was the greatest ever recorded by a challenger. Yet the Americans needed only one more win to extend their 132-year hold on the cup.

Still adamant he could turn things around, Bertrand successfully rallied his men, and *Australia II* scored a two-minute victory in race five. The Aussies then turned the match on its head by taking out race six by another record margin – this time it was three minutes and 25 seconds. Suddenly it was 3–3. The final race would decide whether history's longest winning streak would continue, and whether the Auld Mug would remain bolted to its podium in the NYYC's trophy cabinet.

Only twice before had the Americans come so close to losing the cup – in 1920 Sir Thomas Lipton's challenger *Shamrock* won the first two races in a best-of-five series, before the defender, *Resolute*, won the last three. And in 1934 another British challenger, *Endeavour*, won the first two races in a best-of-seven series, before the defender, *Rainbow*, won the next four.

The tension around Newport was palpable. Threats were made against the safety of *Australia II*'s skipper, his crew and their boat. 'We had armed guards brought in,' Bertrand explained to Collins. 'Australians were no longer welcome in the bars around Newport. Things had turned ugly because it was a billion-dollar industry in Newport and they'd had it for all of those years.'

The deciding race began at 1.05 pm on 26 September 1983. It was the early hours of the morning in Australia, yet millions of Aussies, including Prime Minister Bob Hawke, found themselves glued to their television sets, feverishly barracking for *Australia II* to pull off one of the great sporting upsets. They watched as *Liberty* opened what appeared to be a match-winning one-minute lead, nearing the halfway point in what would prove to be a race of more than four hours, due to the light winds.

Just when it seemed all was lost for *Australia II*, Bertrand took his boat out to the right of *Liberty*, chasing some elusive breeze. With luck and skill playing equal roles, Bertrand achieved his desired outcome. All of a sudden, *Australia II*'s sails bulged as it found a fluky pocket of the wind, and the boat took off, sailing right past Conner and his men, who tried desperately to change their position once they realised they were in trouble.

By the time the yachts rounded the last marker, the challenger was 21 seconds in front. As Hawke and his fellow Aussies roared at their television sets, *Australia II* pulled away during the final tacking duel and crossed the line 41 seconds in front. The NYYC's 132-year hold on the America's Cup was over. A host of polls in the years since have confirmed that Australians believe the America's Cup win in 1983 to be the great sporting achievement in the nation's history.

It was dark by the time Bertrand and his crew arrived back at their Newport dock, but there were countless Aussie family members, friends and supporters there to greet them. Hugs and kisses were dished out, and a beaming Bond was in the thick of it. In countless lounge rooms across Australia, bleary-eyed people punched the air with delight. While being interviewed on a Channel Nine breakfast television program in the hours after the historic victory, Hawke, who had champagne in his hair and was wearing a garish jacket covered in Australian flags, delivered one of the most oft-repeated quotes of his prime ministership: 'I tell you what, any boss who sacks a worker for not turning up today is a bum!'

The Auld Mug – and the 4-foot-long bolt that had held it in place at the NYYC – were handed to Bond two days after the final race. The presentation was made during a function at Marble House, one of Newport's most famous mansions, owned by the Vanderbilt family, a clan that played a key role in the early years of the America's Cup. Bond jokingly declared that he would rename the trophy the Australia's Cup. His only disappointment was that he had not been allowed to use his golden wrench to free the cup from its previous home.

The first American to lose the Auld Mug, Conner was understandably shattered. But he took the loss with grace, as *Sports Illustrated* writer Craig Neff recounted when he profiled Conner four years later:

> No one who watched his last press conference in Newport's dingy Armory on Sept. 26, 1983, is likely to forget the sight: Conner alone and exposed under blinding TV lights, tears running down his tanned cheeks, an incongruously jaunty straw hat jammed squarely on his large head. At that point it was painfully clear that the burden Conner had carried through the long, bitter summer was too much for any one person, even Conner. The old joke – if the America's Cup were ever lost it would be replaced on its pedestal in the New York Yacht Club by the head of the skipper who lost it – wasn't so funny, after all. 'It's kind of ironic,' says Conner now. 'One year you do a fantastic job and win and you get 50 job-well-done letters. Then you lose and you get stacks of letters about what a nice job you did. I actually got more credit for losing than I did for winning.'

In contrast, Bond, Bertrand and the rest of their crew, including Lexcen, arrived home to a tickertape parade and numerous receptions hosted by politicians and businesses figures. Not only had they scored an extraordinary sporting victory, but they had also delivered an enormous economic boost to the nation. As the holder of the Auld Mug, Australia had won the right to host the 1987 America's Cup, and it proved to be a boon for the Royal Perth Yacht Club, the cities of Perth and Fremantle and the state of Western Australia. The festivities and competition began when the challenger and defender series commenced on 5 October 1986. For the first time, the Americans had to take part in the Louis Vuitton Cup, which meant there was a very real chance that they would not feature in the final battle for the America's Cup.

But Dennis Conner had not spent the years since *Liberty*'s shock loss sitting around bemoaning his fate. He had begun his journey to redemption by returning home to San Diego, California, where he initially based his new Sail America syndicate at the carpet and drapery business that he owned. He soon teamed up with the San Diego Yacht Club – the place where he had learnt to sail – then raised million of dollars so he could build three new boats, the fastest of which, *Stars & Stripes*, he sailed in the Louis Vuitton Cup, which was held on a stretch of water off Fremantle called Gage Roads.

Although *Stars & Stripes* was backed by a huge budget and featured all the latest technology, Conner and his team met some very stiff competition in the challenger series, which featured 12 syndicates' boats from six nations. In something of a surprise, Conner's greatest threat proved not to be one of the other five American syndicates. (One of the best-funded of them, which was trying to win back the cup for the NYYC, was knocked out very early in the preliminary rounds.) Rather, it was the sole New Zealand entry, *Kiwi Magic*, that gave Conner the most sleepless nights.

Kiwi Magic won 33 of its 34 preliminary races, a record that included two victories over *Stars & Stripes*. The yacht from New Zealand was both fast and controversial. The first America's Cup boat to be built from fibreglass rather than aluminium, the boat was nicknamed 'Plastic Fantastic', and Conner was convinced that it broke the rules. At one stage, he told a press conference: 'Why would you [build a fibreglass boat] unless you wanted to cheat?' But *Kiwi Magic* was given the all clear and won every race of its semi-final against *French Kiss*. The right to challenge the Australians came down to a best-of-seven series between the New Zealanders and *Stars & Stripes*.

As it turned out, Conner should not have been so worried. His boat proved to be more reliable than its Kiwi rival, and his years of America's Cup experience gave him a further advantage. *Stars & Stripes* duly won the Louis Vuitton Cup, defeating *Kiwi Magic* 4–1. Now it was time for the rivalry between the United States and Australia to spark up once more.

In something of a shock, however, *Stars & Stripes* did not come up against Bond's entry in the defender series, *Australia IV*. (A boat named *Australia III* had also been built, but it had been beaten during testing by *Australia IV*.) Although Bond's yacht was again designed by the now legendary Ben Lexcen, it lacked the technological advantages that had powered *Australia II* to victory in 1983. *Australia II*'s secret weapons – its hull shape and its much-talked-about winged keel – had since then been embraced by just about every syndicate in the defender and challenger series. There was also no John Bertrand, who had decided to quit while he was ahead.

His replacement, Olympic sailor Colin Beashel, was a very talented helmsman in his own right. He had skippered *Australia III* to victory in a 12-metre World Championship regatta that was held on the America's Cup course in 1986, but he wasn't able to guide *Australia IV* into the deciding series against *Stars & Stripes*. Instead, *Kookaburra III*, which was also representing the Royal Perth Yacht Club, won the defender series. It was skippered by renowned 18-foot skiff sailor and designer Iain Murray and funded by Perth department store magnate Kevin Parry. In all, four Aussie syndicates had entered the battle to defend the cup. *Kookaburra III* and *Australia IV* qualified for the best-of-nine-race final, but Murray's team emphatically earned the right to represent the home nation by winning the first five races straight.

A fast boat manned by a talented crew, *Kookaburra III* was given a reasonable chance of keeping the America's Cup in Australia.

But Conner was a man on a mission. With the winds off Fremantle favouring the challenger, *Stars & Stripes* dominated from the start of the first race and went on to win the best-of-seven match 4–0. As Sarah Ballard wrote in *Sports Illustrated*: '*Stars & Stripes* had led *Kooka III* around every mark in every race of the America's Cup series. The last 12-meter to do that was Bus Mosbacher's *Intrepid* in 1967. The *Stars & Stripes* campaign, meaning all of it – the sailing, the science and the shoreside support – was, in the end, so thoroughly right and so devastatingly effective that it served to dull the pain of Australia's heartbreaking loss of the trophy it took so long to win.'

By the time *Stars & Stripes* crossed the line in the fourth race and won back the America's Cup, Conner had surprised many by endearing himself to the Australian crowds. His charm offensive had been a deliberate ploy, backed by a public-relations guru, and it worked, ensuring that Conner and his men faced none of the animosity and threats that had been directed at Bertrand and his crew back in 1983. As Ballard added in her report: 'the affection was real and it was fully expressed by a sign held by one of the thousands of Aussies who came to Fremantle the last day to welcome home the victor and the vanquished, WELL DONE DENNIS, YOU "BASTARD" it read. The quotation marks around the epithet were in the shape of hearts.'

Conner was a hero again. When he returned to the United States he was feted on numerous occasions, with President Ronald Reagan even hosting a function at the White House in his honour. A picture of Conner holding the cup with Reagan graced the cover of *Sports Illustrated*, accompanied by the headline: 'Aye, Aye, Sir!'

Conner reflected on his roller-coaster ride when he addressed a business lunch in Sydney in 2002: 'Me losing after 132 years was the best thing that ever happened to the America's Cup and the best thing that ever happened to Dennis Conner. Before the win by the

AUSTRALIA *vs* THE UNITED STATES

Australians, the America's Cup was only big in the minds of the yachties, but the rest of the world didn't know or care about it at all. But when we lost it... it was a little bit like losing the Panama Canal – suddenly everyone appreciated it. If I hadn't lost it, there never would have been the national effort to get it back in Fremantle, and without that there never would have been the ticker-tape parade up Fifth Avenue in New York, lunch with the President at the White House and all the doors of opportunity that it opened...'

But Conner never raced against an Australian boat in the America's Cup again. The great rivalry between the United States and the Aussies faded away, as other countries – New Zealand and Switzerland, in particular – entered the race for the Auld Mug and won it, and bitter fighting broke out over what type of boats should be raced. The rivalry looked like resuming in 1995, when John Bertrand played a key role in putting together the One Australia syndicate. Even after the syndicate's fastest yacht broke in half and sank, the Aussie team still made the final of the Louis Vuitton Cup in its back-up boat. But *One Australia* was beaten 5–1 in the final by the New Zealand entry *Black Magic*. The Kiwis then went on to become the second syndicate from the southern hemisphere to steal the cup from Conner. However, the 1995 America's Cup regatta was not a nailbiter like 1983. *Kiwi Magic* dominated every race against Conner's boat *Young America*, winning the best-of-nine series 5–0.

These days, the America's Cup has become dominated by billionaires rather than multi-millionaires, so unless Gina Rinehart develops a passion for sailing, it is unlikely that the rivalry between Australia and the United States will be rekindled any time soon. But while it lasted, it was a battle that elevated the status of the Auld Mug around the globe and gave many Aussie sports fans a highlight that remains unsurpassed.

AUSTRALIA vs UNITED STATES, YACHTING (1962–1987)

1962: *Weatherly* (USA) defeated *Gretel* (Australia) 4–1

1967: *Intrepid* (USA) defeated *Dame Pattie* (Australia) 4–0

1970: *Intrepid* (USA) defeated *Gretel II* (Australia) 4–1

1974: *Courageous* (USA) defeated *Southern Cross* (Australia) 4–0

1977: *Courageous* (USA) defeated *Australia* (Australia) 4–0

1980: *Freedom* (USA) defeated *Australia* (Australia) 4–0

1983: *Australia II* (Australia) defeated *Liberty* (USA) 4–3

1987: *Stars & Stripes* (USA) defeated *Kookaburra III* (Australia) 4–0

The Australian Diamonds celebrate winning the 2011 Constellation Cup against New Zealand's Silver Ferns.

NETBALL
Australia *vs* New Zealand

IN THE PAST TWO decades, the rivalry between the Australian Diamonds and the New Zealand Silver Ferns has become the stuff of legend. There have been games decided in double-overtime, heartbreaking misses and numerous buzzer-beating goals. The nations have met in the finals of four successive World Championships, with the games decided by an average margin of just two goals. The Diamonds and the Silver Ferns have also met in each of the gold medal matches since netball was first included in the Commonwealth Games, in Malaysia in 1998. The average margin in those games has been only three goals. As veteran News Limited sports journalist Ron Reed wrote in the aftermath of the Diamonds' win over the Silver Ferns in the 2011 World Championships: '[T]he Australian and New Zealand netball teams have developed a rivalry of an intensity that compares with just about anything else in Australian sport, including Ashes cricket.'

The netball rivalry between Australia and New Zealand dates back to 20 August 1938, when the nations met in what is regarded as the first international netball match. The contest took place outdoors on a patch of turf near the Melbourne Zoo. At that stage, the sport was widely known as 'women's basketball', and its rules were yet to be standardised – for instance, matches were contested between teams of seven players in Australia and teams of nine players in New

Zealand. Many other discrepancies had developed in other parts of the world since the sport was first played in the late 19th century.

Netball's origins can indeed be traced back to the invention of basketball by James Naismith in 1891. A Canadian immigrant, Naismith was teaching physical education at a Young Men's Christian Association (YMCA) school in Springfield, Massachusetts, and came up with the sport in response to calls for the development of a strenuous indoor game that would keep the local men fit during the region's bitter winters. The name 'basketball' refers to the peach baskets that were used as goals during the early matches at the YMCA gym where Naismith taught.

In the years after basketball was first played, a number of female teachers decided to develop versions of the game that they believed would be better suited to women. In the conservative southern American states, the rules were particularly restrictive, while in the some of the northern states, the regulations were slightly more relaxed. In the late 1890s, an American teacher took one version of women's basketball to Great Britain, where the sport was soon refined to suit the local tastes.

If you've ever watched a game of modern netball, which is played at a blistering pace, and wondered why on earth the sport has been designed to be so hard on players' knees and ankles, academic Tracy Taylor has the answer. As she explained in an essay titled 'Gendering Sport: The Development of Netball in Australia':

> Rules were ... devised to accommodate the restrictive female dress of the day, as women's long skirts made dribbling the ball and lengthy passes difficult. In consequence, the court was divided into three equal parts, with players based respectively in one of these three sections and no dribbling was permitted. The rules did not permit players to travel the full length of the

court as women were still considered frail creatures who were not capable of physical exertion without harm ... The lower level of strenuous physical activity and absence of any sanctioned body contact was perceived as a distinct advantage for women's basketball. It was a sport that women could play and still remain graceful and ladylike.

The later introduction of the rule that stipulated players could only handle the ball for three seconds was driven by similar intentions. Basically, netball was designed as a passing game, in which the ball could move up and down the court without the participants breaking into a sweat. In that sense, netball is like the QWERTY keyboard, which was designed to slow down typists in order to prevent jamming of the keys when they worked at speed. These days, people have adapted so that they can type very quickly using a QWERTY keyboard. Similarly, netball's rules were originally designed to ensure that the players did not have be very athletic, yet it has developed into a highly athletic and entertaining sport.

In the United States, the regulations governing women's basketball were gradually relaxed, so that today women and men use the same rules (although the state of Iowa sanctioned a form of women's basketball until 1994). As a result, the sport Australians know today as netball has never taken off in the United States. The refinements to the rules of basketball that led to the creation of netball took place in Great Britain, specifically, at Martina Bergman-Osterberg's Physical Training College at Dartford, in Kent. As Queenslanders Ian Jobling and Pamela Barham explained in their essay, 'The Development of Netball and the All-Australia Women's Basketball Association: 1891–1939', the size of the ball was reduced 'to the same dimensions as a regulation football (soccer) to avoid the need for a special ball. Rings were reduced accordingly, to their present size (15 inches or

380 mm diameter). Nets were added and posts were raised to their present height of 10 feet (3.05 metres). Thus, netball in Great Britain was born.'

Netball – under the guise of women's basketball – arrived in Australia and New Zealand in the early 1900s. (The sport was known as 'netball' in Great Britain from 1901, yet in Australia it was not until 1970 that the name 'women's basketball' was replaced. It was a long overdue change, as countless women were by then playing genuine American basketball.) The sport was most likely brought to the southern hemisphere by female teachers who emigrated from Great Britain. As in the rest of the world, the sport was tailored to suit the conservative social conventions of the time.

In her essay, Taylor wrote:

> The 1930 minutes of an Executive meeting of the AAWBA [All-Australia Women's Basketball Association] stated that, 'our girls should always be well presented and demonstrate good manners in public'. In a 1931 Executive meeting of the AAWBA a motion was passed that required players to be silent during the course of a game. The documented discussion, which accompanied the motion, affirmed that the executive felt that women's basketball should be designated as a silent game where only the captain was allowed to speak. The Executive stated that they did not think it was 'lady-like' for players to shout and carry on while engaging in the sport. Accordingly, the rules of the game were changed to meet expectations about proper conduct of women in a public forum.

It was not until 1960 that a standard set of rules for netball was agreed upon by a range of Commonwealth nations, including Great Britain, Australia, New Zealand and South Africa. This is the key reason why the sport had been around for more than four decades before the first international match was held. Even that inaugural contest between Australia and New Zealand in 1938 took months to organise, due to the bickering over which regulations should govern it. In the end, the Kiwis charitably agreed to travel across the ditch to Melbourne for a match that was held during the All-Australian Women's Basketball Carnival; the local players, judged to have performed best during the carnival – the All-Australian team – represented Australia.

The New Zealanders also agreed to play under rules that were more familiar to the Aussies. Not only did netball in New Zealand feature nine players per team rather than seven, but the Kiwis also played on larger courts and used a lighter ball than was common in Australia. And these weren't the only differences. In New Zealand, netball matches began with the type of centre pass that is used in the game today, while matches in Australia began with a centre bounce, a bit like that used in Aussie rules, although on a smaller scale.

So the first international netball match – and the contest that ignited netball's greatest rivalry – began with the two centres crouching low to the ground as the umpire leaned forward and slammed the ball into the turf. What followed demonstrated the benefit of playing under rules with which you are familiar. Victorian Dot Middleton lunged forward and grabbed the ball, then immediately began to stand up, collecting her unsuspecting New Zealand opponent, Muriel Boswell, in the face and breaking her nose. 'The Australian girl, her head came up, connected with my nose, and that was the end of my first game,' Boswell told *The Age* in 2006.

New Zealand's afternoon failed to improve; Australia led by 14 goals at half-time, then won 40–11. Nevertheless, the newspaper reports published in the days after the game suggested that the match was more closely fought than the score suggests. In fact, New Zealand was left to rue some terrible shooting after hitting the target with just 11 of their 33 shots at goal.

Yet the Kiwis were not without a decent excuse. First, they were used to playing with a larger goal ring, and second, in New Zealand the ring was placed against the goal post, whereas in Australia it was 6 inches out from the post. Despite all that, netball's first international match paved the way for the standardisation of the sport's rules around the globe, which included the adoption of the seven-a-side format.

In fact, the Kiwis subsequently invited Australia and England to play in a seven-a-side tournament in New Zealand in 1940, and the nations planned for a complete set of international rules to be agreed upon then. But the beginning of the Second World War forced the postponement of the tournament, and it wasn't until 1948 that Australia and New Zealand met for a second time.

Australia toured New Zealand in August and September 1948, playing 23 matches, including three international games against the Silver Ferns. Australia won each of the internationals by an average margin of 21 goals. Although domestic netball in New Zealand was played on a nine-a-side basis until 1956, the series in 1948 featured only seven players per team.

Another long gap between matches then ensued, with 12 years elapsing before the Silver Ferns travelled across the Tasman in 1960 for a three-match series. It was during this series that the rivalry was well and truly ignited. The flame was lit when New Zealand caused a boilover by winning the first game, in Adelaide, by nine goals. The shock of being beaten by the Silver Ferns for the first time sparked the Diamonds into action. They won the last two matches, played in Melbourne and Sydney, yet both were very close. Five goals separated the teams in the second game, while the third was decided by just one, with Australia winning 46–45.

AUSTRALIA vs NEW ZEALAND

After the official rules for netball were finally agreed upon in 1961, the first World Netball Championships were held in England in 1963. The 11-team tournament was conducted on a round-robin basis, with all the teams playing each other. No final was played; the winner was the team that finished atop the ladder. Australia, coached by Lorna McConchie and captained by Joyce Brown (who later became a very successful national coach), cruised through its early matches, defeating Sri Lanka 82–12 and Wales 94–7. But its run towards the title was almost upended by New Zealand. In a thrilling game, the lead changed on numerous occasions before Australia prevailed by a goal, 37–36. The Diamonds then won the remainder of their ten matches, ending the tournament with an unbeaten record and claiming the first world title. Almost every international netball championship held since then, whether for a world title or a Commonwealth Games gold medal, has been a two-horse race between Australia and New Zealand.

It was four years later, at the end of the second World Netball Championships, played in Perth, that the next chapter of the Diamonds vs Silver Ferns rivalry was written. As was the case at the first world titles, the tournament was a round-robin affair, although this time it featured only eight teams. The organisers decided to create some drama by fixturing the Australia–New Zealand game in the final round of matches. As expected, both teams won their first six games, which meant their clash became a play-off for the title of world champion. Australia went into the match as favourite, but New Zealand silenced the pro-Aussie crowd by scoring a six-goal win. Silver Fern Joan Harnett was named player of the tournament.

The rivalry was next put to the test when Australia played a two-match international series in New Zealand in 1969. The Diamonds won the first game, in Wellington, by ten goals, then lost the second, in Dunedin, by four. Such twists and turns have been a defining feature of the seven-decade netball rivalry between the nations.

Beginning in December 1970, the third World Netball Championships were held in Kingston, Jamaica, which meant an arduous multi-stop flight for the players from Australia and New Zealand. Nevertheless, the two teams swept all before them during their early rounds. Once again it was a round-robin tournament, and once again the two netball superpowers were drawn to play each other in the final round. As in 1967, both teams went into the match undefeated, so the winner would be crowned world champion. The only difference this time around was the result. Australia, led by its captain and star defender, Gaye Teede, won by six goals.

Australia did not play another international match until the fourth World Netball Championships, held in New Zealand in August and September 1975. Most of the Diamonds' matches were one-sided; they scored a 74-goal win over Papua New Guinea and a 55-goal victory over Singapore, although they beat England by only five. The majority of New Zealand's games were also one-sided, but the Silver Ferns cost themselves any chance of winning the title when they suffered an upset loss to England. Still, the tournament finished with a bang, as the now traditional last-round match between the Kiwis and Australia went down to the wire. The scores were tied at 34–34 when the final whistle blew, but the result was enough to hand the Aussies their third world championship from four attempts. Australia's star player was its captain and goal shooter, Margaret Caldow, whose international career spanned 17 years. At the end of the tournament Caldow was named captain of the 'World Team'.

The next Australia–New Zealand match took place at the fifth World Netball Championships, which featured 12 teams and were played in Port of Spain, Trinidad and Tobago, in 1979. This time, the match between the top-ranked nations occurred in the eighth round of the tournament rather than in the final round. Again under the captaincy of Caldow, the Diamonds defeated their arch-rivals by two goals. The Australian players rejoiced, believing their victory over the Silver Ferns would ensure that they won the tournament. But the following day they were beaten by two goals by the home side, Trinidad and Tobago, in a major upset. When New Zealand then beat Trinidad and Tobago a couple of days later, the organisers were forced to declare that the tournament had finished as a three-way tie.

The rivalry between the Diamonds and Silver Ferns continued during the 1980s. New Zealand won five matches in a row against Australia in 1981 and 1982, only to have the Diamonds strike back and defeat their nemesis in what proved to be the deciding match of the 1983 World Netball Championships, held in Singapore.

Australia fielded a very strong team through the mid-1980s, with tireless centre Jill McIntosh and shooter Anne Sargeant (who captained the Diamonds for six years) leading the way. But after 1983 it was the Silver Ferns who earned a reputation for delivering when it mattered most. They beat the Diamonds by four goals in the final of the Australia Games at Melbourne's Festival Hall in 1985, and later that year they were again too good – although this time the margin was only two goals – when the teams met in the final of the World Games in London (a quadrennial festival featuring international sports that are not part of the Olympics). Although netball is no longer part of the World Games line-up, the sport was included in the program in 1985, 1989 (held in Karlsruhe, Germany) and 1993 (The Hague, Netherlands). Australia and New Zealand met in the gold medal match on each occasion, the Silver Ferns winning the first two and the Diamonds claiming the third.

New Zealand continued its big-game dominance of Australia when the seventh World Netball Championships were held in Glasgow, Scotland, in 1987 (the last world championships to be held outdoors). Captained by Leigh Gibbs and coached by Lois Muir, the Silver Ferns team that contested the tournament is remembered as one of the most talented combinations in netball history. The New Zealanders were far too good for the Diamonds when they met in the eighth round, winning 39–28. It was not a good tournament for the Australians, who the previous day had suffered a one-goal loss to Trinidad and Tobago. The Silver Ferns duly won the world title, finishing the tournament unbeaten. The Diamonds and Trinidad and Tobago were awarded equal second place.

The Silver Ferns won all three matches when the Diamonds toured New Zealand in 1989, but the first indication that the tables were turning again came when the teams met in a demonstration match at the 1990 Commonwealth Games, held in Auckland. Australia emerged victorious by a whopping 18 goals, and then took that form into the eighth World Netball Championships, held at the Sydney Entertainment Centre in 1991.

For the first time, the competing teams were divided into two groups and the tournament featured semi-finals and a final, which was quite a contrast to the simple round-robin format that had been used since 1963. As the top-ranked teams, Australia and New Zealand were placed in different groups. Without the Silver Ferns to worry them, the Diamonds barnstormed through their preliminary matches, their results including a 27-goal win over England and a 107–10 defeat of Sri Lanka. Their semi-final against Jamaica was a harder-fought affair, but the Aussie team still managed to win by six goals. Predictably, New Zealand defeated England in the other semi-final, which set up a much-anticipated final between the best teams in the world.

This game would prove to be such a brilliant contest that it is often quoted as being among the top five international netball matches ever played. The Silver Ferns led 41–40 at three-quarter time, and the game was in the balance right to the end. Australia opened a 53–51 lead with just over a minute to go, before New Zealand narrowed the margin to one goal with 30 seconds remaining.

With a big audience watching the match on ABC TV and Aussie Prime Minister Bob Hawke cheering in the stands, the Diamonds had the centre pass. They tried to flip the ball around and run down the clock, but Silver Ferns defender Waimarama Taumaunu cut off a pass. With about 15 seconds to go, Taumaunu dished the ball off to a teammate, yet the next pass into the goal-ring was a wild one, and Australian defender Roselee Jencke was able to pick it off.

Urged on by a screaming crowd, the Diamonds rushed the ball up the court, the final whistle sounding as a pass found Vicky Wilson by herself inside Australia's goal-ring. Wilson shot the goal but it did not count, and the final score was 53–52.

The excitement got the better of former Australian player Anne Sargeant, who was providing special comments for the ABC's television coverage. 'Australia! Yes!' Sargeant yelled as Wilson and her teammates began jumping up and down with delight. Soon the Diamonds' coach, Joyce Brown, was on the court, hugging her players. Up in the stands, Hawke, wearing a huge grin, clapped wildly. 'Your heart goes out to New Zealand, who led for so much of the game,' said ABC commentator Steve Robilliard, remembering that the match was also being screened across the ditch.

The Diamonds' victory meant they were now the outright winners of seven of the nine world championships played. The triumph in Sydney was also Australia's 19th consecutive win, a run of success that had begun more than a year before. The Diamonds would eventually win 37 straight matches, their streak including a clean sweep of New Zealand in the three-match Kleenex Cup that was played in Melbourne, Sydney and Adelaide a year after the world championships. All up, Australia's winning run lasted from the time it beat England in Melbourne on 17 June 1990 to its three-goal win over New Zealand in the second game of the Milo Series, played in the Kiwi town of Palmerston North on 21 May 1994. Predictably, it was the Silver Ferns who finally reminded the Diamonds what defeat tasted like, their breakthrough win coming in the third and final game of the Milo Series, played in Auckland.

The Diamonds soon regained their verve. Coached by Jill McIntosh and captained by Michelle Fielke, Australia did not lose another game prior to the 1995 World Netball Championships, which were held in the English city of Birmingham. The tournament was notable for two important firsts: South Africa fielded a team, having been allowed to re-enter the global sporting world following the end of apartheid; and the South Africans upset the netball world order by defeating the Silver Ferns in the first round of the preliminary matches. That loss meant the Silver Ferns were placed in the same pool as Australia for the second round of matches, so they had to do battle a week before the final. Yet they put on a show that was worthy of a championship decider, with the Diamonds winning by a goal, 45–44.

'Victory came in the last three minutes,' read the match report in Melbourne's *Age* newspaper. 'The teams were locked at 15–15 at the first break; NZ led 19–16 at half-time. The advantage then changed several times, with NZ 43–42 ahead with three minutes to spare. In a frantic finish, Australia netted three goals to NZ's one.'

Coach Jill McIntosh described the Diamonds' win as 'up there with the best of them'. But success had come at a huge cost, as 30-year-old champion shooter Vicky Wilson suffered a serious knee injury when she was bumped to the floor just before half-time. At the time, it was feared that the injury would end Wilson's international career. 'Tears are just continually rolling down her face,' Wilson's teammate Carley Baker told reporters after the match. 'She has no idea where her future lies. She knows there is nothing we can do for her and nothing she can do for herself. It's devastating.' Wilson's state of mind had improved by the time the Diamonds thrashed South Africa in the final, and she watched on from the sidelines with a smile on her face.

By the end of the 1995 world championships, the Diamonds were compiling another impressive winning streak, having scored 17 consecutive victories since their loss to New Zealand in May 1994. This run of success reached 26 straight wins, before Australia suffered an upset two-goal loss during a tour of Jamaica in February 1998. But the Diamonds then won their following 17 matches, which included numerous defeats of New Zealand.

In fact, the period from 1995 to 1999 featured some of the most one-sided Diamonds–Silver Ferns matches in the history of the great rivalry. Australia won all three contests in the 1996 Milo Cup (played in Sydney, Melbourne and Adelaide) by an average margin of 16 goals. Australia's tour of New Zealand in 1998 produced three similarly one-sided games, the Diamonds winning the first by 11 goals, the second by nine and the third by four. One reason for Australia's continued dominance was Wilson's effort in defying the team doctor's initial diagnosis and returning to the court for Australia a year after undergoing reconstructive surgery on her knee.

In 1998 netball was included as an official sport at the Commonwealth Games for the first time, and although South Africa and England both fielded strong teams, it was Australia and New Zealand that met in the gold medal match at the Stadium Juara in Kuala Lumpur. Stung into action by their recent poor form against the Diamonds, the Silver Ferns put up a brave fight. But Australia proved too polished when it mattered most, Wilson erasing her painful memories of 1995 by leading the Diamonds a 42–39 victory.

'SIMPLY THE BEST!' shouted the headline in the *Herald Sun* a day after the match. 'If there was any question whether Australia was still netball's powerhouse, it was answered once and for all, with Commonwealth Games gold,' read the accompanying report. 'Down by three goals with just 10 minutes to go, the world's most dominant team fought back to write itself into the history books...'

Wilson, who had burst into tears at the final whistle, said it was 'one of the toughest games' she had played. 'I tried not to think about losing,' she added. 'I just kept track of the clock and the centre passes. I knew we had to go goal for goal.'

Diamonds coach Jill McIntosh was similarly effusive: 'I had complete faith in them. I have seen them do it all before. I have seen them 11 goals down and come back so I knew they could do it. This victory is up there with the best. It is the first gold for netball and we wanted to create history. This is as good as the world champs victory... all the tours and preparation are worth it just for this one moment.'

Five months after the Commonwealth Games, New Zealand finally broke its almost-five-year drought against Australia. The Silver Ferns' 12-goal win in the first game of the Fisher & Paykel Cup, played in Christchurch, was their first victory over the Diamonds since May 1994.

But Australia was back to its best by the time the 10th World Netball Championships began in Christchurch, New Zealand, in September 1999 – not that the Kiwi press shared that view. 'The Jill McIntosh-coached Australian side were seen by many as past their peak, and... they were even derided as "Jill's Geriatrics",' read a review of the tournament on the TVNZ website. The Diamonds were never seriously threatened during the preliminary matches, and cruised past England in their semi-final. Spurred on by passionate home crowds, the Silver Ferns were similarly impressive, setting up a mouth-watering final against Australia by battling past Jamaica in their semi.

It proved to be yet another classic contest. New Zealand led by two goals at half-time, and the Silver Ferns appeared to have the world title in the bag when they led by six goals at three-quarter time. Under pressure to inspire a revival, McIntosh made a huge call during the break when she decided to bench Wilson, her captain and champion shooter, and replace her with the far less experienced Jenny Borlase.

The change paid off, as Australia staged one of its greatest comebacks, scoring 14 goals to seven in the final quarter. In a frantic finish, scores were level when the Diamonds' 21-year-old goal attack, Sharelle McMahon, received the ball with just one second left on the game clock. She quickly flung the ball towards the target and it sailed through the ring as the clock ticked down to zero, her accurate shot handing Australia an unbelievable 42–41 victory.

McMahon told her former teammate Liz Ellis in the book *Netball Heroes*: 'I don't really remember what was going through my head when I shot that goal. When [New Zealand's] Donna Loffhagen took her last shot, I remember thinking we were going to lose. But we got the rebound from Donna's shot, and I snapped out of that and back into playing. When the ball was in my hands I didn't know there was only one second left – I was just playing netball.'

McMahon's heroics meant the Diamonds had won their eighth world championship, in the process breaking the Silver Ferns' hearts yet again. McIntosh, meanwhile, was now a supercoach. 'Vicky Wilson had only one shot at goal in that third quarter, which was highly unlike her, so the decision was quite easy,' McIntosh explained in *Netball Heroes*. 'Jenny was pumped and ready and came on and turned it around. And I was lucky. We got out of it and so everyone thinks you're a hero for doing it.'

Three years later, in August 2002, the two teams put on another brilliant show when they met in the gold medal match at the Manchester Commonwealth Games. The Silver Ferns were now a far stronger team thanks to the inclusion of Irene van Dyk, the former captain of South Africa who had emigrated to New Zealand. Van Dyk made her first appearance for New Zealand in a major tournament at the games, and her prowess in attack proved invaluable – she finished as the leading scorer in the competition.

Her great form meant New Zealand went into the gold medal match with plenty of confidence, and the Silver Ferns controlled large parts of a seesawing game. They initially jumped out to a seven-goal lead, only to see Australia hit back and edge in front. New Zealand then opened up a three-goal advantage halfway through the final quarter and was still two goals in front with two minutes to play.

However, the Diamonds proved nerveless in the closing stages. After the margin had been narrowed to one goal, Aussie shooter Catherine Cox – who was actually born in New Zealand – netted a long-range goal with 20 seconds to go, levelling the scores at 46–46 and sending the match into extra-time.

Australia opened a two-goal buffer early in the first seven-minute period of extra-time, but New Zealand responded, with van Dyk nailing three successive goals to give the Silver Ferns the lead. In a major shock, van Dyk – the most accurate shooter in the world – then missed a relatively easy shot, and soon afterwards Cox showed nerves of steel to nail a goal from the outer region of the goal circle. The scores were tied at the end of the first period of extra-time.

Remarkably, they were still tied – this time at 55–55 – when the whistle blew to end the second period of extra-time, and so the match entered a period of sudden-death extra-time in which the first team to open a two-goal buffer would be the winner. As at the world championships in 1999, Australian goal attack Sharelle McMahon was the hero, slotting the goals that handed the Diamonds a two-goal buffer and the gold medal.

'What a great feeling to win a gold medal like that,' McMahon said shortly after the match had reached its dramatic conclusion. 'That game felt like it went on forever. This game did come down to one goal, but really it is a team sport, and Catherine [Cox] was sinking some really important goals through the final seven minutes. If she wasn't sinking those long bombs we really wouldn't have a had a chance.'

In the wake of the 2002 Commonwealth Games, many of the New Zealanders no doubt wondered if they were ever going to defeat Australia in a major championship again. 'All the losses that you go through make you stronger,' the Silver Ferns' captain at the time, Anna Rowberry, said in *Netball Heroes*. 'It makes you tough. When you go through all that pain, you don't want to go through it all again.'

As it turned out, New Zealand had to wait less than a year to gain some revenge. The Diamonds and Silver Ferns both qualified for the final of the 11th World Netball Championships, held in Kingston, Jamaica, in July 2003. The final match of the tournament was a typical Australia–New Zealand encounter: fast, skilful, fearfully competitive and very close. This time around, the Silver Ferns finally kept their composure when everything was on the line. Having led at every break, they refused to buckle in the face of a late comeback from the Diamonds, winning 49–47.

Australian defender Liz Ellis had been unable to curtail the influence of Irene van Dyk, whose brilliant shooting was the difference between the two sides. Her accuracy meant the Silver Ferns converted 90 per cent of their shots; by contrast, Australia's shooters converted only 70 per cent of theirs.

'This is the best moment of my netball career – it's just overwhelming,' Rowberry exclaimed during the celebrations. 'I couldn't have asked for anything more. We share this gold medal with so many people back home – so many players that have been so close in Manchester, Birmingham and Kuala Lumpur, and all our families back home. We share this moment with them.'

New Zealand's win broke the Diamonds' run of 38 consecutive victories at world championships, a streak dating back to their loss to the Silver Ferns in Glasgow in 1987. It was a disappointing end to the international careers of Australia's captain, Kathryn Harby-Williams, and coach, Jill McIntosh, who both retired after the game. 'It's the end of an era, so it would have been nice to go out on a positive note, but it wasn't to be,' Harby-Williams told the media at the post-match press conference.

The pair had been at the heart of a moment of controversy during the third quarter, when McIntosh decided to take Harby-Williams, who was playing goal defence, out of the game. At the time, McIntosh felt her skipper was not doing enough to slow down the delivery to van Dyk, but she later admitted in *Netball Heroes* that benching Harby-Williams was a mistake:

> I've thought about it a lot and in hindsight I would still have brought Janine [Ilitch] on but I wouldn't have taken Kathryn off – I would have played her somewhere else. You do what you think at the time is best for the team. You do what you think is going to win that match. You can't let your heart rule your head in situations like that. But while none of that came into it at the time, it certainly did afterwards. And I thought, 'Goodness, what have I done?' But I knew I did it for every right reason at the time.

The Silver Ferns' breakthrough win over Australia in Jamaica began a period in which they had an edge over the Diamonds. In 2004 and

2005 New Zealand won six of its eight matches against Australia, and the domination continued in the 2006 Commonwealth Games, held in Melbourne. Cheered on by parochial home crowds, the Diamonds – now coached by Norma Plummer and led on the court by stand-in captain Sharelle McMahon, since the permanent team captain, Liz Ellis, was sidelined by a knee reconstruction – suffered an early shock when they were held to a draw by Jamaica during the preliminary rounds. But they recovered to easily defeat England in their semi-final and progress to the gold medal match. New Zealand had progressed to the deciding game without a hiccup, and it was clear that the Silver Ferns were at the top of their game when they thrashed Jamaica by 20 goals in their semi-final.

That performance proved to be a sign of things to come, as New Zealand quickly silenced the home crowd by taking an early lead, then held the Diamonds at bay for the remainder of the game, securing the gold medal with a five-goal win. In the aftermath of New Zealand's win, *The Age*'s Linda Pearce summed up what the result meant for the balance of power in international netball:

> The era of Australia's netball dominance officially closed at the 2003 world championships and, yesterday, its last major title fell into New Zealand's eager hands. Yet yesterday's gold-medal match also confirmed that while Australia may be in the unfamiliar role of pursuer, it is just a couple of breaths behind.
>
> New Zealand won yet another absorbing trans-Tasman final 60-55 at Vodafone Arena to relegate the two-time defending champion to Commonwealth Games silver for the first time. It was, captain Sharelle McMahon said, a 'devastating' result for Australia, which has lost wing attack Natalie Avellino to international retirement and may yet find that defenders Janine Ilitch and Alison Broadbent go the same way.

The gold medal playoffs in the previous two games could hardly have been more dramatic, with a one-goal win to Australia in Kuala Lumpur in 1998 and the double-overtime drama of Manchester four years ago contributing so much to the build-up this time. Although not as tight, the match was closer than anticipated, and did not disappoint.

It included one stretch of 16 unbroken centre passes, and the quarter-time deficit was also the final margin. Australia had one more attempt at goal overall but, for all its tenacity and desperation to keep it's unbeaten Games record intact, could not trim the difference to below three goals after falling behind by seven early in the game.

'We certainly had our chances, and you can claw a few things back but you can't then give away some easy passes I felt we should have nailed,' coach Norma Plummer said. 'But in the end that could be the pressure of the game, and so congratulations to New Zealand, a well-deserved win.'

History suggested that Australia was never going to be on the back foot for long, so it was no surprise that the Diamonds were reinvigorated by the time the 12th World Netball Championships were held in Auckland, New Zealand, in 2007. Australia crushed its meagre opposition in the preliminary matches, defeating Scotland 93–20 and the Cook Islands 90–22 en route to a semi-final clash with England. The Diamonds won that game by 18 goals, setting up yet another championship decider against the Silver Ferns.

With five minutes to go in the final, just one goal separated the teams, and with a big crowd cheering on the New Zealanders, it seemed the home side was set to overrun its arch-enemy. But, as in the Commonwealth Games in Melbourne, it was the home side that faltered. With the results of 2003 and 2006 burning in the back of their minds, the Diamonds surged away in the closing stages and won by four goals.

It was a particularly emotional result for veteran Australian defender and team captain Liz Ellis, who had rebounded from her serious knee injury to win back her place in the team. The victory was the full-stop to her career that Ellis had been craving, and in the days following the match she announced her retirement from international netball. ABC radio's *PM* program summed up her decision thus: 'If Liz Ellis were a male, and played cricket, she'd be up there in the national consciousness with Steve Waugh or Ricky Ponting. As it is, she's a netballer, and she's neither wealthy nor super-famous. Liz Ellis retired today after leading the national team to a World Championship victory in Auckland on Saturday. She represented Australia in a record 122 test matches over 15 years, she won three world championships, two Commonwealth Games gold medals and four national trophies along the way.'

Ellis was in the commentary box working for Channel Ten when the Diamonds and the Silver Ferns met in their next championship decider. The game in question was the gold medal match at the 2010 Commonwealth Games, in Delhi, India. During the previous months, the Australia–New Zealand netball rivalry had received formal recognition when the governors-general of the two nations came together and created the Constellation Cup, a striking Southern Cross-inspired trophy that was to be awarded to the winner of an annual series.

When the first Constellation Cup match was played in Adelaide, the Kiwi governor-general, Sir Anand Satyanand, stated: 'Almost 80 years ago, Lord Bledisloe, one of my predecessors as Governor-General, gifted the cup that bears his name and which has come to symbolise rivalry on the rugby field between Australia and New Zealand. The Constellation Cup will provide an equally enduring focus for netballers on both sides of the Tasman and recognise the wide participation in the sport.' Led by captain Sharelle McMahon, the Diamonds won the game, while the next two matches, played in New Zealand, were split. As a result, the Australians were able to place the newly minted cup in their trophy cabinet before heading off to the Delhi Commonwealth Games.

As great as so many of the previous clashes between Australia and New Zealand had been, the gold medal match in Delhi trumped them all for drama. The Diamonds began well, twice opening four-goal leads in the second quarter. But the Silver Ferns suddenly took control of the match, and by midway through the final quarter they led 40–33.

With her team seemingly down and out, Australian coach Norma Plummer brought champion shooter Catherine Cox, whose form had not been good enough to command a place in the starting seven, into the game. Cox helped ignite a remarkable comeback, and Australia scored 14 of the next 21 goals. With the scores tied at 47–47, Cox had a chance to win the game for the Diamonds in the dying seconds, but she missed and the game went into extra-time.

The teams traded goals during the first seven-minute period of extra-time, and the scores were still tied at the end of it. Only seconds remained in the second period of extra-time when New Zealand shooter Maria Tutaia, who proved a superb foil for the legendary Irene van Dyk, produced her first heroic act, calmly levelling the scores. After 14 minutes of extra-time, the score was now 58–58.

It was time for sudden death – the first team to open a two-goal lead would win the gold medal. Australia scored first, then Cox had her second chance to seal victory for the Diamonds. But she missed once more. The Silver Ferns soon levelled the scores yet again, and the game rolled on. Fully eight minutes of sudden-death extra-time

AUSTRALIA *vs* NEW ZEALAND

were played before Tutaia wrote herself into Kiwi sporting folklore by nailing successive goals.

When the second of them went through the ring, the Silver Ferns collapsed in a jubilant heap on the court. The Diamonds could not hide their devastation, and their tears flowed freely as disappointment coursed through their aching bodies. Having lasted 82 minutes, this was the longest international netball match ever played (a regular netball match consists of four 15-minute quarters). Watched by hundreds of thousands of people in both nations, it was also a brilliant advertisement for both the sport, and for the incredible rivalry between the Diamonds and the Silver Ferns.

Journalist Peter Hanlon captured the essence of the occasion in his report for *The Age*:

> Fittingly for the two nations that are invariably left standing when the music stops and the duel for netball's major prize begins, Australia and New Zealand contested the last gold medal of Delhi's Games last night. So shattered were the Diamonds in defeat, their part in perhaps the greatest contest of these Games was lost to them, too.
>
> Ascendant in the first half, seemingly beaten by a Silver Ferns surge in the second, Australia clawed back a seven-goal last-quarter deficit to send the decider into extra time, then double overtime.
>
> Baskets were traded for another eight nerve-jangling minutes before the magnificent Maria Tutaia drained the winner, settling the issue 66–64 and leaving the Silver Ferns' saviour hoping her parents back home had survived watching it.
>
> Sharelle McMahon, Australia's veteran captain, felt like double extra time had gone 'for a million years'. Thirteen years an international, she rated it the toughest final of her career. 'I'm

really struggling to put a positive spin on this at the moment.'

None were hurting more than her great mate and shooting partner Catherine Cox, who fought back tears and tried vainly to cling to teammates' consoling words that the two long-range victory chances she missed weren't the only reason all were feeling so miserable.

'It's gut-wrenching to know I had an opportunity to win the game,' Cox said of misses in the dying seconds of normal time, and again early in double overtime when a two-goal lead would have brought a golden end and redemption for the loss to New Zealand in the Melbourne 2006 final.

'Four years now we have to wait for another shot at it, [and] we were waiting four years from the last one.'

These great sporting rivals meet regularly, but only in Commonwealth Games and world championships does defeat truly burn. Asked if she had felt worse after a loss, coach Norma Plummer said: 'We don't have too many, [but] I'm not feeling too good at the moment.' She sympathised with Cox, pointing to a centre-pass break and a stepping penalty as just two of many less-glaring but equally-costly errors. McMahon concurred. 'I can go through all the mistakes I made and let you know which one might have caused the loss.'

After all that excitement and drama, no one was surprised when the next major championship game between the Diamonds and Silver Ferns, the final of the 2011 World Netball Championships, in Singapore, was another classic. Australia went into the match desperate to avenge the result in Delhi. Six members of the team that lost at the Commonwealth Games remained in the Diamonds' squad (a ruptured Achilles tendon meant McMahon wasn't one of them), while Plummer was still the coach.

AUSTRALIA vs NEW ZEALAND

New Zealand dominated the early going, van Dyk's 17 goals from 17 attempts helping her team snare a six-goal half-time lead. But Plummer made a game-changing move when she took Cox out of the game and replaced her with 23-year-old Caitlin Bassett, who had played only five international matches before the tournament. Bassett spearheaded Australia's revival, her two goals in the final minute of regular time drawing the Diamonds level. She even had the chance to win the match in the frantic final seconds, but missed, which meant yet another big game between Australia and New Zealand would be settled in extra-time.

Maria Tutaia had the chance to slot the winning goal with just a minute remaining in extra-time, but she was unable to match her heroics in Delhi, the ball bouncing off the ring and landing in the hands of a Diamonds defender. Australia spirited the ball forward and Bassett capped off a remarkable effort by slotting the winning goal.

'I didn't even know it was the last goal, it was only when I heard the cheer,' Bassett said as the celebrations began. 'I wanted Australia to win but I never dreamed I would be the one out there.'

Australia's tenth world title, which elevated the team back above New Zealand to number one in the international rankings, was certainly a case of sweet revenge. 'The one I was happiest for was probably Natty,' Plummer said, referring to her run-all-game centre, Natalie von Bertouch, who assumed the captaincy after McMahon was injured. 'I know after the Comm Games ... we caught up a couple of months later and she told me she was still that gutted, she really took it to heart. I was just so pleased that she got the win as captain.'

Von Bertouch herself added: 'There couldn't be anything better. We just kept fighting back and they kept pulling away and we kept fighting again. It just came down to who was in front when the whistle blew.'

Australia capped off a great 2011 by retaining the Constellation Cup. But no team dominates the rivalry between the Diamonds and Silver Ferns for long. When the 2012 Constellation Cup rolled around, the Silver Ferns won the opening game, in Melbourne, by two goals, then surged to a 16-goal lead early in the second match, in Auckland, before the Diamonds' Bassett inspired another extraordinary comeback.

Having started the game on the bench, Bassett was brought on at the start of the third quarter, again replacing Catherine Cox, who was struggling in her 100th international match. After shooting 19 goals in the second half, Bassett had the chance to send the contest into extra-time, but her shot missed and the Silver Ferns won by the narrowest of margins, 50–49.

In an illustration of how much the rivalry has captured the public's imagination in New Zealand, a sell-out crowd of almost 9000 people had crammed into Vector Arena to watch the game – the largest crowd to ever attend a netball match in New Zealand – and the locals headed home happy as the Silver Ferns took possession of the Constellation Cup for the first time. It was also New Zealand's first series win over the Diamonds in eight years – a remarkable feat, when you consider how even the rivalry has been throughout its long history.

True to form, Australia hit back to win the third match, played at Canterbury Arena in Christchurch, by six goals. 'It's got this special magic dust spread over the whole game when we play the Ferns,' the Diamonds new coach, Lisa Alexander, had told *The Age* prior to the start of the series. 'It's just incredibly exciting.'

Indeed, the rivalry between the Diamonds and the Silver Ferns consistently delivers skill and drama of the highest order. Not only is it the greatest rivalry in netball, but it might also just be the greatest rivalry in all of Australian sport.

AUSTRALIA vs NEW ZEALAND, NETBALL (1938–2012)

Matches played: 103
Australia wins: 64
New Zealand wins: 45

World Netball Championships victories
Australia: 10: 1963, 1971, 1975, 1979 (joint winners), 1983, 1991, 1995, 1999, 2007, 2011
New Zealand: 4: 1967, 1979 (joint winners), 1987, 2003

Commonwealth Games gold medals
Australia: 2: 1998, 2002
New Zealand: 2: 2006, 2010

Queenslander Wally Lewis and New South Welshman Mark Geyer square off during game two of the 1991 State of Origin series at the Sydney Football Stadium.

RUGBY LEAGUE
New South Wales *vs* Queensland

IN HIS FINAL PRESS conference before the first game of the 2012 rugby league State of Origin series between New South Wales and Queensland, Blues coach Ricky Stuart was asked how he felt about the fact that the Maroons had won the previous six series. 'I hate it,' Stuart replied. 'I can't describe to you how much I hate it. Are you allowed to print "fuck"?'

'Why not?' the journalist retorted with a chuckle.

'Well, I fucking hate it,' Stuart said.

He might not be one of the world's great orators, but that afternoon Stuart perfectly summed up the animosity that has made New South Wales vs Queensland one of the most compelling rivalries in Australian sport. In fact, the depth of feeling that underpins the rivalry might well be unmatched in any of the nation's other great sporting rivalries.

Queensland coach Mal Meninga provided another example the year before Stuart's outburst. Responding to media speculation about a range of issues, including his coaching ability, Meninga decided to tee off at the 'rats and filth that tried to poison a monumental team with lies, personal attacks, arrogance and disrespect'.

The rugby league rivalry between New South Wales and Queensland was transformed into its modern incarnation by a change in the rules used to determine which players were eligible to play for each state. Before 1980, players were required to represent the state in which they were currently playing, meaning that Queenslanders who were playing for clubs in New South Wales had to line up for the Blues, and players registered with clubs in Queensland were only eligible to play for the Maroons. The new rules, which relied on each player's state of origin, enabled him to represent his home state. This was defined as the state in which he first played rugby league, which for most players is the same one that they were born in.

So big have matches between New South Wales and Queensland become since this rule change that it is easy to ignore what went on before that Waterloo moment. But the modern rivalry between the Blues and the Maroons is indeed built on strong foundations, on a history of battles dating back to the first year the professional code was played in Australia.

The inaugural rugby league match between New South Wales and Queensland was held at the Agricultural Ground in Sydney on 11 July 1908. The local team consisted of the best players from the newly formed New South Wales Rugby Football League. Many of them had previously been stars in the Sydney rugby union competition but had switched codes so they could be paid to play (the split between rugby union and rugby league occurred because the men who governed union insisted on their sport remaining amateur). In contrast, the Queensland team was a somewhat ragtag line-up, largely because a similar semi-professional club competition did not begin in Brisbane until the following year.

Predictably, New South Wales won by a large margin – 43–0 – with superstar sharpshooter Herbert Henry 'Dally' Messenger (one of the highest-profile players to switch from rugby union to league) kicking eight goals. A 'large attendance' apparently watched the game, but the newspaper articles written at the time suggest that no one who watched the game believed they had seen the birth of a great rivalry.

'It was a lamentable display by Queensland, and, with a few exceptions, the Northerners' showing was far below the usual standard,' read the match report in the *Sydney Morning Herald*. 'The features of the local player were the utter unselfishness of the men and their magnificent combination and condition.' Although terribly one-sided, the match did have some unusual highlights. 'Deane raised a hearty laugh by taking an opponent by the legs and retaining hold of his captive's nether extremities as if he had a wheelbarrow, at the same time playing the ball with his feet to a companion.'

Between 1908 and 1921, New South Wales and Queensland met 22 times, and the Blues won them all. The Maroons broke their drought when they scored a 25–9 victory in Sydney in 1922. That win paved the way for the Queenslanders to comprehensively turn the tables.

The Maroons beat the Blues three times in 1923, then whitewashed another three-match series the following year. League fans in Queensland couldn't get enough of this dominance over the men from south of the border, and 30,000 of them turned up to see the Maroons score a 23–15 win in the first state game of the 1925 season. In all, Queensland and New South Wales did battle five times that year, with the first three played during the initial part of the season. The Maroons won games one and two, before the Blues finally gave their fans something to cheer about by winning game three, at the Sydney Cricket Ground.

But Queensland soon regained its edge and demonstrated its remarkable depth of talent. As Jack Gallaway explained in *Origin: Rugby League's Greatest Contest 1980–2002*: 'Later in the season, the New South Wales team journeyed to Brisbane for a two-game series. The Maroons won the first encounter 26 points to 8, and immediately after this game twenty-two Queenslanders left for a seven-week tour of New Zealand. What might well be called Queensland's "thirds" met the Blues a few days later and scored 32 points to their opponents' 13.'

Queensland continued its remarkable run of success over in New Zealand. The Maroons lost their first match against the Kiwi national team, but rebounded to win the second and third games. They also won each of the seven matches they played against provincial teams. 'The Queenslanders played eighteen representative games that season and they lost only two,' Gallaway wrote. 'The Maroons were the undisputed Australasian Rugby League Champions.'

Once the Maroons returned from New Zealand, a chain of events occurred that would fuel the rivalry between Queensland and New South Wales for years to come. Australia's national team, the Kangaroos, was scheduled to tour England in late 1925. After such a dominant season, Queensland's rugby league community eagerly awaited the selection of the touring squad, confident that most of its members would be Maroons. But no squad was ever selected.

In a huge shock, the Australian Rugby League Board of Control announced that the English Rugby League had decided to invite New Zealand to tour instead. The Aussie administrators insisted that the English believed the Kiwis would make more competitive opposition. According to Galloway:

> [N]o Queenslander believed the story for a moment. No Queenslander ever would. The disappointed Maroons were certain that the cancellation of the Kangaroo tour had been a New South Wales initiative, and it was a blow to Queensland pride which could never be forgotten and would certainly never be forgotten ... To Queenslanders, the true reason for the cancellation was plain to see. The New South Wales Rugby League simply could not tolerate the thought of an Australian

team that contained a majority of Maroons. In Queensland, this gross act created a distaste for everything for which the Blue guernsey stands.

Another development that fuelled the rivalry between the states was the decision by the New South Wales government to legalise poker machines for registered clubs in 1956. The New South Wales Rugby League (NSWRL) clubs made the most of the decision, acquiring their own poker machines, which were soon generating huge amounts of cash. That money was then used to launch recruiting raids, with Queenslanders the principal targets.

News of recruiters from New South Wales crossing the border with suitcases full of banknotes provoked an outcry in Queensland, where fans of the Maroons knew their clubs were not taking part in a fair fight. Poker machines were still illegal in Queensland, so the Brisbane-based clubs were unable to match the extraordinary contracts being offered by the raiders from the south. It was not long before the trickle of Queenslanders defecting to clubs in New South Wales became a flood. And to rub salt into the wound, these players were soon lining up in blue jerseys against the Maroons. Legendary prop forward Arthur 'Artie' Beetson was among the players whose careers followed such a path. A man who declared in his autobiography, *Big Artie*, that 'I always considered myself a Queenslander', Beetson ended up playing 17 games for New South Wales between 1966 and 1980.

It was hardly a surprise that the emigration of talent to New South Wales meant the annual state matches between the Blues and Queensland became increasingly one-sided. Between 1970 and 1979, for example, the Blues won 25 of the 29 games played. The Maroons won just two matches during that times; the other two were drawn. When asked to appear at the launch of Winfield's sponsorship of the Queensland state league, comedian Paul Hogan – a New South Welshman who later found global fame thanks to the *Crocodile Dundee* movies – poured scorn on the situation by saying: 'Every time Queensland produces a good footballer, he finishes up being processed through a New South Wales poker machine.'

By the end of the 1970s, even Blues supporters were finding the matches a bore. Galloway wrote: 'In Sydney, the annual games were being played before smaller crowds than those attending unimportant club fixtures. The major Sydney clubs begrudged the allocation of weekend fixture dates for the interstate contests. They complained bitterly about the risks that their highly priced players ran of injury, and... so as not to interfere with the Sydney competition, interstate games were downgraded to mid-week fixtures, and to emphasise Sydney's lack of interest most of them were played in Brisbane.'

A number of people, the most prominent of them being Queensland Rugby League chairman Ron McAuliffe, who was a Labor senator at the time, started campaigning for the introduction of 'state of origin' rules to decide who played for the Blues and who ran out for the Maroons. McAuliffe was following on from former New South Wales, Queensland and Australia centre Jack Reardon, who had first raised the idea in 1964.

Such rules had already been introduced into Australian Rules football, with great effect, in 1977. The heartland of Aussie Rules is Melbourne, and even though poker machines remained illegal in Victoria, the 12 clubs that made up the Victorian Football League (VFL) had enough clout to consistently poach players from the code's other hotbeds, the South Australian and Western Australian leagues. Prior to 1977, these players would then represent Victoria against their home states.

As did Queenslanders, the South Australian and Western Australian publics hated seeing their favourite sons wearing

Victoria's 'Big V' jumper, and after much public pressure the first Aussie Rules State of Origin game was played at Subiaco Oval, in Perth, on 8 October 1977. To the delight of Western Australia's football community, the local team, known as the Sandgropers (a sandgroper is a type of burrowing insect found in Western Australia), won by 94 points. The result was in stark contrast to the match between Victoria and Western Australia that had been played under the old rules in late June 1977. Victoria won that match by 63 points, thanks largely to the efforts of some westerners who would, later that year, tear Victoria to shreds.

Western Australia's success piqued the interest of McAuliffe. He soon organised to discuss the State of Origin concept with VFL boss Dr Allen Aylett. McAuliffe was convinced he was onto something, and when Queensland was thrashed by New South Wales in both rugby league state games in 1979 – the scores were 30–5 and 31–7 – it was clear that something had to be done. Countless people had their say, including many Brisbane-based journalists. 'Being beaten is bad enough, but being beaten by your own men has a ring of betrayal about it,' Hugh Lunn wrote in *The Australian*.

McAuliffe began campaigning for a State of Origin game to be played between the Maroons and Blues in 1980. As Ian Heads and David Middleton described in *A Centenary of Rugby League: 1908–2008*, McAuliffe believed that State of Origin:

> [N]ot only offered the remedy for ailing interstate football, but ... could also provide the opportunity for Queensland rugby league to regain its lost prestige. In lengthy conversations with NSWRL executive director Kevin Humphreys, the senator's arguments ultimately proved persuasive. McAuliffe had read the mood of Queensland's football public and was so confident he could convince the NSWRL to give their approval for the third game of

the 1980 interstate series to be played under state of origin rules that he instructed the QRL to promote the Origin game and sell tickets to the public even before the final nod was given. The idea that Queensland could call on their 'lost tribe' of stars who were playing for Sydney clubs, if only for one night, generated wild excitement throughout the northern state.

The agreement reached between McAuliffe and Humphreys was that the first two representative matches in 1980 would be played under the old eligibility rules, but if one team or other won both of them, thus securing a series victory, the third game would be conducted under State of Origin rules. Humphreys also insisted that a representative from the NSWRL would supervise the Sydney-based Maroons while they were with the Queensland team to 'protect the interests of both the New South Wales Rugby League and the clubs to which they contracted'.

It was a case of more of the same old one-sided stuff in the first two games of the 1980 representative season. Heads and Middleton explained: 'NSW, bolstered by Queensland-born players Kerry Boustead, Rod Morris and John Lang, wrapped up the series in two games. They overpowered the Maroons at Lang Park, and then cruised to victory before a paltry crowd of 1638 at Leichhardt Oval [in Sydney]. The Leichardt crowd figure was acutely embarrassing to the NSWRL and convinced the game's administrators that the third game of the series should be played on a State of Origin basis.'

Not everyone was happy about the experiment. Former New South Wales and Australia star Bob Fulton described it as 'rugby league's non-event of the century'. Fulton was adamant it would 'achieve absolutely nothing'. Such rubbishing of the concept made McAuliffe nervous. What if no one turned up? What if Queensland's bolstered squad, which featured seven Sydney-based players, still couldn't beat the Blues? What if the players didn't take the match seriously? This final question was much debated in the lead-up to the match. The previous time that rugby league had pitted club teammates against each other was when Australia played 'The Rest' in a charity match at Manly's Brookvale Oval in 1974. That game was notable for its lack of physical intensity, and many pundits believed the State of Origin game would pan out the same way.

But most of McAuliffe's fears were cast aside when a sell-out crowd of more than 33,000 packed into Brisbane's Lang Park for the first official State of Origin game on Tuesday, 8 July 1980. A guttural roar echoed around the stadium as Beetson, who had been appointed Queensland captain, led the Maroons onto the park. It was a grand occasion for the 35-year-old. With his professional football career in its final throes – it would prove to be his last season with his NSWRL club, Parramatta – he had finally been granted the chance to pull on the famous Maroon jersey.

As much as Beetson was renowned for his toughness, New South Wales captain Tommy Raudonikis boasted a similar reputation, and the presence of both men ensured that the contest was no exhibition match. 'Nothing was ever easy when you were up against a side that included Tommy,' Beetson wrote in his autobiography. 'As I have said of him many times, he would start a fight in a phone box. Yes, [the first State of Origin game] lined clubmates against clubmates, but the truth is – despite the pre-match cynicism of some critics – that no one was ever going to take it easy.'

Beetson settled the issue of whether players from the same club were prepared to have a go at each other when he crunched his Parramatta teammate Mick Cronin twice during the second half. He also directed plenty of aggression towards Steve Edge, another Parramatta man who was playing for New South Wales. 'To put it bluntly, I kicked the shit out of him in the scrums,' Beetson wrote.

'They were real scrums back then, of course, and the fans never got to see a lot of what was going on. Often, it was akin to war as the forwards kicked and scrambled and heaved in pursuit of the ball.'

In fact, Beetson tackled the whole match with an intensity that suggested his life depended on a Queensland win. The game was less than a minute old when he landed his first high shot on Blues front-rower Gary Hambly. Although Billy Thompson, the English referee brought out to Australia to oversee the contest, saw no need to award a penalty, Beetson had demonstrated how seriously he was taking the contest.

Big Artie continued in that vein for the entire 80 minutes, inspiring his team and the passionate crowd by landing blows on numerous New South Welshmen. The most brutal was the punch he threw at second-rower Graeme Wynn 27 minutes into the first half, which sparked an all-in brawl. Queensland league legend Dick 'Tosser' Turner watched the incident with pride, as he recounted in Beetson's book. 'The punch Arthur fired at Wynn inflamed the game,' Turner said. 'If it had been anyone other than Arthur Beetson it would not have had the same significance. The moment that Arthur stood up to be counted against this enemy of ours was the most important event in the history of the state of origin.'

Along with the countless spotfires that ignited throughout the match, there was also some decent football played. New South Wales winger Greg Brentnall scored the first State of Origin try when he made the most of some great creativity from Cronin. But Queensland replied when Chris 'Choppy' Close turned his opponent Steve Rogers inside out – 'a classic piece of work, made against one of the greatest of all defensive centres', according to Beetson – then dished the ball off to Kerry Boustead, who scored in the corner. Some accurate kicking from Mal Meninga handed the Maroons at 9–5 lead at the break.

When Close, who was later awarded the man-of-the-match award, scored in the 54th minute, Queensland's lead was out to 18–5. Raudonikis crossed for the Blues with 20 minutes remaining, but Queensland never looked like losing. A chant of 'Artie, Artie' echoed around Lang Park during the dying minutes as an almighty celebration began at the ground and around the Sunshine State. The final whistle confirmed a 20–10 victory for Queensland, and the Maroon army soon poured onto the field, many of its members taking the chance to slap Big Artie on the back.

'THANKS A MILLION, ARTIE', read the headline the following day in the *Courier-Mail*. The 1980 edition of the *Big League Annual* also paid a glowing tribute to Beetson's performance that night: 'As captain, he stood 10 feet tall on the night of July 8. It was Beetson at his best. Arthur shrugged off the years and played with the zest of a teenager just entering the big arena instead of a veteran just quitting.' As part of a deal struck between the players from both sides and the game's administrators, Beetson and his man shared 10 per cent of the gate takings as reward for their triumph. Given the big crowd that had turned out, each winning player pocketed $2000.

Although 'Origin I', as it is now known, was a great success – from a Queensland standpoint, anyway – the structure put in place for the 1981 representative series was the same as 1980's. The traditional eligibility criteria were to be used for the first two matches, and if one team or other won both games, the third match would become Origin II.

Beetston, who had moved back to Brisbane as captain–coach of local club Redcliffe, was appointed Queensland captain–coach for games one and two. He led from the front, throwing his 36-year-old frame into contest after contest, but New South Wales – bolstered by a number of players who would have been running around for Queensland under State of Origin rules – wrapped up the series in straight sets. The Blues won the first match, at Lang Park, 10–2, and the second, which drew a paltry 6268 people to Leichhardt Oval, 22–9. But those defeats had a silver lining for Queensland and for representative rugby league in Australia, as they resulted in State of Origin rules being adopted for the third Blues vs Maroons clash of the season.

Another huge crowd packed into Brisbane's Lang Park for Origin II. Queensland's team was bolstered by the inclusion of four New South Wales-based players – winger Mitch Brennan (South Sydney), second-rower Paul McCabe (Easts) and front-rowers Rod Morris (Balmain) and Paul Khan (Cronulla) – but the big difference from the year before was that Beetson did not lead the Maroons onto the field. Having suffered a badly cut eye in the weeks leading up to the game, he decided to coach from the sidelines, thus ensuring that his Origin playing career ended with a 100 per cent strike rate – one game, one win. With Beetson directing traffic from the bench, Queensland was led into battle by 21-year-old sensation Wally Lewis, who had made a big impression in Origin I in 1980. New South Wales was captained by veteran Cronulla centre Steve Rogers.

An all-in brawl erupted during the opening stages, and it was New South Wales that found its groove after the dust settled. The Blues raced to a 15–0 lead thanks to two tries from Eric Grothe and another that was scored by his Parramatta clubmate Mick Cronin. Grothe's first try, which he scored after intercepting a Queensland pass and dashing 90 metres, remains one of the great Origin efforts. Although the Maroons hit back just before half-time, New South Wales enjoyed a commanding 15–5 lead at the break.

The game changed completely in the second half. Shortly after the resumption, Lewis brought the partisan crowd to his feet when he dodged his way through the Blues' defence and scored a brilliant try. His heroics inspired his fellow Maroons, and they ended up scoring

17 unanswered points in the second half. The final whistle signalled a 22–15 victory for the home side, a result that kicked off yet another XXXX-fuelled party across Queensland. Chris Close won the man-of-the-match award, as he had in Origin I.

Close's performances in the first two Origin games were certainly impressive. But after rugby league's administrators came to their senses in 1982 and decided that all New South Wales and Queensland matches should involve teams selected using State of Origin rules, it was Wally Lewis who emerged as the game's biggest star. In all, Lewis captained the Maroons for 11 seasons between 1981 and 1991, and in that time he would lead Queensland to seven series victories.

By the time Lewis retired, he had earned the nicknames 'the King' and 'the Emperor of Lang Park'. But his team's era of dominance actually began with a loss in the opening game of the first true State of Origin series, which was played before a typically parochial crowd in Brisbane on 1 June 1982.

As it turned out, the loss helped the Maroons in the long run: it encouraged McAuliffe to attack the NSWRL clubs for not allowing the star Queenslanders on their books to be released for a training camp the week before the match. This had meant Queensland coach Arthur Beetson had only four days to prepare his men for game one. In contrast, the New South Wales squad had been training together, under the watchful eye of Frank Stanton, for two and a half weeks prior to their victory. 'I will ask for wider access to our selected Sydney players next year,' McAuliffe said. 'They should be available to us in a live-in situation in Brisbane for a week before the match and allowed to return home for their club matches at the weekend.'

Stirred up by the controversy, the Maroons hit back and won game two, with Paul 'Fatty' Vautin scoring the match-winning try in the 11–7 victory. That clash, also at Lang Park, was notable for the man-of-the-match performance of veteran front-rower Rod Morris, who had only recently decided to make a comeback after a short retirement. It was also notable for the way that Queensland-based referee Barry Gomersall often allowed Morris and his fellow heavy-hitters to escape penalty, despite their clear determination to rough up their New South Wales opponents. This time, it was the Blues' officials wearing angry faces after the final whistle.

But in a win for the code, league fans were soon bursting with excitement at the prospect of a series decider. Game three was played before over 20,000 people at the Sydney Cricket Ground, and it became famous for two things in particular: the brilliance of Wally Lewis and the extraordinary clanger involving Blues players Phil Sigsworth and Phil Duke (who had been called up from the Moree Boomerangs after starring in the annual New South Wales Country vs New South Wales City match) that enabled Lewis to score the series-winning try.

The bungled play began when Sigsworth trapped a kick from Lewis. Aware that Lewis was charging towards him, Sigsworth hurriedly dished the ball backwards to Duke in the in-goal area. Caught off-guard, Duke fumbled and Lewis calmly dashed up to him, picked up the ball, then touched it on the ground. It was one of the simplest tries he scored in his career, but it meant so much.

A short time later, Lewis and his teammates were celebrating Queensland's first series win over New South Wales since 1959. For Lewis, the deciding match in the 1982 series set him on course for a dream run. He was named best player in five of his next six Origin games, earning the adulation of the Queensland public and grudging respect from his New South Wales opponents.

Lewis was just one of many reasons why the Maroons dominated the early years of State of Origin. Another was the coercive people-management skills of McAuliffe, who was the most powerful man in rugby league for a brief time after Humphreys was caught up in a corruption scandal. McAuliffe insisted that the Brisbane-based players selected for the Maroons sign a form declaring that they would not transfer to a NSWRL club in the future.

This approach helped stem the flood of players heading south, but it almost blew up in McAuliffe's face on one famous occasion, which was detailed in Brisbane's *Courier-Mail*: 'Just hours before the opening game of the first-ever Origin series in 1982, four Queensland players were facing the sack for refusing to comply with a QRL direction to sign loyalty agreements. Rod Morris, Gene Miles, Colin Scott and Mark Murray were summoned to team manager Dick Turner's room and told there were four players ready, willing and able to take their places. One by one, they signed "under duress".'

Lewis was among the great players who committed to staying in Queensland. He played for local clubs Fortitude Valley and Wynnum-Manly before becoming the inaugural captain of the Brisbane Broncos in 1988.

The captain and coach combination of Lewis and Beetson ended up leading Queensland to 2–1 series wins in 1982, 1983 and 1984. Each series produced moments of brilliance and madness, although none was more controversial than the elbow that Blues second-rower Les Boyd landed on Queensland forward Darryl Brohman in the opening match of the 1983 series. The blow shattered Brohman's jaw, sidelining him for the rest of the season. Having been tipped to play for Australia that year, he was denied the chance to represent his nation, and he ended up making just one more appearance for Queensland, three years later.

Boyd was cited by the NSWRL judiciary and handed a 12-month suspension, which cost him the chance to add to the 17 games he had already played for Australia. He later claimed that the Sydney-based Australian selectors Ernie Hammerton, Les Cowie and Peter McLean had told him to do whatever was required to make sure no Queenslanders were in the Australian side. The matter didn't end with Boyd's suspension, however, as Brohman sued him for damages (the case was settled out of court). In fact, the matter has never really ended, as Brohman and Boyd have continued to trade blows through the media in the three decades since their infamous on-field altercation.

After Queensland's series wins in 1982 and 1983, many league fans and pundits wondered where New South Wales was ever going to find the passion and toughness to match the marauding Maroons over an entire series. At that stage, it seemed that State of Origin football meant more to the Maroons and their army of supporters, who had suffered through so many thrashings during the 1960s and '70s. The 1984 series at least demonstrated that the New South Wales fans had the passion for Origin footy. Even though Queensland scored an easy win in game one, around 30,000 people braved pouring rain to watch game two, played at the Sydney Cricket Ground.

For the men who had breathed life into the Origin concept, it was a landmark occasion. 'I looked around the ground that night and I thought to myself, "Well, we've made it,"' Beetson recalled in *A Centenary of Rugby League*. 'If Sydney could turn out like this and support the Blues the way they were, we had got there. There was no longer any doubt. Nobody could remember an interstate game in Sydney drawing such interest, and none of us could see any reason why it wouldn't continue to be like that.'

Despite the Blues army turning out in such force, Queensland still won, with Lewis, Close and Meninga doing much of the damage. The result meant the Maroons had beaten New South Wales in three straight series for the first time since 1925. But when Des Morris replaced Beetson as Queensland coach, a turning of the tables occurred. The Blues notched their first series win in 1985, a result that hurt the Queenslanders so much that they dumped Morris and replaced him with Wayne Bennett. A year later New South Wales went one better, scoring a 3–0 clean sweep.

The first match of the 1985 series looked set to be a grinding slog after heavy rain lashed Brisbane in the lead-up to the game. But some bad weather wasn't going to distract the New South Wales boys from the task at hand. Thanks to the passion of their skipper Steve Mortimer, they now had a harder edge. As explained by Ian Heads and David Middleton: 'There is a famous story of [Mortimer] demanding that the New South Wales team bus be stopped in Caxton Street, the hostile marshalling point for Queensland barrackers just up the road from Lang Park, while he revved up the team. "Look at the faces," he said to his teammates. "They hate us. They think we're no good." More than anyone, Mortimer was responsible for raising the levels of passion among New South Wales players to match those of the Maroons.'

The star of the game in question was Blues centre Michael O'Connor, who thrived in the wet and muddy conditions. A former rugby union player who had made 13 appearances for the Wallabies before defecting to league, O'Connor produced one of the greatest Origin debuts, scoring all of the Blues' points (two tries and five goals) in their 18–2 win.

Almost 40,000 people crammed into the Sydney Cricket Ground two weeks later to see New South Wales claim its first series victory. Five-eighth Brett Kenny scored the try that clinched the Blues' 21–14 victory, and there were extraordinary scenes after the whistle, with Mortimer chaired from the field amid the jubilation.

However, more fuel was soon poured on the rivalry between the Blues and the Maroons. The Australian team travelled to New Zealand for a Test series during the six-week break between the second and third Origin games. At the time, New South Wales coach Terry Fearnley was also the national coach. He drew claims of bias when he axed four Queensland players from the Australian squad prior to the second Test. Fearnley's decision came back to haunt him when the third Origin game was played at Lang Park. Not only did the fired-up Queensland side easily win, but Greg Dowling, one of the Maroons' players dropped from the Australian team, also gave Fearnley a fearful spray while pointing at the scoreboard late in the second half. The ugly incident led to the Australian Rugby League changing its rules so that a serving Origin coach could not also coach the Kangaroos.

The Queenslanders didn't do much pointing at the scoreboard the year after. Although the greatest margin in the three games was six points, New South Wales' new coach, Ron Wiley, and skipper Wayne Pearce had the last laugh when they won all three games. As Pearce told *Fox Sports* some years later:

> We went into 1986 with a lot of emotion there. It was just a really tough contest. What I recall is the intensity of the matches. It was just great to be a part of that series. It was the first-ever whitewash in Origin history – it was a buzz, it was fantastic. The win has even more merit given there were two games up there at Lang Park. It was an intimidating environment. You go there in the bus and it gets halfway down the hill to the oval in Caxton Street and it gets rocked by passionate Queensland supporters who have been drinking. They come out, give it a rock and let you know you're in enemy territory. Their idea was to intimidate you, but it actually pumped you up. It got you fully aroused so you knew you had to be on your best effort to win the match.

New South Wales made it four wins on the trot when it defeated Queensland 20–16 in the first game of the 1987 series at Lang Park. That match was notable for two things: the match-winning try scored by New South Wales Blues forward Mark McGaw in the dying minutes, and the Origin debuts of Allan 'Alfie' Langer (Maroons) and Andrew 'ET' Ettingshausen (Blues). Both made a big impression that night, and both would become Origin legends over the course of the following decade.

In the days after the first game of the 1987 series, however, Langer and his fellow Maroons found themselves staring a crisis in the face. With a hat-trick of series defeats looming, Queensland coach Wayne Bennett didn't pull any punches. 'He made it clear to everyone that basically if we didn't win game two, [and] therefore lost that series, heads would roll, and for a lot of us it would be the end of our Origin series,' Maroons great Gary Belcher recalled in an interview with *Fox Sports* in 2011. 'Wayne said he'd finish up his coaching with Queensland at that point, too, if we lost. There was a lot on the line.'

More than 40,000 fans turned out in their raincoats for game two, which proved to be the last Origin match played at the Sydney Cricket Ground (the Sydney Football Stadium was opened the following year). The pro-Blues crowd saw Peter Sterling produce a man-of-the-match performance, but their team lost to an inspired Queensland outfit, which refused to wilt in the driving rain and ankle-deep mud. Wally Lewis was as inspirational as ever in the 8–6 triumph, but he had many helpers. 'The thing I remember most is [that] "Fatty" Vautin was all over the place, making amazing amounts of tackles and chasing everything,' said Belcher, who laid a crucial tackle on New South Wales playmaker Cliff Lyon, which prevented the Blues from taking the lead.

It all came down to game three, at Lang Park, and it proved to be an edge-of-your-seat clash. Youngster Alfie Langer engineered two brilliant tries for Queensland, but New South Wales stayed in touch, thanks to a David Boyle try and two goals from Michael O'Connor. When O'Connor was ruled offside late in the first half and Dale

Shearer kicked the Maroons to a 10–8 lead, no one at the ground thought too much about it, but that accurate penalty kick would be the last score of the night. Nevertheless, the second half was gripping from start to finish, with heroes aplenty on both sides.

Queensland won the game – and its fourth Origin series – thanks to its never-say-die attitude, although it had a few doses of luck to boot. Belcher was the morale officer during the closing stages, yelling out the Maroons' war-cry – 'Queenslander!' – at every opportunity. Lewis and Langer provided the class, with Lewis pulling off one of the most important tackles of the night when he stopped a surging O'Connor in his tracks. Langer proved so cool and constructive in a crisis that he was awarded the man-of-the-match honour in just his third Origin game, the first of many for him. 'He came into the side for game one and, dead-set, we thought it was almost criminal to throw a kid of that size into that arena because he was just so small,' Belcher said. 'But right from the go he was magnificent. He won us all over from the minute he took the field.'

Queensland and New South Wales later played a fourth Origin game for the year when they clashed in an exhibition match before 12,000 people at Long Beach in California. Peter Sterling led the Blues to a 30–18 victory in a contest that featured little of the passion and ferocity for which Origin matches are renowned. Given that the Blues won the game, New South Wales officials and supporters believe the match should be counted as an official Origin match. Not surprisingly, Queenslanders are adamant that the match was nothing more than a casual kick-around and should not be counted in the head-to-head record.

During the months after rugby league's American experiment, the dynamic of the New South Wales–Queensland rivalry changed again when the Brisbane Broncos were formed and admitted into the NSWRL. In Australian Rules, the advent of a national competition was already killing off State of Origin football. Whereas Western Australians and South Australians had once ardently followed their state teams, they shifted their allegiance to the West Coast Eagles, the Fremantle Dockers, the Adelaide Crows and the Port Adelaide Power as they joined the Australian Football League between 1987 and 1997. Eventually, the lack of fan support for state games, as well as an increasing reluctance on the part of clubs to release their players for such matches, resulted in State of Origin being axed from the AFL's calendar.

But no such thing happened when the Broncos came into the NSWRL. With Wally Lewis as the inaugural Broncos captain, Queenslanders began rabidly supporting both them and the Maroons. And the players remained desperate to play in State of Origin games, largely because they remained the number-one route to selection in the Australian team.

Queenslanders' continuing passion for their State of Origin team was demonstrated during the second game of the 1988 series, played at Lang Park. With New South Wales leading 6–4 with 18 minutes remaining in the match, an all-in brawl of the sort that Origin is famous for, broke out. In the aftermath of the fight, Lewis was sent to the sinbin for dissent by referee Mick Stone. A chant of 'Send Stone off!' soon began echoing around the stadium as thousands of people stamped their feet in protest.

The situation then turned even uglier when Queensland fans began hurling beer cans onto the field. Play was halted while the debris was cleared, with the Maroons using the break and the crowd noise to gee themselves up. A minute after the game restarted, Queensland prop Sam Backo handed the home side the lead. When Lewis returned to the game, he delighted the XXXX-fuelled crowd by leading his team to a 16–6 victory, which sealed another series win for the men in maroon. Three weeks later Queensland made it a clean sweep when they defeated the Blues 38–22 at the Sydney Cricket Ground.

With Bennett wanting to concentrate on coaching the Broncos, Beetson returned to head up Queensland's 1989 campaign. New South Wales also went for experience at the top, appointing five-time premiership coach Jack Gibson, a man known as 'the Supercoach', to lead their campaign. Funnily enough, Beetson and Gibson were great mates.

Gibson faced a massive challenge. New South Wales Origin stars Peter Sterling, Brett Kenny and Wayne Pearce had all retired from representative football, so he was forced to pick a young squad that included a host of debutants. Given all that, and the fact that Lewis was in career-best form, few people were surprised when the Maroons whitewashed the Blues for the second straight year.

'That 1989 Queensland team was as near to perfect as you could get, the greatest Origin side of my experience,' Beetson wrote in *Big Artie*. 'It was well balanced, with power and speed.'

But it wasn't as if the Maroons just turned up and claimed the trophy. Their effort in game two is one of the legendary performances in Queensland league history. Beetson recorded his impressions in his book:

> That night, NSW front-rower Peter Kelly, in my view, was given a licence to commit mayhem. We were battered from pillar to post, yet still won the game, with Wally Lewis scoring a famous late try to kick us away to a match-winning 16–6 lead. Afterwards, our dressing room was like the casualty room at a large hospital. Alfie Langer had been forced off the field after 18 minutes with a fractured shinbone, Mal Meninga after 29 minutes with a fractured eye socket. Paul Vautin, who'd dislocated an elbow, wasn't able to come back in the second half, while Michael Hancock, who

did a collarbone... came off after 57 minutes. Five minutes from the end, Bob Lindner was carried off with a broken leg. There was no fifth replacement, just 12 blokes out there defending their honour, and their pride in the jumper. Game two ranks as my favourite win as coach. And Wally was the finest Origin player I saw.

By the end of the 1989 series, Queensland had won eight matches in succession. 'I congratulate Queensland,' Gibson said at the time. 'We've run second to a champion team. That's really all I found out.' For his part, Beetson never blamed Gibson for the mayhem caused by Kelly in game two. Rather, he believed Kelly had been wound up before the match by a couple of other Blues officials.

Again under the leadership of Gibson, New South Wales dug deep and won the 1990 series, which was the first losing Origin campaign that Beetson had been part of. The ruthless nature of Queensland's administrators was then laid bare when they controversially replaced Beetson with a new coach who wasn't even from Queensland. In fact, he wasn't even from Australia. Nevertheless, the wise words of New Zealander Graham Lowe had the desired effect on the Maroons players, who took out the 1991 series, although not without a serious fight.

Queensland won the first game at home, then New South Wales literally came out swinging in the second match, played at the Sydney Football Stadium, with giant second-rower Mark Geyer (195 centimetres and 114 kilograms) leading the way. Geyer's forearm to the head of Maroons' hooker Steve 'Boxhead' Walters right on half-time resembled the sort of move seen in WWE wrestling. The incident sparked a wild all-in brawl that had the crowd roaring and referee David Manson looking more and more concerned as it escalated.

The league fans watching the Channel Nine coverage at home saw bodies flying everywhere as the excitement built in commentator Ray 'Rabs' Warren's voice. 'There's a bit of a punch-up,' Warren said. 'Players coming in from all over now. And still going. Let's stay with it and see what happens out of this.'

The fight soon stopped, but Manson then found himself standing between Geyer and a fuming Wally Lewis, who eyeballed each other and stomped the turf like bulls ready to charge. Just when the referee thought he had the situation under control, Lewis rushed at Geyer, pushing him in the chest. Geyer responded by shaping up. Manson, who looked like a grasshopper compared to the warring footballers, showed he was not short on courage by immediately standing between the pair.

'I just waited for one of them to throw a punch,' Queensland team member Kevin Walters remembered in his book *Brave Hearts*. 'Fortunately neither did. But, gee, it looked as if they were going to, and I think they both wanted to, but sanity prevailed and they both held back. It would have been a good knuckle, actually, because MG's supposed to be able to throw 'em all right and Wally certainly can.'

The stoush, which was made famous by the newspaper photographs of Lewis and Geyer eyeballing each other while Benny Elias looked on, was listed as one of the Top 10 State of Origin moments when the centenary of Australian rugby league was celebrated in 2008.

It was a case of more of the same at the start of the second half. Geyer cleaned up Queensland fullback Paul Hauff with a swinging elbow, sparking another bust-up. Manson refused to send Geyer from the field, but his wild night would later win him a five-match suspension.

The closing stages of the game were equally dramatic, although it was skill rather than brute force that had the fans captivated. Queensland was four points in front with only a few minutes to go when New South Wales centre Mark McGaw crashed over for a try and levelled the scores at 12–12. With rain belting down, Blues star Michael O'Connor stepped up to take the conversion kick from out on the sideline. O'Connor looked to be staring down an all-but-impossible task, but he brought the huge crowd to life by coolly booting the ball straight through the uprights, handing New South Wales a famous 14–12 win.

Two weeks later, the series was decided before a packed house at Lang Park in Brisbane. Ten minutes prior to kick-off, the big pro-Maroons crowd was sent into a frenzy when it was announced that the match would be Wally Lewis's last State of Origin appearance for Queensland. Lewis had been widely tipped to retire from representative football but had kept his intentions to himself until game day.

'I told [Queensland team manager Dick] "Tosser Turner" just before I went out to toss the coin,' Lewis recalled in an interview with *The Australian* some years later. 'So absolutely no one knew about it. I hadn't even told my wife about it.' The announcement came as a shock to Lewis's teammates. 'The first time they were told about it was around the same time – just before kick-off and just before the crowd was told,' he explained. 'I left the dressing room, as captain, to go out and toss the coin, and Dick told the players after I'd left the room.'

The match itself was a gripping contest, with the margin between the sides never more than four points. Queensland led 8–4 at half-time, but the Blues grabbed the ascendancy by scoring twice early in the second half (neither try was converted) to take a 12–8 lead. As the contest edged into its dying minutes, Lewis urged his men to keep attacking, and the Maroons fans roared their team on. They were out of their seats when Steve Walters broke through the Blues' defence and charged down the field, setting up a try for substitute Dale Shearer and tying the scores.

In a situation remarkably similar to the close of game two, Mal Meninga, who had missed his previous seven kicks at goal, then slotted an extremely tough conversion and handed Queensland what proved to be a match-winning 14–12 lead. Lewis was able to end his representative career by holding aloft the State of Origin shield. He was given a standing ovation when he completed a lap of honour before his adoring Lang Park faithful.

By the end of the 1991 series, Queensland had won seven of the ten State of Origin series played. However, Lewis's retirement paved the way for New South Wales to enjoy a golden era of its own. The Blues, under the coaching of Phil Gould, won five out of six series between 1992 and 1997, with Benny Elias, Ricky Stuart, Andrew Ettingshausen, Laurie Daley, Brad Fittler and Andrew Johns among the key contributors.

The era contained many highlights for Blues fans: there was Daley's deft grubber kick that led to a try for Andrew Ettingshausen in the 1992 series decider; there was the tremendous defensive effort in the second half of game one in 1993, which was led by Ian Roberts, who had to be substituted close to the finish because he was suffering exhaustion; there was the 14–0 win in game two of the 1994 series, which was played in front of more than 87,000 people at the Melbourne Cricket Ground; and there was the 3–0 series whitewash in 1996, which was notable for the fact that the Blues used the same squad in each match.

And for fans of the biff, there was plenty of that as well. New South Wales prop Paul 'the Chief' Harragon and Queensland's Martin Bella threw punches galore at each other during the third game of the 1993 series, and television commentator Darrell Eastlake added to his fan base by declaring, 'Nothing wrong with that, two men having a go!'

The fisticuffs between Harragon and Bella meant few people noticed that Elias and Steve Walters were having their own box-on, which was almost as wild.

Despite all those crazy happenings, it wasn't until 1996 that a player was sent off for the rest of a match. The man who earned that dubious honour was Queenslander Paul Greenhill, who was marched from the field after delivering a 'coat-hanger' to Harragon.

A year later, after tough-as-nails former player Tom Raudonikis took over as New South Wales coach, he and his men came up with their famous 'Cattle Dog' rallying cry while enjoying a team bonding session at the Coogee Bay Hotel, in Sydney. The Maroons already had their 'Queenslander!' cry, which their players would yell to stir their passion. 'Cattle Dog' became the Blues' version; the words were chosen after Raudonikis told his players that, during fights, 'once I latched onto their leg, I was like a cattle dog. I wouldn't let go.' Its very mention often sparked a stoush, as Raudonikis recalled during an interview with *Rugby League Week*:

> In that third game in 1997 we were in a bit of a hole, so I sent out the call and the reaction was just fantastic. [Mark] Spud Carroll went berserk and starting jobbing blokes. When the call came out, [Steven] 'Beaver' Menzies popped his head up and said, 'Oh, no. Not the dreaded cattle dog.' But Spud and the boys had already started. It was just phenomenal. Andrew Johns came off worse for wear because Jamie Goddard got him with a right hand but the cattle dog toughness showed out in him because he had 18 stitches in a mouth wound and went back out.

Queenslanders did have a few reasons to smile during the mid-1990s. Among them was the extraordinary comeback in game one of the 1994 series at the Sydney Football Stadium. At the 75-minute mark, New South Wales led 12–4 and fans were starting to trickle out of the stands to beat the traffic. A converted try to Willie Carne narrowed the gap to 12–10, before a famous attacking surge from the Maroons finished with Mark Coyne scoring the match-winning try.

'Coyne's try deserves capitals. Coyne's Try,' wrote Will Swanton in the *Sydney Morning Herald*. 'It was the 79th minute. NSW leading 12–10. The ball sailed through 10 sets of hands, from the right side of the field to the left and back to Coyne's wing on the right in 26 frenzied seconds that secured the greatest and most dramatic Origin comeback of them all.' On Channel Nine's coverage, Ray Warren yelled, 'That's not a try, it's a miracle!'

Wally Lewis, who was in the second year of his short stint as Queensland coach, leapt in the air and started hugging his assistants. Steve Renouf was the man whose burst of speed had set the passage of play in motion, then Coyne beat two New South Welshman to get the ball over the line at the finish. Coyne told *The Sydney Morning Herald* in 2010: 'I could see the numbers lining up for us. I thought I'd be a chance. It was all a bit chaotic but I remember thinking everything was falling into place for us even before it happened. It felt like we might just get there, and we did ... it still gets a run on TV and I still love seeing it. People are still telling me where they were when it happened. Honestly, five times a week, that still happens ... it was an unbelievable way to win a game.'

Fans of the Maroons also love recalling their team's whitewash of the Blues in 1995. Queensland's success in that series was remarkable for a number of reasons. The battle over the rights to televise elite rugby league in Australia, nowadays referred to as 'the Super League war', had exploded earlier that year. It soon emerged that Rupert Murdoch's News Limited was attempting to form a breakaway club competition, to be titled the Super League.

NEW SOUTH WALES vs QUEENSLAND

A number of clubs were immediately linked to the new competition, and the Australian Rugby League responded by banning their players from taking part in the 1995 State of Origin series. The Brisbane Broncos were not only linked to Super League, but they also had most of Queensland's best players on their books. With those players banned from Origin, the Maroons' selectors were forced to assemble a ragtag squad of Queenslanders from clubs loyal to the ARL. Disgusted with the situation, Wayne Bennett, who had been appointed Maroons coach, quit the position. Former Queensland player Paul 'Fatty' Vautin, who had been working as a television pundit and had little coaching experience, was handed the job.

After such a shocking build-up, the expectation was that Queensland would be hammered in all three games. But Vautin's men caused a huge boilover in the first match, played at the Sydney Football Stadium in early May. Captained by South Queensland Crushers second-rower Trevor 'the Axe' Gillmeister, the Maroons won a very defensive yet gripping game 2–0.

Later that month the Queenslanders completed one of the greatest upsets in rugby league history when they wrapped up the series by scoring a 20–12 victory in game two, held at the Melbourne Cricket Ground. That match was notable for the brawl that broke out at the first scrum. It all started when the New South Welshmen decided to go on the attack after one of the Maroons had bellowed a 'Queenslander!' rallying cry. Players brawled all over the field as many of the Victorians in the crowd watched on bemused. Manly teammates John Hopoate (New South Wales) and Danny Moore (Queensland) put on the most brutal show, with punches flying thick and fast.

There were similar fracas in game three at Lang Park, the most infamous occurring after Queenslander Tony Hearn headbutted New South Wales prop Mark Carroll, which led Carroll to unleash a flurry of punches towards Hearn's head. But it was Hearn who was smiling at the finish. Queensland won game three 24–16 and secured a thoroughly improbable clean sweep.

After losing the 1996 and 1997 series, the Maroons regained their verve when the National Rugby League – formed in the wake of the Super League war – began in 1998. Under the guidance of Wayne Bennett, Queensland snatched a one-point win in the opening game, at the Sydney Football Stadium. Five-eighth Kevin Walters, whose wife, Kim, had died of breast cancer earlier in the year, was the hero. He later wrote in *Brave Hearts*:

> With 90 seconds left on the clock we were five points down and struggling deep in our territory. 'What the hell,' I thought as the ball shot to me on the first tackle. I reefed that ball upfield. The NSW defence was caught offguard by my kick so early in the tackle count. Ben Ikin, chasing hard, gathered the ball on the first bounce on the halfway line. It went to Darren Smith, to Tonie Carroll who crashed over for a try. One point behind with the conversion to come. As the siren rang, Darren Lockyer kicked the goal. Queensland 24 – NSW 23. In the exultant celebrations that followed the miracle win ... I thought of my conversations with Kim and saluted the stars.

Laurie Daley put on a clinic in game two, played in Brisbane, guiding the Blues to a series-levelling win. But Queensland rebounded to win the decider, which was held back at the Sydney Football Stadium. 'Gorden Tallis, Shane Webcke, Darren and Jason Smith had the measure of the NSW forwards,' Walters recalled, 'with Gorden having one of his great tearaway games.'

Little separated Queensland and New South Wales the following season. The Maroons won the first match by one point, then the Blues made a lighting start to the second, with Robbie Ross scoring after only 42 seconds. Retiring skipper Laurie Daley then scored the last try of the match, which New South Wales won by four points.

'I just remember feeling excited, knowing that I didn't want to leave anything in the tank,' Daley told *Fox Sports* a decade later. 'It was a matter of going out there and giving it your all ... knowing that you were never going to play in Sydney again. I wanted to thank everyone who supported my career and fortunately we got the win with a really strong performance.'

The third game ended in a 10–10 draw and the series was tied, which meant Queensland retained the shield for another season. New South Wales greats Paul Harragon, Andrew Ettingshausen and Daley all quit representative football following that series, leading some pundits to claim that the Blues would struggle in 2000. The series was indeed one-sided, yet it was the Maroons that copped a hiding.

Queensland's campaign began poorly, with Tallis sent off in the opening game for calling referee Bill Harrigan a cheat; the northerners went on to lose that game and the other two as well. The dominant Blues, coached by Wayne Pearce, saved their best form for the final game, which they won 56–16. As a team, New South Wales broke a number of Origin records in that match, including the highest score and greatest winning margin. But it was centre Ryan Girdler who attracted the most headlines. He scored 32 points (three tries and ten goals) in an extraordinary effort that stands, when judged by figures alone, as the greatest individual performance in Origin history.

Wayne Bennett returned to the position of Queensland coach in 2001 and was given the task of restoring the state's pride after the whitewash the previous year. He inspired the Maroons to an impressive victory in game one, but the Blues hit back to easily win game two. With his squad hit hard by a series of injuries to key players, Bennett decided to do some left-field recruiting for game three.

At that time, one of Bennett's favourite players, halfback Alfie Langer, was living in England and playing for the Warrington Wolves. He had not run out for Queensland since 1998. And he was almost 35 years old. None of that fazed Bennett. The coaching legend phoned Langer and asked him if he would come home and make a one-off appearance for the Maroons. 'Hey, coach, why did it take you so long to call?' was Langer's reply. He was in.

Steve Crawley explained what happened next in an article published in the *Sydney Morning Herald*:

> Queensland Rugby League chairman John McDonald was packed off on Wednesday to solve the question of eligibility but under strict instructions not to release the name of the player, only that he was English-based and had a clearance from his club. This was, after all, still a secret. McDonald returned with a smile broader than the Big Pineapple, suggesting the ARL had thought the player to be Hull's Jason Smith. So Warrington knew, the Queensland selectors and board of directors knew, the Bennetts, [Ben] Ikin, plus Allan and Janine Langer, and yet until yesterday the secret didn't escape a coup in itself. The cloak-and-dagger went right down to Langer being booked London–Singapore–Brisbane under a false name. He told airline crew on QF 521 he was coming home for a little break. Some holiday. At 34 years and 336 days, he becomes the third-oldest player to represent at Origin level, behind Queensland's first captain, Arthur Beetson (35 years, 163 days), in 1980 and New South Wales winger John Ferguson (34 years, 348 days) in 1989. What a chapter in Origin lore.

Langer spoke to Crawley shortly after touching down in Sydney. 'I haven't been able to tell anyone,' he admitted. 'Not even my parents. Dad's going to have a heart attack when he hears the news. I wish the game was tomorrow. I just want to play.'

Langer's reputation as a footballing genius was confirmed when he guided the Maroons to a 40–14 win in front of almost 50,000 roaring Queenslanders at the redeveloped Lang Park in Brisbane. The following day, Sydney's *Daily Telegraph* featured a picture of Langer on its front cover accompanied by the headline: 'BLOODY ALF. You flew 16,981km to break our hearts. Now, please go back to England.'

Bennett ended up enticing Langer to return to Australia on a full-time basis in 2002. He played one last season for the Brisbane Broncos and made three more appearances for Queensland. True to form, he helped the Maroons retain the Origin shield. He was just a month shy of his 36th birthday when he produced a man-of-the-match performance in the deciding match of the 2002 series, which ended in an 18–18 draw.

The Blues turned the tables by taking back the shield in 2003, and a year later they brought back a hero of their own midway through their campaign. Although Brad Fittler was still playing club football in 2004, he had not been part of an Origin series since 2001. But a scarcity of five-eighths led New South Wales coach Phil Gould to sound out Fittler in the lead-up to game two.

'I called Freddie's girlfriend Marie Liarris this morning,' Gould explained to the *Sydney Morning Herald*. 'Brad wasn't there; he was out . . . at the beach. I said to Marie, "Has he got any old pairs of Origin socks in his drawer?" She said she'd love to see him play Origin again.' Fittler rang Gould as soon as he returned home. 'If you want me to play, I'll play,' he said. The Blues' boss was happy to tell the media that he was hoping Fittler's return would be as successful as Langer's shock comeback for Queensland three years earlier.

It didn't work out that way in game two, which New South Wales lost by four points. But Fittler wound back the clock in game three, scoring the final try of the match as the Blues regained the Origin title with a 36–16 victory. 'As if scripted, Fittler charged down a Darren Lockyer chip, regained the ball, which bounced into his safe hands, and raced across the line with his left arm raised in celebration,' read the AAP match report.

Afterwards, Fittler, who grew up in a low-income, single-parent household in western Sydney, and then became the highest-paid rugby league player in the world, told the media: 'I've had a fairytale run my whole life.' In the following day's *Sydney Morning Herald*, league legend Roy Masters wrote: 'You could almost feel the pixie dust shower down and magic wands flicker across the land as the fairytale became complete.'

New South Wales had plenty of reasons to celebrate. The Blues had now won 11 Origin series to the Maroons' tally of ten. Their dreams having come true, both Gould and Fittler retired from their respective positions after the celebrations had died down.

A similar story played out in 2005, when much-admired New South Wales player Andrew Johns, who had only recently recovered from a broken jaw and had not played an Origin match since 2003, was a late call-up for game two. With his team trailling 1–0 in the series, Johns silenced his doubters by earning the man-of-the-match award as the Blues levelled things up with a 32–22 win. Three weeks later Johns produced another masterful performance as the Blues scored a 22-point victory before a hostile crowd in Brisbane and celebrated their third consecutive series win. As AAP summed up the contest:

NEW SOUTH WALES vs QUEENSLAND

It was blue murder – a night most of the 52,496 fans will want to forget as the Blues notched their biggest ever Origin victory on Queensland soil. Only one previous NSW side – the 1994 Phil Gould–Laurie Daley outfit – had fought back from 1–0 down ... to win the series. It puts NSW up 12 series to 10 and gives them a 37–36 edge in head-to-head in the 25th anniversary year. Again the destroyer was champion halfback Andrew Johns. Johns, who overcame a knee scare early in the game, followed up his sublime second game effort in Sydney with another commanding performance that surely must have buried critics who have hedged at putting him in the same class as Wally Lewis.

The New South Wales players, their coach, Ricky Stuart, and their fans celebrated long and hard after the 2005 triumph. It was just as well: so dominant was Queensland during the following seven seasons that the 2013 Blues squad found itself staring at the prospect of an eighth straight series defeat.

The Maroons' great era began in the third and deciding game of the 2006 series, which was played at Melbourne's Etihad Stadium. Queensland trailed 14–4 with ten minutes to go, but the men in maroon pulled off one of their trademark comebacks, running in two late tries as the supposedly neutral Victorians in the crowd roared them on. Queensland captain Darren Lockyer scored the match-winner after making the most of a wayward pass from New South Wales' Brett Hodgson. Lockyer not only held the Origin shield aloft that night, but he was also voted man of the match and man of the series.

Eleven months later Lockyer was again in the thick of the action when another clanger from the Blues – this one committed by Jarryd Hayne – enabled him to score a crucial try in the Maroons' 25–18 victory in game one. Queensland then wrapped up the series by winning the second game as well, a feat it repeated in 2009 and 2010. In fact, the Maroons whitewashed the latter of those series.

There were times during these years when New South Wales proved its own worst enemy. In 2010 the Blues fought hard in game one, losing a classic match 28–24. But their chances of levelling the series nosedived after dynamic centre Timana Tahu, whose heritage is Māori and Aboriginal, accused former halfback Andrew Johns of directing racist remarks towards him during the training camp prior to game two. Tahu quit the team and headed home, and New South Wales was duly thrashed 34–6 a few days later. Tahu and Johns, who had been teammates at Newcastle in the years preceding their spat, were later reunited at the club after patching up their differences.

Few such dramas hit the Queensland camp during its winning run, which was powered by the skill, athleticism and toughness of many great players. For many years Lockyer stood head and shoulders above them all, but he had plenty of brilliant helpers. There was North Queensland Cowboys' superstar Johnathan Thurston – a two-time winner of the Wally Lewis Medal, awarded to the player of the series – whose accurate kicking was crucial in many victories. Thurston was the only Maroons player to line up in every origin match between 2006 and 2012.

There was also Melbourne Storm playmaker Cameron Smith. Voted player of the series in 2007 and 2011, Smith took over the captaincy from Lockyer in 2012 and continued to lead by example. He was ably supported by another Melbourne Storm man, Billy Slater, who first shot to prominence when he scored one of Origin's most spectacular individual tries at Suncorp Stadium (the new name for Lang Park) in 2004. Slater's moment of magic began when he sharked a Lockyer chip-kick. He kicked the ball himself, then scooted past

Blues fullback Anthony Minichiello, grabbed the ball and touched it down. Slater came of age during the Maroons' period of domination, scoring the series-winning try in 2008 and winning the Wally Lewis Medal in 2010.

The Maroons also benefitted from some controversial recruiting. They were allowed to claim super-talented back Greg Inglis as their own, despite the fact that Inglis had grown up in the New South Wales town of Bowraville and was a prominent player while a student at Newcastle's Hunter Sports High. Inglis was allowed to play for Queensland because he had moved north as a teenager and was ruled to have played his first 'serious' football matches while attending Wavell State High School in Brisbane.

Inglis sent New South Wales officials into a fury when he scored two tries on debut for the Maroons, then scored another two in his second Origin game. He was the leading point-scorer in the 2007 Origin series and was awarded the Wally Lewis Medal after being voted the best player in the 2009 series. In 2012 he became the leading try-scorer in Origin history.

Other players to have qualified for the Maroons despite having spent their earliest days outside Queensland were legendary prop Petero Civoniceva, who was born in Fiji, Brad Thorn, Tonie Carroll and Karmichael Hunt, who were born in New Zealand, and Neville Costigan and Adrian Lam, who both entered the world in Rabaul in Papua New Guinea.

'They are thieves in the night,' New South Wales legend Benny Elias wailed in a story published in Sydney's *Daily Telegraph* that discussed how many 'ring-ins' have played for the Maroons over the years. 'And they blatantly do it in front of our faces. The Queenslanders would cheat, lie and steal to win an Origin series. They just don't care. They sell their scruples to win a series over NSW. Unbelievable. Origin means more to them than a state election, it means more to them than anything. They talk about their Queensland passion and they have had some great players over the years. But a lot of them were born outside Queensland.'

New South Wales has also done its share of recruiting over the years. Champion Blues player Peter Sterling was born in Toowoomba, while Steve Rogers, who became a star for New South Wales in the 1980s, was born in Sydney but began his league career on Queensland's Gold Coast. There are countless similar stories, but in 2012 the Australian Rugby League commission attempted to put a stop to the questioning of player eligibility when it introduced a multi-step process to determine a player's Origin status. The new criterion takes many factors into account, including a player's birthplace, where he went to school and in which state he first played the game at under-15 level.

Another issue that has riled league fans in both states in recent years is Victoria's efforts to pinch a piece of the New South Wales vs Queensland rivalry. Victoria's major events and tourism bodies have offered millions of dollars in inducements to try to secure an Origin match in Melbourne each year. The Victorians' motivations are clear: they want to boost the state's tourist numbers by enticing thousands of Queenslanders and New South Welshmen to travel south for the big game.

League blogger Jeff Wall has been among the most vocal opponents of staging matches down south. 'The game is not in [such dire straights] that it has to sell off a precious asset for a couple of million dollars, without any evidence of wider long term benefit,' Wall wrote. 'It should not have done so in the past – and it must not do so in the future.' And it's fair to say that Victorian sports minister Hugh Delahunty – a former Australian Rules player for Essendon – didn't exactly help his state's cause when, in the lead-up to game one of the 2012 series, at Melbourne's Etihad Stadium, he declared that he was looking forward to the big clash between 'Queensland and New Zealand'.

In any case, the Queensland players, coaches and supporters who travelled south for that game went home happy, as they have from so many Origin matches over the years. Despite having been well beaten by the Blues in general play, the Maroons scored an 18–10 victory, thanks largely to a very contentious try awarded to Inglis. 'They have had the rub of the green all night,' an outraged New South Wales captain Paul Gallen said afterwards. 'This is ridiculous. This is getting out of control.'

New South Wales hit back and won the second game in Sydney, setting up yet another series decider at Brisbane's cauldron of passion. In one of the greatest contests in the history of the New South Wales–Queensland rivalry, which was watched by a television audience of more than four million people, the Maroons won by a single point after halfback Cooper Cronk slotted a field goal from 40 metres out in the dying minutes.

'The pride and the passion within this Queensland team ... we had a few hurdles to get over during the week, we lost a few key men, but found a way to win, which is an indication of our spirit,' exclaimed Petero Civoniceva, who retired from representative football after the match.

The days when it was believed that Origin meant more to Queenslanders are long gone. 'We worked so hard as a group, it's just shattering,' was the reaction of New South Wales' five-eighth Todd Carney to the Blues' seventh series loss on the trot. 'I've never experienced this or felt like this after a game. It's heartbreaking.'

From humble beginnings, the rivalry between the Blues and the Maroons has become a juggernaut. These days, the passion, aggression and sublime skill on show in the annual State of Origin series not only captivates the people of New South Wales and

US *vs* THEM

Queensland, but it has also become a must-see for sports fans around the nation.

NEW SOUTH WALES vs QUEENSLAND, RUGBY LEAGUE (1980–2012)

Matches played: 94 (including exhibition match in the United States in 1987)
New South Wales wins: 43
Queensland wins: 51

State of Origin series wins
New South Wales: 12: 1985–86, 1990, 1992–94, 1996–97, 2000, 2003–05
Queensland: 17: 1982–84, 1987–89, 1991, 1995, 1998, 2001, 2006–12
Tied series: 2: 1999, 2002

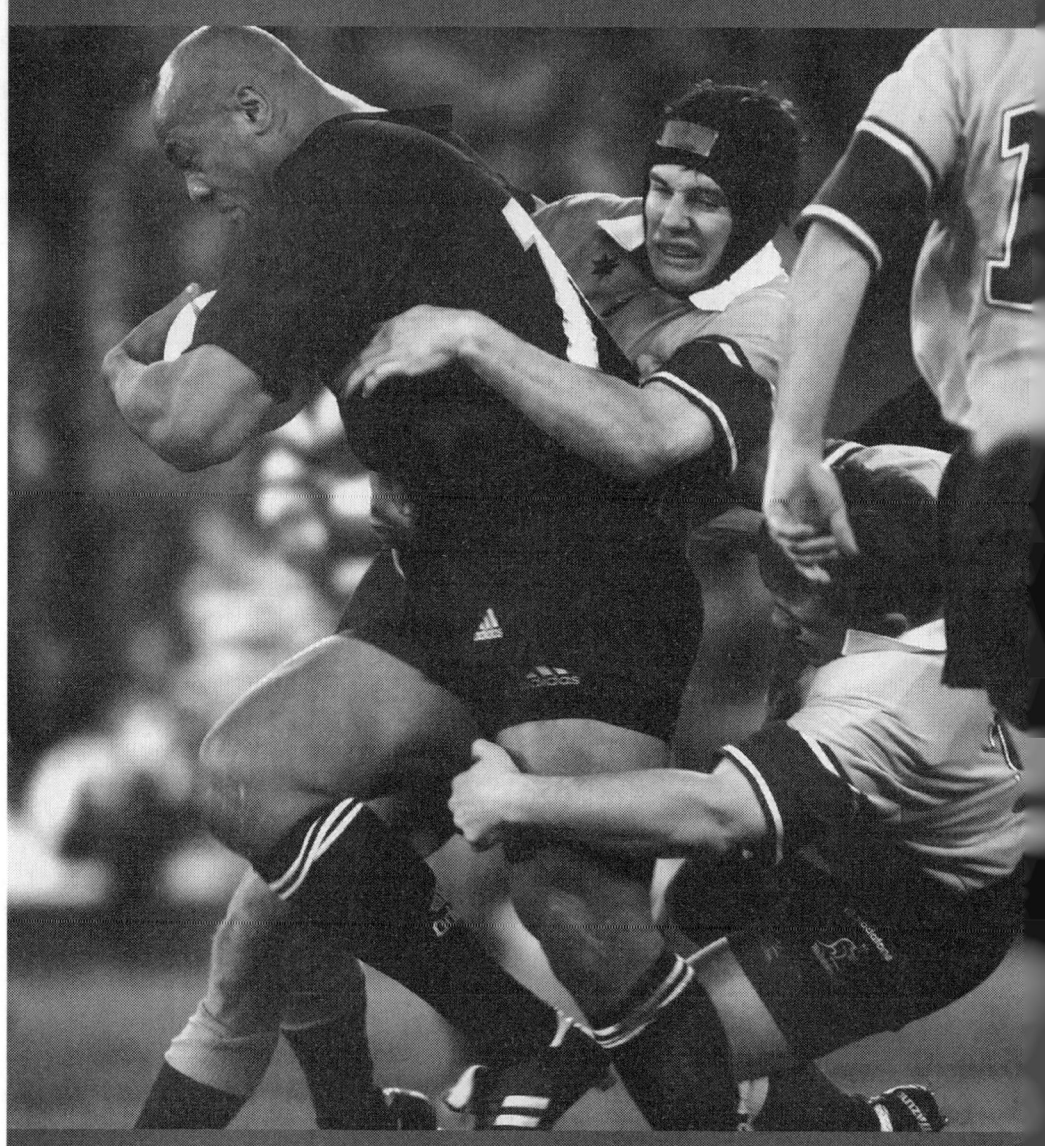

New Zealand rugby player Jonah Lomu tries to break a tackle from Australia's Stephen Larkham during the 2000 Bledisloe Cup match at Stadium Australia in Sydney.

RUGBY UNION
Australia *vs* New Zealand

BOASTING A MUCH LARGER landmass, a far bigger economy and many more people than its neighbour across the ditch, Australia is often portrayed as being New Zealand's dominant older sibling. But when it comes to rugby, the situation is reversed. By the end of 2012, the All Blacks had won 99 of their 146 Test matches against the Wallabies, a winning percentage of 67.8. And New Zealand's domination over Australia on the pitch has been especially pronounced in recent years, with the All Blacks taking out ten consecutive Bledisloe Cup series between 2003 and 2012.

Although the century-long rivalry between the All Blacks and the Wallabies has not been particularly even, it has provided some of the greatest moments in Aussie sport. Highlights include the so-called 'greatest game of rugby ever played', which drew a crowd of almost 110,000 people to Sydney's Olympic Stadium and was decided by a late piece of brilliance from legendary All Black Jonah Lomu, and the 1991 and 2003 World Cup semi-finals, in which the Wallabies, rank underdogs before both games, scored famous victories.

The rugby rivalry between the two nations began in 1882, when a team from the New South Wales Rugby Union (NSWRU, known then as the Southern Rugby Union) toured New Zealand and took on a number of provincial sides. The New South Wales side was captained by University of Sydney skipper Ted Raper, a big, strong man who was regarded as having a 'great strength and power'. Raper died only two years later, at the age of 26, after contracting typhoid. His efforts on the tour of New Zealand were referred to in his obituary, published in the *Sydney Morning Herald* on 18 February 1884: 'He made hosts of friends among the hospitable inhabitants of Maoriland by the way in which he piloted his men through that hard-fought campaign, representing them as worthily in social circles as he did in the field.'

In the decades prior to that tour, Aussies had been introduced to the sport of rugby by British settlers. The University of Sydney Rugby Club – the oldest rugby club outside England – was formed in 1863. In Australia, the animosity between the colonists in New South Wales and Victoria meant that while rugby quickly became popular in Sydney it was largely ignored in Melbourne, where locals preferred their own code of football, then known as Victorian Rules.

In New Zealand, the events that led to the introduction of rugby and the way it spread throughout the nation were far different. As Sean Davies explained on *BBC Sport*'s website in 2003:

> Few politicians can have had more of an impact on the fate of their country than Sir David Monro – the Speaker in the New Zealand House of Representatives – when he chose to send his son to England to complete his education. Charles John Monro discovered rugby at London's Christ College, and on his return to Nelson he staged New Zealand's first game. Nelson Town met Nelson College on 14 May, 1870, the Town triumphing by two goals to nil, instigating a game that would become a national obsession and come to dominate the country's sporting passions. The game appealed to the Kiwi psyche and quickly spread, the native Maoris finding a particular empathy with the sport's warrior ethos.

AUSTRALIA vs NEW ZEALAND

New Zealand's rugby dominance over Australia was established when a Kiwi team toured New South Wales in 1884. The touring side, which featured mostly Māori players and was known as 'New Zealand Natives', was a brilliant combination. It won each of its nine matches, scoring 176 points while conceding only 17.

Not only did the New Zealanders prove far too good for lesser teams such as Cumberland County and the Combined Suburbs XV, but they also thrashed New South Wales on two occasions at the Sydney Cricket Ground, 11–0 in the first match and 21–2 in the second. Spectators at the matches were dazzled by the Māori war dance staged by the Kiwis before each match. As explained on the official All Blacks website: 'The centrality of the haka within All Black rugby tradition is not a recent development. Since the original [team] led by Joseph Warbrick, the haka has been closely associated with New Zealand rugby. Its mystique has evolved along with the fierce determination, commitment and high level skill which has been the hallmark of New Zealand's National game.'

The development of rugby in New Zealand took a big step forward when a national governing body, the New Zealand Rugby Football Union (NZRFU), was formed in 1892. The following year, renowned Māori player Thomas Rangiwahia Ellison (who was also the first Māori solicitor in New Zealand) suggested that Kiwi national teams should wear a black jersey with a silver fern on the breast. This was quickly adopted and soon led to New Zealand teams becoming known as the All Blacks, although it took some years for the nickname to catch on. According to the website Rugby Football History, the *Express & Echo* newspaper in the English city of Devon appears to have been the 'first to use the term All Blacks when it recorded the day the 1905 touring side beat Devon 55–4 in their first game: "The All Blacks, as they are styled by reason of their sable and unrelieved costume, were under the guidance of their captain, and their fine physique favourably impressed the spectators.'"

A year after the NZRFU was established, its members selected a squad that embarked on a ten-game tour of Australia. Most of the matches were played in New South Wales but a few took place in Queensland, where rugby was slowly overtaking Victorian Rules as the most popular football code. Once again, the All Blacks were almost unstoppable. Captained by Ellison, they won each of their matches in Queensland, impressing the large crowds that turned out to watch their skill and flair. 'The visitors' play was splendid, their passing, punting and drop-kicking being a treat to witness,' wrote the correspondent for the *Sydney Mail* after New Zealand had beaten a Queensland Rugby Union (QRU) representative team 36–0. 'They outclassed Queensland in every point of the game.' The All Blacks' only blemish on the tour was a 25–3 loss to New South Wales, although they avenged that defeat by scoring a 16–0 victory over New South Wales in the final match of the tour.

Between 1894 and 1901, the All Blacks played matches at home against New South Wales and Queensland and also toured both colonies. During that period, New Zealand added to its already impressive record, winning 12 matches and losing just three. Despite the success of the Kiwi national team, it took until 1899 for New South Wales and Queensland to come together and select an Australian national squad.

After playing its inaugural Test series against a touring Great Britain team (Australia won the first game but lost the next three), Australia finally played its first Test match against New Zealand in 1903. The game took place at the Sydney Cricket Ground and created such excitement among the local sports fans that a crowd of more than 30,000 turned up to see it. (The crowds for the New Zealand versus New South Wales games had usually been fewer than 10,000 people).

AUSTRALIA vs NEW ZEALAND

At the time, Test matches in Australia were organised by the host state's governing body, so the NSWRU organised matches in Sydney and the QRU organised those that took place in Brisbane; a national governing body, the Australian Rugby Union (ARU), was not established until 1947. As a result, the Australian players wore the light-blue jerseys usually sported by New South Wales when they took on New Zealand for the first time, and the Aussies were referred to in newspaper reports as the 'Blues'. The NSWRU also organised all of the Australian's team's overseas tours. When Australia played matches in Brisbane, however, the players wore Queensland's maroon jerseys.

The All Blacks, meanwhile, went into the match in brilliant form. They had won all their previous eight matches on the tour, scoring 242 points and conceding only ten. But because the All Blacks squad contained a number of players over the age of 30, some of the media coverage in the lead-up to the Test match suggested that Australia was not without a chance of causing an upset. A report in the weekly sports newspaper *The Referee* put things in perspective: 'If there be one thing more than another of which New Zealanders are proud, it is their ability as rugby footballers. The average New Zealander, in speaking of Australians [when playing against England] at cricket, uses the pronoun "we". In football, however, he is careful to differentiate. And, as he is cock of the walk in the latter game, his view is correct and his pride quite excusable.'

When the time came for action, New Zealand's players performed the haka, then their captain, James Duncan, won the toss and elected to run with the breeze. The All Blacks took a 3–0 lead when fullback Billy Wallace landed a penalty goal after eight minutes of play, and the visitors were never headed from there. In front 7–3 at half-time, New Zealand scored 15 unanswered points in the second half and won 22–3. As rugby guru Peter Jenkins described in his book *Wallaby*

223

Gold, the All Blacks had perfected a number of skills rarely seen in rugby nowadays: 'In the second half, the New Zealand forwards, employing the popular tactic of dribbling, ball at toe, with clever foot passes frustrating the defence, were causing the Australians problems.'

Although it proved to be a relatively one-sided affair, the match was not without controversy. All Blacks winger Opai Asher was awarded a try early in the second half even though the ball appeared to slip from his grasp when he was tackled by Australian winger Chris White. Later in the game, the Aussies stopped playing when it appeared that another All Blacks winger, Duncan McGregor, had stepped over the sideline. But the touch umpire was unmoved, so McGregor scooted down the field and scored under the posts.

More than two years passed before Australia and New Zealand played their second Test match. This time the venue was Tahuna Park in the Kiwi city of Dunedin, but the result was much the same: the All Blacks won 14–3.

A further two years later, in 1907, the nations took part in their first Test series. The first match was held at the Sydney Cricket Ground, the second at the Brisbane Cricket Ground and the third back at the Sydney Cricket Ground. True to form, the All Blacks cantered to victory in the first two matches. However, Australia, which had recently adopted the nickname 'the Wallabies', fought back strongly in the Third Test, avoiding a loss for the first time in a match against New Zealand by holding out for a 5–5 draw.

By the time the All Blacks arrived in Australia for a three-Test series in 1910, the sport of rugby had been split in two by the fight over whether players should be amateurs or professionals. In short, rugby union's administrators were adamant that players should not be paid to play (rugby would not embrace professionalism until 1995), so a number of English working-class footballers and businessmen combined to establish rugby league in Great Britain around the start of the 20th century. From its beginnings, rugby league was fully professional – with players not only paid to play but clubs also able to command fees for transferring players between clubs.

As had happened in Britain, the establishment of rugby league in the southern hemisphere resulted in many great union players quitting the code. As explained on the official website of the Australian Rugby Union, the greatest change occurred after the Wallabies had visited Great Britain in 1908. The tour 'coincided with the London Olympic Games in which rugby union was a sport. Invited to play, the Australian team won the gold medal by defeating Cornwall, the Champion English team representing England. When the team returned home, eleven of its members were enticed by the money offered to join the newly formed Rugby League.'

Among the Australians to join the league ranks was Herbert Henry 'Dally' Messenger, considered one of the finest players in the nation. Messenger, who played two Tests for the Wallabies and 17 matches for New South Wales before defecting to league, was just 23 when he made his monumental move. Such was the animosity between rugby's warring factions at the time that the rugby union administrators struck Messenger's name from their record books; his achievements were not reinstated to the NSWRU's record books until the centenary of the split, in 2007.

'I don't think anyone would doubt that Dally Messenger is one of the all-time greats of Australian sport,' NSWRU chief executive Fraser Neill said when Messenger's reinstatement was announced. 'Rugby should be proud of the part he played not just in our game but in the overall fabric of sport in this country. He was a class act both on the field and off it, given that even after many years out of the game he never once admonished it. The only pity is that he's not around to witness for himself the game embracing him once again.'

A similar furore had erupted in New Zealand, with a number of All Blacks defecting to league. This meant that two weakened teams contested the three-match Test series in Australia in 1910. All the Tests were played at the Sydney Cricket Ground, and the teams had just one day of rest between the first two.

The short break seemed to suit Australia, as a far more purposeful Aussie team showed up for the second match. The Wallabies were not just competitive, but they finally also recorded their first victory over New Zealand by scoring an 11–0 victory. The match report in the following day's *Sydney Morning Herald* read:

> Undoubtedly the light-blue side was the best team on the day, from start to finish the game being in their favour. They were attacking practically all the time, and were seldom called on to defend for more than a few minutes. With the wind in their favour they only scored 3 points; but in the second half, when it was thought they would have to look to their lines of defence, they had a better time than before. The forwards got possession of the ball in almost every scrum, and on the line-out were also more prominent than their opponents. These advantages gave the backs innumerable opportunities to storm the New Zealand line, and right well did they do their part. They were sure in handling the ball, and combined brilliantly and effectively in attack. The defence, too, left nothing to be desired, Dwyer again performing in his usual first-class style, and proving himself one of the greatest full-backs we have seen. Prentice was next in order of merit in this department, and several times saved splendidly. The remaining backs also made no mistakes, and the whole division showed some of the brightest flashes that an Australian side has ever put forth.

Australia's dominance was short-lived, as New Zealand bounced back to easily win the third game by 15 points. The All Blacks then won the first two games of the three-Test series that was played in New Zealand in 1913, meaning they had won eight of their 11 Tests against the Wallabies.

Australia narrowed the gap and injected new life into the rivalry by scoring a 16–5 win in the Third Test, played at Lancaster Park in Christchurch. It was New Zealand's first loss at home for 19 years. Yet the outbreak of the First World War meant that a team named 'Australia' would not win another Test match until 1929.

As were most other sports, rugby union was shut down during the war, and it recommenced only slowly after the conflict ended. A lack of people and finance meant that the Queensland Rugby Union stayed in recess during most of the 1920s, and as a result, New South Wales represented Australia in international rugby on its own between 1920 and 1929. The Waratahs, as the team was now nicknamed, played matches against New Zealand, New Zealand Māori (a team made up of only Māori players), South Africa, Ireland, Wales, Scotland, England and France, and all these contests were eventually awarded Test status.

Not surprisingly, New South Wales struggled to match the might of the All Blacks when the teams met in a three-Test series at the Sydney Cricket Ground in July and August of 1920. New Zealand won all three matches, although the Waratahs did show enough to suggest that they might cause a few upsets in the future.

And that was exactly what happened. Using its revolutionary style of open, running rugby, New South Wales turned heads by defeating the All Blacks 17–0 in Christchurch in 1921. The Waratahs backed up that result by scoring a 2–1 win in the three-Test series they played against the All Blacks in 1922. It was the first time the Waratahs had scored a series win over New Zealand. A report about the Third Test was published in the *Sydney Morning Herald* on 8 August 1922:

> New South Wales won by eight points to six after a game which will be memorable to all those who witnessed it, if for nothing else than the sheer intensity with which it was waged. How wonderfully well matched the two teams have been can be gauged from the fact that in the three test fixtures the total points scored have been 41 by New South Wales as against 40 by the Dominion players. The match yesterday was scarcely worthy of the occasion. It was by no means brilliantly spectacular, and the spectators were favoured with few of the finer and more scientific aspects of the old Rugby game. Too much depended upon the ultimate result for risks to be taken by either side. Consequently it developed into a desperate, gruelling struggle, in which the rival packs dominated the play. Strangely enough the whole of the points were scored in the first half hour of the match.

All up, New South Wales and New Zealand contested 24 Test matches between 1920 and 1928, with the matches often drawing crowds of around 15,000; the fact that the teams met so often only added to ferocity of the rivalry that developed. As they had in matches against the Wallabies, however, the All Blacks held the upper hand overall, winning 18 of the matches. New South Wales also played seven Tests against the New Zealand Māori team during the same period, winning four and losing three. Those matches were often high-scoring and highly entertaining affairs, with both teams often scoring 20 points or more.

In 1928 the Queensland Rugby Union reformed and restarted its club competition, which paved the way for the selection of the first Australian team since 1914. Around the same time, the New

South Wales and Queensland Rugby Unions decided that the new Wallabies team needed its own jersey, and it was agreed that the Australian amateur representative colours of green and gold would be adopted. As explained on the ARU's website:

> In 1929 when New Zealand toured Australia, the first official Australian jersey was introduced – an emerald green jersey with the Australian Coat of Arms and green leg socks with green and gold bars on the top. There were variations in 1933, 1937 and 1938. In 1933, when Australia toured South Africa for the first time, the Wallabies wore sky blue with the Australian Coat of Arms because ... both countries played in dark green jerseys. (This courtesy was reciprocated by South Africa who wore white jerseys for test matches when Australia toured South Africa in 1953.) When South Africa toured Australia in 1937, the Australian jersey was changed to white with green and gold hoops. In 1938 when Australia played New Zealand, the Australian jersey was changed to gold with a dark green hoop – because it had been suggested that there was too much similarity between the dark green of Australia and the black of New Zealand. The change to gold in 1961 was also to avoid any clash with South Africa. It has remained predominantly gold ever since.

The rivalry between the Wallabies and the All Blacks resumed when the teams contested a three-Test series in Sydney and Brisbane in July 1929. Given that New South Wales had been reasonably competitive against New Zealand over the previous eight years, Aussie rugby fans held high hopes that the combination of the best New South Welshman and Queenslanders would be a decent match for the All Blacks. Their hopes were realised when Australia scored narrow victories in all three Tests: 9–8, 17–9 and 15–13.

Another crucial element was added to the rivalry in 1931 when the New Zealand governor-general, Lord Bledisloe, donated a large silver trophy to be awarded to the winner of each Wallabies vs All Blacks Test series.

The first battle for what became known as the Bledisloe Cup took place when New Zealand played a three-Test series in Australia in 1932. The Wallabies won the first Test, at the Sydney Cricket Ground, but the All Blacks squared the series with a dominant performance in the second Test, at the Exhibition Ground in Brisbane. New Zealand then won the deciding match 21–13. As the *Brisbane Courier* reported:

> Australia was outplayed, back and forward, and New Zealand's win was just as convincing as the success in the second Test at Brisbane, where the All Blacks scored 21 points to 3. The attendance was announced officially at 29,553 ... the New Zealand combination has developed sufficiently to have taught lessons to our men. Most vital is the lesson that forwards, if they must have speed and ability to handle, must also do their share of solid rucking. That was the finest feature of the form of the All Black forwards. They shone brilliantly in the open, moving into line with the backs, and they scored four of the side's five tries. They proved magnificent ruckers, often overwhelming the Australian pack after a scrum or line out, and robbing our men of the ball.

Australia claimed the Bledisloe Cup for the first time when it won the two-Test series played at the Sydney Cricket Ground in 1934 – the Wallabies won the first match 25–11, while the second was a 3–3 draw – but the All Blacks then won both series played before the outbreak of the Second World War. It would not be until 1949 that the Bledisloe Cup returned to Australian hands.

AUSTRALIA vs NEW ZEALAND

The members of the 1949 Wallabies team achieved fame by defeating the All Blacks in two Tests on their home turf. Upon their return, the Wallabies were feted at a series of receptions, while the *Sydney Morning Herald* published a triumphant article under the headline 'Giant Cup Here'. Next to the article was a picture of the NSWRU secretary standing next to the enormous trophy. The article read: 'Weighing 153lb and needing two men to carry it, the giant Bledisloe Cup was brought back to Australia yesterday by the victorious Wallabies. They beat New Zealand in both Rugby Union Tests, to regain the trophy that was last held by Australia in 1934. Four feet high and nearly three feet wide, the cup ... is insured for £350 in New Zealand. Taken to the NSW Rugby Union's rooms when the team reached Sydney by air yesterday, the cup was placed in the charge of the Union's secretary, Mr A. Marks.'

It was just as well the Australian rugby community had a decent party after the Wallabies reclaimed the Bledisloe Cup. New Zealand won it back by clean-sweeping the three-Test series played in Sydney and Brisbane in 1951. The All Blacks then held the cup for 28 years.

Although New Zealand won the vast majority of Test matches between 1951 and 1979, the fierce rivalry between the All Blacks and the Wallabies never waned. In fact, the animosity between the teams reached a new height when much-admired Australian captain Ken Catchpole had his career cruelly cut short when he was seriously injured by legendary All Blacks lock Colin 'Pinetree' Meads during the second Test of 1968.

Earlier in his career, Catchpole had earned the distinction of captaining the Wallabies in his debut match, played against Fiji. As Huw Richards explained in his book *A Game for Hooligans: A History of Rugby Union*: 'After three matches against Fiji, 21-year-old Ken Catchpole captained the tour of South Africa and was hailed by selector Wally Meagher... as "the greatest scrum-half we've ever had". Few opinions differed from Meagher's.'

Catchpole ended up leading the Wallabies in 13 of his 27 Tests, and he would have made more appearances for Australia had Meads not maimed him. The infamous incident, which took place at the Sydney Cricket Ground, occurred when Catchpole was pinned under a ruck. Meads grabbed Catchpole's leg, wrenching it until the Australian's hamstring had been torn from the bone. 'I was driven into a splits position under enormous pressure,' Catchpole said some years later. 'I could feel the muscles stretch like rubber bands reaching the end of their elasticity and snapping. It really hurt, then the whole area went numb. I knew it was something serious.' Carried from the field, Catchpole never played another game of rugby.

The incident didn't do much harm to Meads' reputation. In 1999 the New Zealand *Rugby Monthly* magazine proclaimed him the New Zealand Player of the Century, and he became Sir Colin Meads when was knighted for his services to the game in 2009. The New Zealand website *Rugby Museum* describes him thus:

> Throughout the 1960s, a golden era in All Black rugby, Meads became the personification of the New Zealand style of the game. He was rugged and uncompromising and as the All Black prototype he quickly became a genuine folk hero. A farming product of backblocks New Zealand, Meads epitomised the nation and the rugby of his era, one which is in stark... contrast to the way the game and society with it has evolved under professionalism. While Meads would never be intimidated and was quick to take action if one of his team-mates was suffering from someone else's illegality, he was never a deliberately dirty player. Such was his power, commitment and determination he never really had to be. As a sporting legend Meads is New

AUSTRALIA vs NEW ZEALAND

Zealand's equivalent of Australia's Sir Donald Bradman or the United States of America's Babe Ruth.

Australian rugby hit its lowest ebb during the early 1970s. As Phil Wilkins explained in the *Sydney Morning Herald* many years later: 'Before Australia toured New Zealand in 1972, coach Bob Templeton learned Test half John Hipwell, centre Geoff Shaw, lineout forward Stuart Gregory, prop David Dunworth and hooker Bruce Taafe were unavailable. The team was beaten in all three Tests and became vilified as the "Woeful Wallabies". A year later, Tonga beat Australia 16–11 in Brisbane. Australian rugby was on its knees. More representative games and more sophisticated coaching were needed. The establishment of a national coaching organisation, headed by former Wallabies centre Dick Marks, was of huge importance.'

The fruits of the rebuilding process were put on show when the Wallabies, having lost the first two Tests, beat the All Blacks at Eden Park in Auckland in 1978. The victory was all the more remarkable because the Australian coach, Daryl Haberecht, suffered a heart attack in the lead-up to the game and was in hospital when it was played. 'We just took over,' then-Wallabies captain Tony Shaw recalled prior to the third Bledisloe Cup Test of 2012. 'Bob Templeton was here and we could have brought him in to coach us. But we thought: "No, f--- it, we know what's wrong, and we know how to fix it." Everyone in New Zealand thought we had no hope. We were copping heaps from the Kiwis, and the press. There was some of the "Awful Aussie, Woeful Wallabies" carry-on that was still around from the 1972 Wallabies tour. Greg Cornelsen scores four tries and the rest is history. A 30–16 win.'

The win in Auckland was Australia's first Test victory over New Zealand since 1964. And the Wallabies' rise back up the charts was capped off when the Wallabies defeated the All Blacks 12–6 before more than 30,000 roaring fans at the Sydney Cricket Ground on 28 July 1979. Because it was a one-off Test, the victory was enough for Australia to take hold of the Bledisloe Cup for the first time since 1951, and the reporting in the aftermath of the game reflected the gravity of the triumph.

'Australia's stunning victory in yesterday's international was possibly the most remarkable of the 15 we have managed in 76 years against the All Blacks,' wrote Evan Whitton in Sydney's *Sun-Herald*. 'Sent out with, on the face of it, the wrong team and the wrong tactics, the Australians overcame all odds. This argues, at the very least, great character, and the 15 players are entitled to every tribute for that.'

Whitton's colleague Jim Webster added: 'Australia pulled off a magnificent win over the New Zealand All Blacks at the SCG yesterday in a Test that will go down as one of the best in this country's Rugby Union history. It is the fist time Australia has defeated the All Blacks in this country since the first Test at this ground in 1934.' After describing how the game unfolded, Webster painted the picture of the scene in the Wallabies' dressing room: 'David Brockhoff, the Australian coach, was tearful afterwards. He smiled, shook countless hands, kissed me on the forehead and his beer went flat as he talked in constant praise of his team.'

The Wallabies' newfound status was further enhanced when they retained the Bledisloe Cup by winning two of the three bruising Tests played in Australia in June and July of 1980. Having won the first Test 13–9, the Wallabies were then defeated 12–9 in the second game. New Zealand entered the third match with a cloud hanging over the fitness of a number of their best players; many of them had suffered a bout of food poisoning that was attributed to dodgy oysters rather than Australian espionage. The All Blacks felt no better after the game, having suffered an emphatic 26–10 defeat.

AUSTRALIA vs NEW ZEALAND

The Wallabies' victory was hailed as another landmark day for a team that was now considered number one in the world. The press sang the praises of rookie winger Peter Grigg, who burst onto the international scene by scoring two tries, while the reporters pointed out that the 16-point differential at the finish set a new record for Australia's greatest winning margin over New Zealand. 'As captain Tony Shaw was hoisted shoulder-high for the lap of honour of the ground after the final whistle, the cheers were for not one, but for all 15 Australian players,' wrote Brian Mossop in the *Sun-Herald*. 'If ever a match was won by a wholehearted team effort, it was this third Test. A reconstructed set of forwards rewarded the selectors for their faith, and the backs underlined their talents with a style and flair seen all too seldom in international rugby.'

After a year of playing other opponents, Australia and New Zealand resumed hostilities when the Wallabies travelled across the Tasman for a three-Test series in July and August 1982. The build-up was marred by infighting in the Australian camp. 'Coach Bob Dwyer's preference of Mark and Glen Ella over Queensland's Paul McLean and Roger Gould for the Brisbane Test against Scotland caused much angst,' Phil Wilkins wrote in the *Sydney Morning Herald* in 2009. 'The Queenslanders were reinstated for the second Test, and Australia squared the series. Subsequently, nine players withdrew from the tour of New Zealand, citing financial difficulties. Remarkably, Mark Ella led a resilient Wallabies side to a 19–16 second Test win in Wellington, only for the Kiwis to win the decider and regain the Bledisloe Cup.'

New Zealand retained the cup when it won the one-off Test played at the Sydney Cricket Ground in August 1983, but Australia's fortunes swung upwards once more when Alan Jones – the man now far better known as a radio broadcaster – took over as coach in 1984. The Wallabies scored a 16–9 victory at the Sydney Cricket Ground in Jones's first Bledisloe Cup match in charge, and they almost pulled off a series win. But despite the efforts of inspirational skipper Andrew Slack, Australian lost the series 2–1 after suffering a one-point defeat in the third Test, also in Sydney.

Jones soon achieved fame as a coach when he guided the Wallabies through a brilliant tour of Great Britain and Ireland. The tour began with Jones instructing his men to write on their arrival cards under the 'Purpose of visit' category: 'Business... because that's what we're here on.' It might seem corny, but the initiative did the trick, as the team achieved a grand slam by defeating England, Ireland, Wales and Scotland in the space of five weeks.

Six months after returning home, the Wallabies travelled to New Zealand for a one-off Test at Auckland's Eden Park. The build-up to the game was marred by protests against the New Zealand Rugby Union's decision to allow the All Blacks to tour South Africa later in the year. (At that time, South Africa had been shut out of most international sport because of the apartheid policies enforced by its white government.) In the end, the game was not interrupted by any incidents, with *Sun-Herald* correspondent Phil Wilkins reporting that 'The police had an extremely easy day. Barely a half a dozen spectators were arrested for trying to reach the playing arena. But twice during the first half, spectators were asked to remain calm while police blew up suspicious objects behind a grandstand.' The Wallabies were outplayed during much of the game, yet they lost by just a point, 10–9, because the home team's fullback, Keiran Crowley, missed six of his eight field-goal attempts.

In August 1986 the Wallabies returned to New Zealand for a three-Test series. Australia won a tough and rugged first Test 13–12, then the All Blacks won the second match, with the score in that game also finishing on 13–12. The scene was set for a mouth-watering Bledisloe Cup decider at that cauldron of passion otherwise known as Eden Park.

Jones and his men became immortal in the eyes of Australian rugby fans when they silenced the 50,000-strong crowd and won the match 22–9, a victory that was described by Jones as 'bigger than anything'. *Sun-Herald* reporter Greg Growden wrote: 'In a gripping International, the Wallabies scored two tries to nil to ensure they were the first Australian team to win in New Zealand since Trevor Allan's 1949 side. The 1986 Wallabies join the 1937 Springboks, 1949 Australians and the 1971 British Lions as the only sides to defeat the mighty All Blacks at home.' By the conclusion of the 2012 Bledisloe Cup series, Australia had still not won another game at Eden Park.

So big was the 1986 triumph considered at the time that Jones was awarded the Coach of the Year title by the Confederation of Australian Sport. However, he later invited ridicule when he suggested that the Wallabies should be allowed to prove they were the best team in the world by touring South Africa and taking on the Springboks (the tour never went ahead).

Despite the backlash triggered by Jones' comments, and by the fact that he had a strained relationship with a number of his players, the coach guided the Wallabies through the first Rugby World Cup, played in Australia and New Zealand in 1987. It was widely expected that the Wallabies and All Blacks would contest the final, but Australia was beaten in the semi-finals by France, and then lost the third-place play-off to Wales. New Zealand claimed the newly minted Webb Ellis Cup (named after William Webb Ellis, the man who, according to the mythical version of the sport's founding, created rugby when he picked up the ball during a football match and ran forwards with it, something that was not permitted at the time) by defeating France 29–9 in the final, played at Eden Park.

Australia and New Zealand did meet in the following World Cup, which was held in Great Britain, Ireland and France in 1991, although in a semi-final rather than the final. Captained by Nick

Farr-Jones and coached for the second time by Bob Dwyer, who had taken over from Alan Jones in 1988, Australia had only just scraped into the clash with the All Blacks. The Wallabies had faced Ireland in the quarter-finals at the home of Irish rugby, Lansdowne Road, in Dublin, and despite two magical tries from winger David Campese, they looked headed for defeat when they trailed 18–15 with only a couple of minutes remaining. But fly-half Michael Lynagh covered himself in glory by scoring a late try, and Australia won 19–18.

The semi-final against New Zealand was also held at Lansdowne Road, and the Wallabies went in as slight underdogs. But Australia began in sensational fashion, with Campese scoring an extraordinary try – later voted the best try of the World Cup – after just six minutes. Campese's effort was described in detail in *The Wallabies: A Definitive History of Test Rugby*: 'A maul followed a lineout win by Australia and Michael Lynagh made inroads before giving the pass to Campese, who had come into the backline from the opposition side. He angled across field and then completely fooled All Blacks' Sean Fitzpatrick, Mark Carter and, particularly, John Kirwan as he accelerated and scored...' Campese set up the Wallabies' second try just before half-time when he evaded a number of tacklers, then flicked a pass over his shoulder to Tom Horan, who sprinted over the line. The Wallabies were never troubled from there, running out 16–6 winners.

As good as Australia was on the attack, its defence was equally impressive, especially when the All Blacks were running with the wind in the second half. New Zealand's only scores were two penalty goals kicked by Grant Fox. 'I have never seen an Australian team defend as well as this side,' remarked former Wallaby Sir Nicholas Shehadie, one of the men responsible for creating the Rugby World Cup, after the game. 'The semi-final between England and Scotland took rugby back 10 years, but this unbelievable Australia–New Zealand match brought it back again. I would say that would be our most significant win ever.' Australia went on and claimed the Webb Ellis Cup for the first time, defeating England 12–6 in the final. Campese was named player of the tournament.

The Wallabies scored another upset victory over the All Blacks in the semi-finals of the 2003 World Cup, held in Australia. Tensions between the rugby communities in the two nations had run high in the two years before the tournament. The chief flare-up occurred when New Zealand was stripped of its right to co-host the World Cup after the New Zealand Rugby Union said it would not agree to the International Rugby Board's demand for 'clean' stadiums (in which only advertising signage approved by the World Cup 'partners' was allowed). Such was the ruckus after the Kiwis were sacked as co-hosts that NZRU boss Malcolm McCaw went as far as intimating that New Zealand was considering boycotting the tournament.

After much chest-beating, the All Blacks did take part, and they blitzed their way through the early rounds, then thrashed South Africa in their quarter-final. Clear favourites to win the title, the All Blacks were expected to be far too good for the home side in their semi-final at Sydney's Olympic Stadium, but the result was in complete contrast to the expectations, with Australia winning 22–10. It was the second straight time that the All Blacks had suffered an upset loss in the semi-finals (they were beaten by France in the semis of the 1999 World Cup), and after the final whistle Wallaby halfback George Gregan sledged his Kiwi counterpart Byron Kelleher, saying: 'Four more years, boys.'

'It was a moment where it was myself and [Kelleher] and I was just directing the comment to Byron, but the camera gets you in that moment and all of a sudden 4.5 million Kiwis thought it was directed at them,' Gregan told the *Sydney Morning Herald* in 2011. '[It was] a bit of fun, a bit of sport ... they've hung on to it, though. They've got long memories.'

A week after defeating New Zealand, the Wallabies lost a gripping final to England at the same venue. Fly-half Johnny Wilkinson was England's hero, slotting the winning drop goal with just 26 seconds remaining in extra-time.

The All Blacks finally gained some World Cup revenge over the Wallabies in 2011, when New Zealand hosted the tournament. As they had in 2003, the teams met in a semi-final, but the result was far different this time around. The match report in *The Australian* read:

> Four and a half million New Zealanders started breathing again after the All Blacks utterly dominated a clueless Wallabies side in a ferocious World Cup semi-final in Auckland. With 24 years having passed since the All Blacks last held aloft the Webb Ellis Cup, and 25 years since the Wallabies last won at Eden Park, one team was going to lay its demons to rest and demonstrably it was New Zealand. Technically, tactically and territorially, the All Blacks were vastly superior to Australia and typically the match ended with the Wallabies scrum in disarray, bulldozed by the NZ forwards who congratulated themselves with a fist-pumping, high-fiving celebration. This 20–6 defeat was one of Australia's worst trans-Tasman performances in years. They seemed to have completely lost faith in their wide attack and were utterly bereft of ideas and the ultimate insult came in the 78th minute when, having failed to score from bash-and-barge rugby, they threw the ball wide to fullback Adam Ashley-Cooper who slipped over and was instantly swarmed upon by the All Blacks defenders.

Gregan, who by this time was retired but was at the game as a spectator, copped plenty of grief from New Zealand fans who remembered his 'four more years' sledge. 'I got plenty of it,' he chuckled the following day. 'I got a song and everything. They spotted me and they were chanting it everywhere.'

There was also plenty of drama during the Bledisloe Cup battles of the 1990s and 2000s. Some of the incidents are remembered for their violence, such as the clash between All Blacks enforcer Richard Loe and Wallabies winger Paul Carozza during the second Test of the 1992 series, played at Ballymore in Brisbane. Carozza had just crossed in the corner to give Australia an 11–7 lead when Loe dived on him and elbowed him in the face, breaking his nose. According to *The Wallabies: A Definitive History of Test Rugby*, Loe's hit on Carozza was 'something more common in American professional wrestling. [It] received universal condemnation but drew no action from New Zealand team management.'

Loe, who was infamous throughout his career for being the dirtiest player in rugby, summed up his thoughts on the incident some years later after being asked if he had apologised to Carozza. 'After it's happened you can't change it,' was Loe's reply. 'So you don't lose too much sleep over it.'

Carozza had the last laugh, however. After being patched up, he played on in the second half and scored another great try in the dying moments, which not only won the game but also reclaimed the Bledisloe Cup for Australia.

In 1996 an Australian was the protagonist in another Bledisloe Cup bust-up in Brisbane. On this occasion, it was Wallaby Michael Brial who copped the wrath of New Zealand rugby fans – but not the referee, who elected not to send him to the sinbin – after he launched an unprovoked attack on champion All Black centre Frank Bunce. A man whose toughness was never doubted, Bunce simply fended off the blows, then helped the All Blacks win the game 32–25.

In the past 25 years a number of other controversial incidents have been sparked by the All Blacks' pre-game war dance, the haka.

Wallabies back-rower Sam Scott-Young was the first to infuriate the New Zealanders when he winked and blew a kiss at his opponents during a haka in 1992. His actions were in direct contravention of the International Rugby Board's rules, which state that opposition teams are expected to stand motionless and make no reaction while the haka is being performed.

Another haka-related drama marred the first Test of the 1996 Bledisloe Cup series. The Wallabies sent the capacity crowd at Athletic Park, in Wellington, into a fit of fury when they refused to stand and watch the haka – no team had ever done this to the All Blacks before. As the New Zealanders began their performance, the Australian players walked to the far side of the pitch and began going through their warm-up routines. The furious All Blacks then racked up their biggest victory over Australia, 43–6. Many of the Wallabies who ignored the haka have since insisted that they did not support the controversial move and that it was the idea of the Australian team's management.

The Wallabies have faced every haka performed in the years since then, although that hasn't stopped a few brave souls from pondering whether the haka is appropriate for the sporting stage. In 2006 the Wallabies' coach, John Connolly, caused a stir when he called on the All Blacks to take the 'murderous' throat-slitting gesture out of the haka. Connolly declared that the throat-slitting part of the performance was sending the wrong message to society. All Blacks coach Graham Henry responded by stating that he believed Connolly was being 'arrogant' and 'pathetic'.

Such arguments haven't stopped the IRB from policing its rules regarding the observation of the haka. As a 2010 article in the *Sydney Morning Herald* explained:

The Wallabies have been warned that disrespecting the All Blacks' haka could result in a fine from the International Rugby Board. The ARU was recently forced to pay a £1000 (NZ$2128) fine to Rugby World Cup Limited after the Wallaroos, Australia's women's rugby team, advanced on the Black Ferns mid-haka before their World Cup pool match in England last month. Shortly after the match, won by New Zealand 32–5, the ARU received a letter from the Women's World Cup tournament director, based at the IRB headquarters in Dublin, explaining that the conduct of the Wallaroos was in breach of tournament rules. The Australian women were found guilty of moving several metres towards the haka. IRB tournament rules dictated that the team facing the haka must stay at least 10 metres on its own side of the halfway line, but the Wallaroos made the mistake of walking beyond that line.

For all the moments of controversy that have fuelled the rivalry between the Wallabies and the All Blacks, there have been many more moments of sporting brilliance during recent decades.

After the Wallabies enjoyed a period of dominance over their greatest rival, winning all three Bledisloe Cup Tests in 1998 and retaining the cup by winning the second of the two Tests played in 1999, the teams did battle in mid-July the following year at Sydney's Olympic Stadium, two months before the 2000 Olympics began. The stadium could then hold 110,000 people (its capacity was reduced to 83,600 after the Olympics), and almost every seat was filled for the clash between Australia and New Zealand, with the final crowd posted at 109,874. The All Blacks launched a blitzkrieg from the opening whistle, racing to a 24–0 lead after eight minutes. Fullback Chris Latham was the only Wallabies player to touch the ball during the onslaught.

But Australia, coached at the time by Rod Macqueen, refused to crumble under the immense pressure. The Wallabies launched a stunning counter-attack that yielded four tries in the following 22 minutes – two to Stirling Mortlock and one each to Latham and Joe Roff. By the half-hour mark, it was 24–24.

The twists and turns continued after the break. New Zealand edged back in front when halfback Justin Marshall ran 40 metres to score a spectacular try, before Australia appeared to be on the verge of a famous victory when halfback George Gregan broke away and set up a try for hooker Jeremy Paul. With only four minutes to play, the Wallabies led 35–34, but the game had one final twist remaining.

With just two minutes left, New Zealand launched a last-ditch attack. All Black back-rower Taine Randell received the ball, drew two Wallabies towards him, then launched a basketball-style pass to the most famous All Black at the time, Jonah Lomu. Having grasped the ball in his giant hands, Lomu charged down the sideline, evading a diving Stephen Larkham. Thousands of New Zealanders jumped for joy in the stands as Lomu calmly pulled up and touched the ball on the ground, in the process handing his team a match-winning 39–35 lead.

The thousands of Australians watching Channel 7's telecast of the match heard the golden voice of Aussie rugby, Gordon Bray, celebrate Randall's pass and Lomu's moment of magic. 'This has been a magnificent comeback by the All Blacks, after all looked lost,' he said, 'and it's that man Jonah Lomu. The human juggernaut.' When interviewed in the New Zealand rooms after the match, Randall exclaimed: 'I have never seen or played in anything like that before.'

Despite losing that extraordinary contest, the Wallabies retained the Bledisloe Cup by scoring a remarkable victory of their own in the second Test, played at Wellington's Westpac Stadium three weeks later. Australia scored two tries and raced to a 12–0 lead after 15 minutes, before the All Blacks scored a pair of tries of their own and grabbed a two-point advantage. From there, both sides traded penalty goals, and New Zealand led 23–21 when the game reached its final minute. With time running out, Wallaby Stephen Larkham sunk his right boot into the ball, and it found touch well into the All Blacks' territory.

The big pro-New Zealand crowd roared at the South African referee, Jonathan Kaplan, to blow his whistle, but he instead ordered that a line-out be formed, which brought a deafening round of boos from All Blacks' supporters and a smile from Kaplan. Still, the All Blacks had the throw and the chance to kill the game. 'If New Zealand won the ball and kicked it dead or knocked on, it was all over,' Kaplan later acknowledged.

But the All Blacks did no such thing. Mark Hammett went for a short throw, but his move backfired as the Australians were able to tap the ball back to George Gregan, who dished off a pass. Suddenly, the Wallabies were on the attack.

'They've got to be careful here about the penalty,' muttered the Kiwi commentator on the New Zealand television broadcast. About ten seconds later, the very same commentator yelled, 'Oh dear, there's the penalty.' And so it was. Kaplan waved his arms to indicate that he had awarded a penalty to the Wallabies. The kick at goal was to be the last act of the match, and would decide the winner.

Such a kick would usually have been taken by Stirling Mortlock, but he had been substituted out of the game due to cramp. 'We got the penalty and I think, "Wow, this is fantastic, where's Sterling?" And I look around and Stirling's not there,' John Eales, the Wallabies' captain at the time, told a TVNZ documentary on the series. 'And Jeremy Paul it was who came up to me and said, "Mate, Sterling's off; it's your kick." So all of a sudden you change from being really

245

excited about it to being a bit anxious about it. But still, look, as a player they're the moments you train for. I kicked a hundred of those as a kid in the backyard, trying to win a Test for Australia.'

As the crowd hooted wildly, Eales sent his kick flying towards the uprights. It started out to the right but swung back beautifully and sailed right between the posts. Eales raised his arms in triumph. 'I'm very, very glad it went over,' he said, 'because I think my life and people's memories of me as a rugby player would have been very different if I had've missed that kick. It would've been, "You're the bloke that missed the kick that cost us the Bledisloe Cup and the Tri-Nations, aren't you?" It could easily have been like that.'

The following year the Wallabies retained the Bledisloe Cup again, thanks to a 29–26 victory over the All Blacks in the Second Test at Sydney's Olympic Stadium, which was also Eales' last game for Australia. Totai Kefu put the Wallabies in front with a memorable last-gasp try that ensured that Eales left the sport on a high.

In all, the Wallabies held the Bledisloe Cup for five consecutive seasons between 1998 and 2002. But after reclaiming the cup in 2003, New Zealand was in no mood to relinquish it. By the end of 2012 – by which time Bledisloe Cup games had also been played in Hong Kong and Tokyo – they had held it for ten straight seasons.

Throughout that period the Wallabies did enjoy some successes, but they seemed unable to stretch their periods of dominance beyond half a game. One such example took place in 2006, when the Wallabies led the All Blacks 20–11 at half-time of their clash at Eden Park. Yet the home side came out firing after the break and won the game 34–27, which secured a 3–0 series win for New Zealand.

But even as they have conceded series after series to the All Blacks, the Wallabies have never stopped taking the fight to their greatest rival. The chief protagonist in recent years has been fly-half (and occasional professional boxer) Quade Cooper, who just happened to spend his first 13 years in New Zealand. Cooper's tangles with All Blacks' skipper Richie McCaw – a god-like figure in the Land of the Long White Cloud – have made him one of the most hated men in New Zealand, up there with Trevor Chappell, who bowled the underarm delivery.

But the All Blacks and their army of supporters have not been riled for long. Their team won 22 of the 28 Bledisloe Cup tests played between 2003 and 2012, along the way racking up some huge points tallies. On one occasion at Eden Park, New Zealand even managed to keep Australia scoreless for the first time in half a century. So the All Blacks' fans have spent far more time celebrating than railing against injustices.

And, to be fair, it has almost always been that way. New Zealand might be a small fish in most departments when compared to Australia, but when it comes to rugby the Kiwis have made beating up on their big brother an artform.

WALLABIES vs ALL BLACKS, RUGBY UNION (1903–2012)

Tests played: 146
Australia wins: 41
New Zealand wins: 99
Draws: 6

Bledisloe Cup series wins

Australia: 12: 1934, 1949, 1979, 1980, 1986, 1992, 1994, 1998–2002
New Zealand: 39: 1932, 1936, 1938, 1946–47, 1951–52, 1955, 1957, 1958, 1962, 1964, 1967–68, 1972, 1974, 1978, 1982, 1984, 1985, 1987–91, 1993, 1995, 1996–97, 2003–12

Statistics at a Glance

HOLDEN vs FORD (1960–2012)
Australian Touring Car Championship/
V8 Supercar Championship Series
Ford: 23 wins: 1964–69, 1973, 1976-77, 1981–82, 1984, 1988–89, 1993, 1995, 1997, 2003–05, 2008–10
Holden: 17 wins: 1970, 1974–75, 1978–80, 1994, 1996, 1998–2002, 2006–07, 2011, 2012

Phillip Island 500/Bathurst 500/Bathurst 1000
Holden: 29 wins: 1968–69, 1972, 1975–76, 1978–80, 1982–84, 1986–87, 1990, 1993, 1995–97, 1999–2005, 2009–12
Ford: 17 wins: 1962–65, 1967, 1979, 1971, 1973–74, 1977, 1981, 1988–89, 1994, 1998, 2006–08

CARLTON vs COLLINGWOOD, AUSTRALIAN RULES (1897–2012)
Matches played: 245
Carlton wins: 125
Collingwood wins: 116
Draws: 4

VFL/AFL premierships

Carlton: 16: 1906–08, 1914–15, 1938, 1945, 1947, 1968, 1970, 1972, 1979, 1981–82, 1987, 1995

Collingwood: 15: 1902–03, 1910, 1917, 1919, 1927–30, 1935–36, 1953, 1958, 1990, 2010

WAYNE CAREY vs GLEN JAKOVICH, AUSTRALIAN RULES

Wayne Carey

Clubs: North Melbourne (1989–2001), Adelaide (2003–04)
Position: Centre half-forward
Matches played: 272
Goals kicked: 727
Premierships: 1996, 1999
Club best-and-fairest awards: 4: 1992–93, 1996, 1998
Number of times selected in All-Australian team: 7: 1993–96, 1998–2000

Glen Jakovich

Club: West Coast (1991–2004)
Position: Centre half-back
Matches played: 276
Goals kicked: 60
Premierships: 1992, 1994
Club best-and-fairest awards: 4: 1993–95, 2000
Number of times selected in All-Australian team: 2: 1994–95

STATISTICS AT A GLANCE

SHANE WARNE vs DARYLL CULLINAN, TEST CRICKET

Shane Warne
Team: Australia
International career span: 1992–2007
Test matches played: 145
Test wickets: 708
Test bowling average: 25.41
Best Test figures: 8 for 71 vs England, 1994
ODI matches played: 194
ODI wickets: 293
ODI bowling average: 25.73
Best ODI figures: 5 for 33 vs West Indies, 1996

Daryll Cullinan
Team: South Africa
International career span: 1993–2000
Test matches played: 70
Test runs: 4554
Test batting average: 44.21
Test average versus Australia: 12.75
Highest Test score: 275* vs New Zealand, 1999 (* denotes not out)
ODI matches played: 138
ODI runs: 3860
ODI batting average: 32.99
Highest ODI score: 124 vs Pakistan, 1996

AUSTRALIA vs ENGLAND, TEST CRICKET (1877–2012)

Tests played: 310
Australia wins: 123

US *vs* THEM

England wins: 100
Draws: 87
Ties: 0

Test series wins

Australia: 31: 1891–92, 1897/–98, 1899, 1901–02, 1902, 1907–08, 1909, 1920–21, 1924–25, 1930, 1934, 1936–37, 1946–47, 1948, 1950–51, 1958–59, 1961, 1964, 1974–75, 1975, 1982–83, 1989, 1990–91, 1993, 1994–95, 1997, 1998–99, 2001, 2002–03, 2006–07

England: 30: 1882–83, 1884, 1884–85, 1886, 1886–87, 1887–88, 1888, 1890, 1893, 1894–95, 1896, 1903–04, 1905, 1911–12, 1912, 1926, 1928–29, 1932–33, 1953, 1954–55, 1956, 1970–71, 1977, 1978–79, 1981, 1985, 1986–87, 2005, 2009, 2010–11

Drawn series: 5: 1938, 1962–63, 1965–66, 1968, 1972

AUSTRALIA vs UNITED STATES, YACHTING (1962–1987)

1962: *Weatherly* (USA) defeated *Gretel* (Australia) 4–1

1967: *Intrepid* (USA) defeated *Dame Pattie* (Australia) 4–0

1970: *Intrepid* (USA) defeated *Gretel II* (Australia) 4–1

1974: *Courageous* (USA) defeated *Southern Cross* (Australia) 4–0

1977: *Courageous* (USA) defeated *Australia* (Australia) 4–0

1980: *Freedom* (USA) defeated *Australia* (Australia) 4–0

1983: *Australia II* (Australia) defeated *Liberty* (USA) 4–3

1987: *Stars & Stripes* (USA) defeated *Kookaburra III* (Australia) 4–0

STATISTICS AT A GLANCE

AUSTRALIA vs NEW ZEALAND, NETBALL (1938–2012)

Matches played: 103
Australia wins: 64
New Zealand wins: 45

World Netball Championships victories

Australia: 10: 1963, 1971, 1975, 1979 (joint winners), 1983, 1991, 1995, 1999, 2007, 2011
New Zealand: 4: 1967, 1979 (joint winners), 1987, 2003

Commonwealth Games gold medals

Australia: 2: 1998, 2002
New Zealand: 2: 2006, 2010

NEW SOUTH WALES vs QUEENSLAND, RUGBY LEAGUE (1980–2012)

Matches played: 94 (including exhibition match in the United States in 1987)
New South Wales wins: 43
Queensland wins: 51

State of Origin series wins

New South Wales: 12: 1985–86, 1990, 1992–94, 1996–97, 2000, 2003–05
Queensland: 17: 1982–84, 1987–89, 1991, 1995, 1998, 2001, 2006–12
Tied series: 2: 1999, 2002

US *vs* THEM

WALLABIES vs ALL BLACKS, RUGBY UNION (1903–2012)
Tests played: 146
Australia wins: 41
New Zealand wins: 99
Draws: 6

Bledisloe Cup series wins
Australia: 12: 1934, 1949, 1979, 1980, 1986, 1992, 1994, 1998–2002
New Zealand: 39: 1932, 1936, 1938, 1946–47, 1951–52, 1955, 1957, 1958, 1962, 1964, 1967–68, 1972, 1974, 1978, 1982, 1984, 1985, 1987–91, 1993, 1995, 1996–97, 2003–12

Acknowledgements

THANKS FIRSTLY TO Craig Collins, key account manager at The Five Mile Press, for coming up with the idea of a book about Australian sporting rivalries, and to commissioning editor Julia Taylor for giving me the opportunity to bring Craig's idea to life. My ever-supportive wife, Zara, played a key role in assisting with the research (she nearly wore out her library card!) and bringing the manuscript up to standard, while Julian Welch did a brilliant job with the editing. A number of my colleagues at AFL Media also came forth with some excellent suggestions on which rivalries to include and why. All the help was greatly appreciated.

References

Bedwell, Steve, *Holden versus Ford: The Cars, The Culture*, The Competition, Rockpool Publishing, 2009

Futon, Colin & Russell, Terry, *Peter Brock: Road to Glory*, Allen & Unwin, 2011

Flanagan, Martin, *1970 and Other Stories of the Australian Game*, Allen & Unwin, 1999

McFarlane, Glenn, *Jock: The Story of Jock McHale, Collingwood's Greatest Coach*, Slattery Media, 2011

McFarlane, Glenn & Roberts, Michael, *The Official Collingwood Illustrated Encyclopedia*, Slattery Media, 2012

Browne, Ashley (editor), *Grand Finals, Volume 1, 1897–1938*, Slattery Media, 2011

Carey, Wayne (with Happell, Charles), *The Truth Hurts*, Pan Macmillan, 2009

Collins, Ben, *Champions: Conversations with Great Players & Coaches of Australian Football*, Slattery Media, 2008

Warne, Shane, *Shane Warne: My Autobiography*, Hodder, 2001

Warne, Shane, *Shane Warne: My Official Illustrated Career*, Cassell Illustrated, 2006

Frith, David, *Australia versus England: A Pictorial History of Every Test Match since 1877*, Penguin, 1990

Haigh, Gideon, *The Big Ship: Warwick Armstrong and the Making of Modern Cricket*, Text, 2001

Rousmaniere, John, *The America's Cup: 1851 to 1983*, Norton, 1983

Collins, Ben, *Book of Success: Prominent Australians Describe How They Achieved Success*, Slattery Media, 2004

Taylor, Tracy, 'Gendering Sport: The Development of Netball In Australia', *Sporting Traditions: Journal of the Australian Society for Sports History*, vol. 18, no. 1, 2001, pp. 57–74.

Ellis, Liz, *Netball Heroes*, Allen & Unwin, 2005

Jobling, Ian & Barham, Pamela, 'The Development of Netball and the All-Australia Women's Basketball Association: 1891–1939', *Sporting Traditions: Journal of the Australian Society for Sports History*, vol. 8, no. 1, 1991, pp. 29–48.

Gallaway, Jack, *Origin: Rugby League's Greatest Contest 1980–2002*, University of Queensland Press, 2003

Beetson, Arthur (with Heads, Ian), *Big Artie: The Autobiography*, ABC Books, 2004

Heads, Ian & Middleton, David, *A Centenary of Rugby League 1908–2008*, Pan Macmillan, 2008

Walters, Kevin, *Brave Hearts*, Ironbark, 1999

Jenkins, Peter & Alvarez, Matthew, *Wallaby Gold*, Random House, 2003

Richards, Huw, *A Game for Hooligans: A History of Rugby Union*, Trafalgar Square, 2008

Howell, Maxwell, Xiw, Lingyu & Wilkes, Bensley, *The Wallabies: A Definitive History of Test Rugby*, GAP Publishing, 2000

Index

Bold refers to image

A

Ablett, Gary 61
Adelaide Football Club 63, 66, 67
Adelaide Oval 99, 101
AFL *see* Australian Football League
Alderman, Terry 113
Alexander, Lisa 174
Allan, Graeme 51
Allan, Kevin 43
Allan, Trevor 237
All-Australian Women's Basketball Association 152
All Blacks **218**, 219–47
Ambrose, Marcus 28, 29
America's Cup **120**, 121–46
AMP Bathurst 100–28
Armstrong 500 7–8
Armstrong, Warwick 96, 117
ARU *see* Australian Rugby Union
Ashes, The **84**, 81, 85–119, 149
Ashman, Rod 52
Asher, Opai 224
Ashley-Cooper, Adam 240
Atherton, Mike 81, 113
Athey, Bill 112
Australia II 134, 135, 137, 138–9, 140
Australian Board for Control for International Cricket *see* Cricket Australia
Australian Cricket Board *see* Cricket Australia
Australian Cricket Team 72–82, 85–97, 98–100, 101–18
Bodyline Series 98–100

Australian Football League 41, 57, 58, 59, 65, 182, 197
Australian Formula 1 Grand Prix 27
Australian Netball Team *see* Diamonds
Australian Rugby League 177–216
Australian Rugby League Board of Control 180
Australian Rugby Union 223, 225, 227–47
Australian Rules Football **32, 56**, 33–82
Australian Touring Car Championship (ATCC) 15, 16, 17, 18, 19, 21, 22, 23, 25, 27, 28
Avellino, Natalie 167
Aylett, Allen 183

B

Backo, Sam 197
Bacquie, Jack 36, 37
Bailey, Graeme 24
Baker, Carley 160
Ballymore 241
Banfield, Drew 63
Bannerman, Charles 88
Barassi, Ron 45, 46, 47
Barham, Pamela 151
Bartlett, Kevin 18
Barton, Edmund 90
Basin Reserve 75
Bassett, Caitlin 173, 174
Bathurst 5, 8, 9–10, 13–30
AMP Bathurst 1000 28
Bathurst 1000 27
Bathurst 1000 27
Baxter, Tom 36, 37
Beashel, Colin 133, 143
Beck, Damon 14
Beechy, Norm 29

Beetson, Arthur 182, 185, 186, 187, 188, 189, 191, 192, 197, 208
Belcher, Gary 195, 196
Bell, Ian 118
Bella, Martin 202–3
Benaud, Richie 105
Bennett, Wayne 193, 195, 197, 205, 206, 207–9
Benson & Hedges World Series Cup 72, 74
Bergman-Osterberg, Martina 151
Bertoch, Natalie van 173
Bertrand, John **120**, 122, 127, 129, 131, 133, 134, 135, 138, 139, 140, 141, 143, 145
Bich, Marcel 126, 127, 128, 131, 134
Blackham, John 92
Blakey, John 59
Bledisloe Cup 219, 230, 231, 233, 235, 237, 240, 241, 242, 243, 246
Bligh, Ivo 93–4
Block, Ken 43
Blues 177–216
Bodyline series 98–100
Bond, Alan **120**, 128, 129, 130, 131, 133, 135, 137, 138, 140, 141, 143
Bond, Colin 12, 19
Boon, David 112
Border, Allan 74, 110–11, 112, 113
Borlase, Jenny 163
Bosustow, Peter 52
Boswell, Muriel 153
Bosworth, Midge 9
Botham, Ian 109, 110, 111, 112
Bousted, Kerry 184, 186
Bowe, John 28

259

Boxing Day Test 73, 77, 78
Boycott, Geoff 106
Boyd, Les 191–2, 195
Boyle, David- 195
Boyle, Harry 92
Bradman, Donald 71, 98, 99, 101, 102, 116, 233
Bray, Gordon 244
Brennan, Mitch 188
Brentnall, Greg 186
Brial, Michael 241
Brisbane Cricket Ground 224
British Motor Corporation 9
Broadbent, Alison 167
Brock, Peter 4, 12, 13–17, 18–20, 21, 22–6, 27, 28, 29
Brock, Phil 18
Brockhoff, David 234
Brohman, Darryl 191–2
Brookvale Oval 185
Brown, Joyce 155, 159
Bunce, Frank 241

C

Caldow, Margaret 156–7
Campese, David 238, 239
CAMS *see* Confederation of Australia Motor Sport
Canterbury Arena 174
Car racing 4, 5–31
Carey, Wayne 56, 57–68
Carlton & United Breweries Series 79
Carlton Football Club 32, 33–55
Carne, Willie 204
Carney, Todd 215
Carozza, Paul 241
Carroll, Mark 203, 205
Carroll, Tonie 206, 213
Carter, Mark 238
Catchpole, Ken 231, 232
Centenary Tests 108
Chappell, Greg 106, 108, 109, 110, 112
Chappell Ian 106, 108
Chappell, Trevor 247
Chifley, Ben 6
Chivas, Doug 14, 16
Civoniceva, Petero 213, 215
Clark, Peter 14
Clark, William 93
Clarke, Michael 115
Clifton, Jeff 46
Clipsal 500 27
Close, Chris 186, 189, 192
Cole, King 87

Collingwood Football Club 32, 33–55, 60
Collins, Ben 58, 61, 65, 129, 138, 139
Collins, Herbie 97
Commonwealth Games 147, 155, 161–2, 164–5, 166–7, 167, 169–72,
Compton, Denis 116
Condon, Pat 44
Confederation of Australian Motor Sport 15, 22
Conner, Dennis 129, 130, 132, 135–6, 138, 140, 141, 142, 143, 144, 145
Connolly, John 242
Constellation Cup 169, 174
Constigan, Neville 213
Cook, Alastair 118
Cooper, Quade 246, 247
Copeland, E. W. 38
Cornelsen, Greg 233
Costello, Army Major Peter 133
Coulthard, George 90
Cowie, Les 191
Cox, Catherine 164, 165, 172, 173, 174
Coyne, Mark 204
Crawley, Steve 208
Cricket 70, 84, 71–119
Cricket Australia 97, 100, 109
Crompton, Neil 42
Cronin, Mick 185, 186, 188
Cronk, Cooper 215
Cronje, Hansie 73, 77
Crow, Jim 87
Crowley, Keiran 236
Cullinan, Daryll 70, 71–82
Cumbes, Jim 116

D

Daicos, Peter 51
Daley, Laurie 202, 206, 207, 211
Darling, Joe 95
Delahunty, Hugh 214
de Villiers, Fanie 78–9
Dexter, Ted 106
Diamonds Netball Team 148, 149–75
Docklands Stadium 80
Donald, Allan 77
Doull, Bruce 52
Dowling, Greg 194
Duke, Phil 190
Duncan, James 223
Dunne, Twiggy 46
Dunworth, David 233

Dwyer, Bob 135, 238
Dyer, Jack 40
Dyk, Irene van 164, 165, 166, 173
Dyson, John 109

E

Eales, John 245, 246
Eastlake, Darrell 202
Eden Park 233, 236, 237, 240, 246
Edgbaston 110, 114
Edge, Steve 185
Edrich, John 107
Elder, Jack 36, 37
Elias, Benny 176, 200, 201, 203, 213
Ella, Mark 235
Ella, Glen 235
Ellis, Liz 163, 165, 167, 168
Ellis, William Webb 237
Ellison, Thomas Rangiwahia 221, 222
England Cricket Team 75, 85–118
Essendon Football Club 53, 65, 66
Etihad Stadium 211, 214
Ettingshausen, Andrew 195, 202, 206

F

Fanning, Fred 44
Farr-Jones, Nick 238
Fearnley, Terry 193–4
Ferguson, John 208
Fesq, Bill 126
Ficker, Bill -127, 128
Fielke, Michelle 160
Fingleton, Jack 99, 101
Firth, Harry 8, 9, 10, 11, 12, 13, 14, 17, 19
Fischer, Syd 134
Fisher & Paykel Cup 162
Fittler, Brad 202, 209–10
Fitzpatrick, Mike 52
Fitzpatrick, Sean 238
Fitzroy Football Club 34, 49
Flanagan, Martin 46, 48
Flintoff, Andrew 114, 115, 117
Footscray Football Club 48
Ford 5–31
    Declining sales 30–31
    Ford Motor Co. of Australia team 8
    Ford performance racing 28
Fox, Grant 238

INDEX

Franklin, Lance 57
Fraser, Douglas 35
French, John 14
Frith, David 88, 96, 113
Fulton, Bob 184

G

Galbally, Frank 46
Gabba 103
Gabelich, Ray 41
Gallagher 500 9, 10,
Gallaway, Jack 179–80, 182
Gallen, Paul 215
Gatting, Michael 73, 112, 113
Geelong Football Club 52, 54, 60, 61, 63, 65
General Motors 5
  establishment in Australia 6
Geoghegan, Ian 16
Geoghegan, Ian and Leo 10, 13
Geyer, Mark **176**, 199–200
Gibbs, Leigh 158
Gibson, Fred 10
Gibson, Jack 197–8
Gilchrist, Adam 77, 116, 117
Gillespie, Doug 35
Gillespie, Jason 114
Gillmeister, Trevor 205
Girdler, Ryan 207
Goddard, Jamie 203
Gomersall, Barry 190
Gooch, Graham 112
Goss, John 18
Gould, Phil 202, 209, 210, 211
Gould, Roger 235
Gower, David 112
Greenhill, Paul 203
Greening, Johnny 46
Gregan, George 239, 240, 244, 245
Grace, W. G. 87, 89, 91, 92, 94, 95
Gregory, Dave 90
Gregory, Stuart 233
Gregory, Syd 95
Greig, Tony 108
Grice, Alan 24, 26,
Grigg, Peter 235
Grimmett, Clarrie 101
Grothe, Eric 188

H

Haberecht, Daryl 233
Hafey, Tom 49, 51, 52, 53
Haigh, Gideon 93
Hambly, Gary 186
Hamilton, Alan 12, 19
Hamilton Football Club 43
Hamilton Imperial Football Club 44
Hammerton, Ernie 191
Hammett, Mark 245
Hammond, Wally 98
Hang Ten 400 19
Hancock, Michael 198
Harby-Williams, Kathryn 166
Hardie-Ferodo 500 11, 14, 16, 19
Hardie-Ferodo 1000 20
Hardy, Jim 127, 128, 131, 132
Harmes, Wayne 49–50
Harmison, Steve 115, 116
Harrigan, Bill 206
Harris, George R. C. 90, 91
Harnett, Joan 155
Harragon, Paul 202–3, 206
Harvey, John 22
Hauff, Paul 200
Hawthorn Football Club 52, 54, 57
Hawke, Bob 139, 140, 159
Hayden, Laurie 138
Hayne, Jarryd 211
Headingley 109
Heads, Ian 183, 184, 193
Healy, Ian 75, 76, 79
Hearn, Tony 205–6
Henry, Graham 242
Hill, Clem 95
Hipwell, John 233
Hobbs, Jack 97
Hobson, Denys 74
Hodgson, Brett 211
Hogan, Paul 182
Hoggard, Matthew 116
Holden 5–31
  General Motors 5, 6, 11
  Holden Motor Body Builders 6
  Holden Dealer Team 11, 16, 17, 18, 19, 22, 23, 24, 25
  Holden Racing Team 26, 27, 28
Hollies, Eric 103
Hood, Ted 125
Hookes, David 108
Hopkins, Ted 47, 48
Hopoate, John 205
Horan, Tom 238
Hughes, Kim 109
Humphreys, Kevin 183, 184, 190
Hunt, Karmichael 213
Hussey, Mike 117

I

Ickx, Jacky 19
Ikin, Ben 208
Ikin, Jack 103
Ilitch, Janine 166, 167
Illingworth, Ray 106
Impalas Cricket Team 72
Indian Cricket Team 72, 76
Ingall, Russell 27
Inglis, Greg 213
International Race Committee 127
International Rugby Board 239, 242, 243
Iverson, Jack 104

J

Jakovich, Glen **56**, 57–68
James Hardie 1000 22, 23, 24
Jane, Bob 8, 9
Jardine, Douglas 98–100, 101
Jencke, Roselee 159
Jenkin, Graeme 45
Jenkins, Peter 223
Jesaulenko, Alex **32**, 45, 47, 49
Jobling, Ian 151
Johns, Andrew 202, 203, 210, 211, 212
Johnson, Dick **4**, 20, 21, 22, 23, 24, 25, 28, 29
Johnston, Wayne 52
Jones, Alan 235, 236, 237, 238
Jones, Ernie 95
Jones, Geraint 115
Jones, Simon 116
Jones, Warren 136, 137
Judge, Ken 64

K

Kangaroos Rugby League Team 180
Kaplan, Johnathan 245
Kasprowicz 114, 115
Kefu, Totai 246
Kelleher, Byron 239
Kelly, Peter 197
Kelly, Rick 29, 30
Kelly, Todd 30
Kemp, Dean 63
Kennedy, Jacqueline 124
Kennedy, John F. 124
Kenner, Ted 44, 78
Kenny, Brett 193, 197
Khan, Paul 188
Kirsten, Gary 78
Kirwan, John 238
Kleenex Cup 159
Kourie, Alan 75

261

Kumble, Anil 104

L
Laker, Jim 104–5
Lam, Adrian 213
Lamb, Alan 72
Lancashire County Cricket Club 116
Lancaster Park 227
Lang, Alex 35
Lang, John 184
Lang Park 184, 185, 187, 188, 189, 193, 194, 195, 197, 200, 201, 205, 209
Langer, Allan 195, 196, 198, 206, 208–10
Langer, Justin 117, 118
Lansdowne Road 238
Larkham, Stephen 218, 244, 245
Larwood, Harold 98, 99, 100, 101
Latham, Chris 243, 244
Lawry, Bill 105, 107
Lee, Brett 114, 115
Lee, Dick 36, 38
Leeds Cricket Ground 98, 103
Leichardt Oval 184, 188
Le Mans Disaster 11
Lever, Peter 107
Lewis, Wally 176, 188, 189, 190, 191, 192, 195, 196, 197, 198, 199–200, 201, 204, 211
Lexcen, Ben 129, 133, 134, 136, 137, 138, 141, 143 *See also* Robert Miller
Lillee, Dennis 108, 109, 110, 112
Lillywhite, James 87–88
Lindner, Bob 198
Lindwall, Ray 102
Lipton, Thomas 122, 139
Lloyd, Matthew 65, 66
Lockyer, Darren 206, 210, 211, 212
Loe, Richard 241
Loffhagen, Donna 163
Lomu, Jonah 218, 219, 244
Lord's Cricket Ground 89, 93, 96, 98, 101, 108, 113, 114
Louis Vuitton Cup 121, 126, 134, 136, 141, 142, 143, 145
Lowe, Graham 199
Lowndes, Craig 28, 29, 30
Lunn, Hugh 183
Lynagh, Michael 238
Lyon, Cliff 195

Lyons, Joseph 100

M
Maclure, Mark 53
Macqueen, Rod 244
Malthouse, Mick 33, 34, 54, 59, 60, 62
Manson, David 176, 199–200
Marcou, Alex 50
Marks, Dick 233
Marsh, Geoff 112
Marsh, Rod 108, 109, 110, 112
Marshall, Justin 244
Martyn, Damien 117
Martyn, Mick 59, 60
Maroons 177–216
Marylebone Cricket Club 93, 100
Masters, Roy 210
Matera, Peter 63
McAuliffe, Ron 182, 183, 184, 189, 190, 191
McCabe, Paul 188
McCaw, Richie 247
McConchie, Lorna 155
McDonald, Fenley John 37
McDonald, John 208
McDermott, Craig 73, 75, 112
McGaw, Mark 194, 200
McGilvray, Alan 107
McGrath, Glenn 81, 113, 114, 117
McGrath, John 66
McGregor, Duncan 224
McHale, Jock 36, 38
McIntosh, Jill 157, 160, 162, 163, 166
McKenna, Guy 59
McKenna, Peter 45, 47, 48, 49
McLean, Paul 235
McLean, Peter 191
McMahon, Sharelle 163, 164, 165, 167, 172, 173
McPhee, Bruce 11
MCC *see* Melbourne Cricket Club
MCG *see* Melbourne Cricket Ground
Meads, Colin 231, 232
Meagher, Wally 232
Meckiff, Ian 105
Melbourne Cricket Club 86, 89, 93
Melbourne Cricket Ground AFL 36, 39, 40, 41, 42, 45, 49, 50, 51, 54, 57, 60, 61, 63, 64, 72, 73, 77, 78, 79, 81, 89

Cricket 88, 94, 96, 97, 101, 104, 105, 107, 110
Rugby League 202, 205
Melbourne Football Club 41, 42, 44, 53, 60
Meninga, Mal -177, 186, 192, 198, 201
Menzies, Sir Robert 124
Menzies, Steve 203
Messenger, Herbert Henry 178, 225
Middleton, David 183, 184, 193
Middleton, Dot 152
Midwinter, Billy 88
Miles, Gene 191
Miller, Jeff 111
Miller, Keith, 102
Miller, Robert 128
Minichiello, Anthony 213
Mitchell, Carleton 124, 125, 126
Moffat, Allan 12, 13, 14, 15, 16, 17, 18, 19, 20, 21, 23
Allan Moffat Racing Team 17
Moffat Ford Dealers Team 19
Moore, Danny 205
Moore, Peter 50, 52, 53
Morris, Arthur 103
Morris, Des 192
Morris, Rod 184, 188, 189, 190, 191
Mortimer, Steve 193
Mortlock, Stirling 244, 245
Mosbacher, Emil 123, 124, 143
Motorsport 4, 5–31
Mount Panorama 8, 9, 10, 13, 15, 16, 18, 19, 20, 21, 22, 23, 25
Muir, Lois 158
Mulholland, Barry 11
Mullagh, Johnny 86–87
Munro, Charles John 220
Munro, David 220
Muralitharan, Muttiah 72
Murdoch, Billy 88–9, 90, 91, 95
Murdoch, Rupert 204
Murphy, Greg 28
Murray, Iain 143
Murray, Mark 191

N
Naismith, James 148
National Rugby League 206
Neill, Fraser 225
New York Yacht Club 121, 122, 123, 124, 127, 128,

INDEX

129, 130, 132, 133, 136, 138, 139, 140, 141, 142
Netball **148**, 149–75
North Melbourne Football Club 49, 51, 57, 59, 60, 63, 64, 65
New South Wales Rugby League **176**, 177–216
New South Wales Rugby Union 219, 223, 225, 231
New Zealand Netball Team *see* Silver Ferns
New Zealand Rugby Football Union 219–47
NSWRL *see* New South Wales Rugby League
NSWRU *see* New South Wales Rugby Union
NZRFU *see* New Zealand Rugby Football Union

O
O'Connor, Michael 193, 195, 196, 200
O'Keefe, Jack 43, 44
O'Reilly, Bill 101
Oldfield, Bert 100
Old Trafford 104, 110, 111, 113, 115
Olympic Games 225
Olympic Staidum 219, 239, 243, 246
Oossanen, Peter van 133, 136, 137
Oval, The 75, 91, 92, 97, 98, 101, 103, 104, 116

P
Packer, Sir Frank 121, 122, 123, 124, 125, 128, 130
Packer, Kerry 109
Pagan, Denis 59, 63, 65
Park, Jim 40
Parkin, David 52
Parr, George 6
Parry, Kevin 143
Patterson, A. B. 90
Patterson, Bill 19
Paul, Jeremy 244, 245
Payne, Alan 122
Pearce, Linda 167
Pearce, Wayne 194, 197, 206
Pearkes, Thomas 122
Peate, Ted 92
Percy, Win 26
Perkins, Larry 22, 27
Phillip Island 7, 8, 9, 29
Picken, Billy 49, 51, 53
Pietersen, Kevin 116

Plummer, Norma 167, 168, 172, 173
Pollock, Graeme 71
Pond, Christopher 86
Ponsford, Bill 97, 98, 101
Ponting, Ricky 114, 169
Pratt, Richard 134
Price, Barry 47, 48
Princes Park 38, 48, 61

Q
Queensland Rugby League 177–216
Queensland Rugby Union 222, 223, 227, 228, 229

R
Racing, car **4**, 5–31
Randell, Taine 244
Raper, Ted 219–20
Raudonikis, Tommy 185, 187, 203
Reagen, Ronald 144
Reardon, Jack 182
Renouf, Steve 204
Reynolds, George 9
Rhodes, Wilfred 96
Richards, Huw 231
Richards, Jim 19, 20, 26
Richards, Lou 52
Richards, Ted 57
Richards, Viv 117
Richardson, Brian -133
Richardson, Vic 106
Richmond Football Club 40, 42, 49, 50
Ridley, Ian 44
Roberts, Ian 202
Roberts, Tony 12
Robilliard, Steve 159
Robins, Noel 130, 131
Roff, Joe 244
Rogers, Steve 186, 188, 214
Rose, Bob 42, 45, 46, 48
Ross, Robbie 207
Rousmaniere, John 123, 126, 128, 135
Rowan, Paddy 38
Rowbery, Anna 165
Rowell, Ted 38
Royal Perth Yacht Club 134, 141, 143
Royal Sydney Yacht Squadron 121, 124
Royal Ulster Yacht Club 122
Rugby League **176**, 177–216
Rugby Union **218**, 219–47
Rugby World Cup **218**, 219, 237, 238, 239, 240

S
Sampson, Brian 18
San Diego Yacht Club 142
Sandown 5, 15, 18, 19
Sargeant, Anne 157, 159
Satyanand, Anand 169
SCG *see* Sydney Cricket Ground
Scarlett, Matthew 65, 66
Scott, Colin 191
Scott-Young, Sam 242
Seddon, Malcolm 38
Seton, Barry 9
Shaw, Alfred 88
Shaw, Geoff 233
Shaw, Tony 51, 52, 53
Shaw, Tony 233, 235
Shearer, Dale 196, 201
Sheehan, Percy 37
Shehadie, Nicholas 238
Sheldon, Ken 50
Sheppard, John 19
Shorten, Jim 45
Sigsworth, Phil 190
Silvagni, Sergio 47
Silver Ferns 149–75
Simpson, Bob 105
Skaife, Mark 26
Slack, Andrew 236
Slater, Billy 212–13
Slater, Michael 72
Sloof, Joop 133, 136
Smith, Cameron 212
Smith, Charlie 6, 7
Smith, Darren 206
Smith, Jason- 206, 208
Smith, Robin 72
Snow, John 106
South African Cricket Team 71, 72, 73, 74, 75, 76, 77, 79, 80, 105
Spiers, Felix William 86
Spofforth, Fred 88–90, 91
Spurr, Dan 136
Sri Lankan Cricket Team 72, 101
St Kilda Football Club 45, 62
Stackpole, Keith 107
Stanton, Frank 189
State of Origin 177–216
Statistics
Australian Rules, Collingwood vs Carlton 55
Australian Rules, Wayne Carey vs Glen Jakovich 68
Cricket, Australia vs England 118–19

263

Cricket, Shane Warne vs
    Daryll Cullinan 82
Motorsport, Holden vs
    Ford 31
Netball, Australia vs New
    Zealand 175
Rugby League, New
    South Wales vs
    Queensland 216
Rugby Union, Australia vs
    New Zealand 247
Yachting, America's Cup,
    Australia vs United
    States 146
Stephens, Olin 124
Stephenson, H. H. 85–6
Sterling, Peter 195, 196, 197, 214
Strauss, Andrew 117
Strickland, Bill 35
Stone, Mick 197
Stuart, Ricky- 177, 202, 211
Sturrock, Jock 123, 124
Stynes, Jim 59
Subiaco Oval 62, 64, 65, 66, 183
Sumich, Peter 59
Suncorp Stadium 212
Sundown, 87
Super League 204–6
Sutcliffe, Herbert 97
Swanton, Will 204
Sydney Cricket Ground
    AFL 64, 72
    Cricket 72, 73, 74, 91, 93, 106,
    Rugby League 179, 190, 192, 193, 195, 197
    Rugby Union 221, 222, 224, 225, 227, 230, 232, 234, 235
Sydney Football Club 54, 57
Sydney Football
    Stadium 195, 199, 203, 205, 206
Sydney University Rugby
    Club 220
Symonds, Andrews 80

T
Taafe, Bruce 233
Tahu, Timana 212
Tahuna Park 224
Tallis, Gorden 206, 207
Tander, Garth 29
Taumaunu, Waimarama 159
Tavare, Chris 111
Taylor, Mark 112, 113
Teede, Gaye 156

Telemachus, Roger 76
Templeton, Bob 233, 233
Thompson, Billy 186
Thompson, Len 46
Thompson, Peter 128
Thomson, Jeff 108, 110–11, 112
Thorn, Brad 213
Thornely, Burt 48
Thurston, Johnathan 212
Titan Cup 76
Tooheys 1000 25
Transvaal Cricket Team 72, 75, 95
Trent Bridge 109, 116
Trott, Harry 95
Trott, Johnathan 118
Trumper, Victor 95
Tuddenham, Des 47
Tudor, Leigh 61
Turner, Dick 186, 191, 201
Turner, Ted 130, 131
Tutaia, Maria 173

V
V8 Supercars 27
V8 Supercars Championship
    Series 28, 29, 30
Valentijn, Johan 129
Vallance, Harry 40
Vaughan, Michael 114, 116
Vautin, Paul 189, 195, 198, 205
Vector Arena 174
Victorian Football
    League 34, 35, 37, 39, 40, 41, 53, 182
Victoria Park 34, 38, 53
Visser, Martin 127
Vodafone Arena 167

W
WACA *see* Western
    Australian Cricket
    Association
Walkinshaw, Tom 23
Wallabies 219–47
Wallace, Billy 223
Walters, Doug 108
Walters, Kevin 200, 206
Walters, Steve 199, 201, 203
Wangaratta Football
    Club 42, 43
Wangaratta Rovers Football
    Club 42
Warbrick, Joseph 221
Ward, Steve 133, 134
Warne, Shane 70, 71–82, 113, 114, 115, 116, 117

Warner, Pelham 99
Warren, Ray 200, 204
Waters, Terry 48
Waugh, Mark 74, 79
Waugh, Steve 74, 75, 80, 112, 113, 169
Waverley Park 59,
Webb Ellis Cup 237, 238
Webcke, Shane 214
Wessels, Keppler 72
West Coast Eagles Football
    Club 54, 57, 60, 61, 63, 64, 66
West, Des 12
Western Australian Cricket
    Association 59, 60, 61, 79, 106
Western Province Cricket
    Team 72
West Indian Cricket
    Team 73
Westpac Stadium 244
Whincup, Jamie 29, 30
White, Chris 224
Wiley, Ron 194
Wilkins, Phil 233
Wilkinson, Johnny 240
Williamson, Mike 45
Willis, Bob 109
Wilson, Vicky 159, 160, 161, 162, 163
Winterbottom, Mark 30
Wisden Cricketers'
    Almanac 76, 101
Woodfull, Bill 98, 99, 101
Wooldrige, Ian 110
World Championships,
    Netball 147, 155, 156–7
World Cup Cricket 72, 79, 81, 112
World Games 157
World Netball
    Championships 154, 155, 156, 157, 158, 160, 161, 162–3, 165–6, 168–9, 172
World Series Cricket 109
World Touring Car
    Championships 24
Worsfold, John 59
Wynn, Graeme 186

Y
Yachting 120, 121–47
YMCA *see* Young Men's
    Christian Association
Young Men's Christian
    Association 148